W9-CLD-301

ENTERED APR 6 1999

Lawful Order

CURRENT ISSUES IN CRIMINAL JUSTICE
VOLUME 23
GARLAND REFERENCE LIBRARY OF SOCIAL SCIENCE
VOLUME 949

CURRENT ISSUES IN CRIMINAL JUSTICE

FRANK P. WILLIAMS III AND MARILYN D. MCSHANE
Series Editors

Lawful Order
A Case Study
of Correctional Crisis
and Reform

Leo Carroll

Columbia College Library
600 South Michigan
Chicago, IL 60605

Garland Publishing, Inc.
A member of the Taylor & Francis Group
New York and London
1998

365.7 C319L

Carroll, Leo.

Lawful order

Copyright © 1998 by Leo Carroll
All rights reserved

Library of Congress Cataloging-in-Publication Data

Carroll, Leo.
    Lawful order : a case study of correctional crisis and reform / by Leo
Carroll.
         p.   cm. — (Garland reference library of social science ; v. 949.
Current issues in criminal justice ; v. 23)
    Includes bibliographical references and index.
    ISBN 0-8153-1617-8 (alk. paper)
    1. Prisons—Government policy—United States. 2. Prisoners—United
States—Social conditions. 3. Prison administration—United States.
4. Prison violence—United States. 5. Prisons—Security measures—United
States.   I. Title. II. Series: Garland reference library of social science ;
v. 949. III. Series: Garland reference library of social science. Current issues
in criminal justice ; v. 23.
HV9304.C365 1998
365'.7'0973—dc21
                                                     97-39224
                                                     CIP

Printed on acid-free, 250-year-life paper
Manufactured in the United States of America

To Jeanne,
With Love and Appreciation.

Contents

List of Figures

Preface

Research for this study, in effect, began over 25 years ago when I spent 15 months as a participant observer in the maximum security prison studying race relations.[1] From that study I had retained all of my field notes, diaries and journals, a number of documents, the transcripts of 12 unstructured formal interviews with inmates, and the tapes of nine similar interviews conducted with staff. These, together with the published work, not to mention a host of vivid memories, proved invaluable sources in reconstructing the history of the period around 1970.

Over the years, although I remained in Rhode Island, my research interests moved away from the prison in part because my relationship to it and its administration changed. For several years I served on the board of directors of a halfway house for ex-felons that was operated by a non-profit group that was often at odds with the department. I also served on several citizens' advisory committees concerned with corrections and testified as an expert witness for the plaintiffs in two cases (neither of which is central to this book) in which the department was a defendant. Early in the history of *Palmigiano v. Garrahy*, I briefed attorneys for the plaintiffs on conditions in the prison, and for two years in the mid-1980s, I attempted to work with the corrections administration in mediating inmate grievances that had been submitted to the local chapter of the ACLU. These various connections provided windows through which I periodically caught glances of the prison system and its operations, but their partisan nature strained my relation with the administration and made it unlikely that I would have received their cooperation to do research had I asked for it, which, in fact, I did not.

In January 1991, a new administration took office and the case appeared to be drawing to a close. It seemed a good time to assess its impact. I contacted J. Michael Keating, Jr., who had been the special master and whom I had known for a number of years, and wrote to Director George Vose asking his cooperation and enclosing a rather formal proposal. Both expressed a willingness to cooperate, and the research began in earnest.

There had been an earlier study that had followed the case through 1985.[2] My intent initially was to broaden the scope of that study somewhat and update it to the termination of the case which, at the time, I thought would be in 1991. Soon after beginning the study, however, I realized—it now seems strange that I did not realize this initially, but I did not—that the case could not be seen as a disjunctive event but had to be seen in context, as part of an evolving pattern in which court intervention may have been the largest but was certainly not the only strand. Thus, with a great deal of reluctance, I moved the starting point back from 1977, when the order was entered, to 1970, the period in which I had studied race relations and during which conditions seemed to be deteriorating, and finally back to 1956 when the prison complex was officially renamed the Adult Correctional Institutions. Luckily, for me at least, the case was not dismissed in 1991 but dragged on until June 1995.

The first 12 to 15 months of research was spent mainly in gathering documentary material. Using the Rhode Island Collection catalogue at the Providence Public Library and the computerized index of the *Providence Journal-Bulletin*, I was able to locate what I think are probably all the news stories, features and editorials mentioning the prisons or the corrections department from 1956 through 1991. At the same time I was clipping current news items from the daily newspapers, something I obsessively continue to do. Even the smallest correctional issues such as a prisoner walking off from a work release detail appear regularly in the *Journal-Bulletin*; thus I developed an extensive file containing somewhere in excess of 5,000 items.

Through Judge Pettine and Special Master Keating, I was able to gain access to the court records which, by the time I began the research, had been moved to the attic of the federal courthouse in Providence. A good number of hours were spent in this musty and dusty attic, rifling through some 20-30 file drawers attempting to separate the wheat from the chaff when I had only a city dweller's sense of what each looked like. In addition to unpublished orders, I was able to retrieve all of the reports submitted to the court by the special masters, briefs submitted by both plaintiffs and defendants, transcripts of some hearings as well as chambers conferences and conference calls, notes kept at meetings, and correspondence among the principal parties. One notable find was the tape-recorded diary kept by Allen Breed during his tenure as special master at the request of the Federal Judicial Center. Permission to use this material was secured from both the Center and Mr. Breed. All of this material was photocopied and returned to the court.

Additional documentary material was found in the State House Library in Providence and supplied by the Department of Corrections. From the former, I secured a number of early reports on the prison by investigative commissions. The material I received from the department is too varied and voluminous to list in full but included annual reports, budgets, investigative commissions, union contracts, statistical reports of various kinds, and policy statements. Of particular value were the very comprehensive and detailed reports of two management consultant teams that were done a decade apart, one in 1977 and the other in 1989.

While gathering this material, I was also reading it quickly and developing short summaries which were then coded into one or more categories and entered into computer files. An editorial from January 21, 1975, for example, was summarized as "unsigned ed. supporting furloughs & work release for lifers proposed by the NPRA [National Prisoners' Reform Association] at legislative forum" and coded with the keywords Media and NPRA. A 63-page report of the special master was summarized as follows: "extensive report dealing with all aspects of the order, comparing 1983 conditions with 1977, and concluding there is substantial compliance with most provisions." This report was then coded in the following categories: master, physical conditions, classification, medical care, programming, and overcrowding. Some materials such as the above-mentioned consultants' reports, each of which ran to two thick volumes, defied such quick reading, easy summary and coding. They were so obviously important, however, that I was unlikely to neglect them.

I began interviewing key participants during the summer of 1992, a process which continued intermittently through 1996. In all, I conducted formal interviews with 36 people. Those interviewed included the judge, the special master, lawyers, past and present directors and their assistants, wardens, correctional officers, prison reformers, inmates and past inmates. Despite my trepidation about past conflicts, only one person refused my request, and most seemed happy to renew our acquaintance and talk about the past. A number of people were interviewed more than once, and several were subjected to my questioning three or four times. All told, I completed 57 interviews totalling approximately 170 hours.

Prior to each interview, I reviewed as much of the relevant documentary material as I could, prepared a list of topics to be covered and arranged them on a yellow legal tablet in what seemed to me a sensible order. Each topic was introduced in an neutral way such as "Do you remember . . . ?"; "What can you tell me about that?" and then allowed to flow as a normal conversation. At first, I was very concerned not to wear out my welcome and anxiously turned the interview to the next topic rather quickly. Gradually, I came to realize that most of the people were enjoying the conversation, and as this became clear I inclined to let them talk until they seemed to have exhausted the topic, at which point I steered the interview back on course. This made the interviews longer and more complex than I had anticipated, as respondents spontaneously connected the topics I raised to things I had not. Some of the information thereby secured was quite rich, but most was not all that germane to my purposes. The process, however, was important for developing rapport and always provided valuable insight into how the person constructed events.

Having recently read documentary material about the events under discussion, I often found myself in the unusual position of having a clearer grasp of events and their chronological order than did the person I was interviewing. Early on this seemed to me an advantage and I would try to assist the recall of a respondent who was struggling to remember the order in which things had occurred. These attempts were coolly received. Those being interviewed seemed to feel that their ownership of the experience was in some way violated by my prompting and that if I knew so much about what had happened, why was I asking them about it. It may also have kindled fears that maybe I was trying to catch them in an error. In any event, after a few uncomfortable experiences in which I sensed the interviewee tighten up in response to my offers of assistance, I resisted my impulse to set things straight and adopted the attitude of one seeking to learn about the prison and its history from those who live it.

All of the interviews were tape-recorded. This may have caused some people to be more tight-lipped than they might otherwise have been, but I do not think it seriously affected what people were willing to convey. I made it clear that the tape could be turned off at any time and that anything they did not wish attributed to them, taped or untaped, would not be. In about half of the interviews, I was asked to "go off the record" for some portion of the time. Usually what was relayed to me at these times were bits of gossip or descriptions of events which, while sensitive, were of purely local interest. One such event was the "nervous breakdown" suffered by an official, but that had never been made public. All of those in a position to know about this told me about it; some of them asked that the tape be turned off, but others described it on tape. All of them asked that I not use the material, however, out of concern for the damage it might do to the individual's reputation, and I have respected those confidences. Although this could have been a difficult decision, it was not; in my judgment this occurrence, while not without an impact at the time, was of little importance in the broader scheme of things.

Six of those interviewed requested that they be permitted to read anything that was attributed to them. I agreed to this with the understanding that I would only make changes to attributions that were inaccurate or that were factually incorrect and that interpretations of the material were mine and mine alone. Three of those to whom I sent materials never replied. The other three pointed out factual errors that were, for the most part, of little or no consequence and easily changed. All three agreed that I had correctly portrayed the big picture and captured its dynamics well. Two of these people are cast in a somewhat unfavorable light in the text, and I think their willingness to cooperate in this project and not to challenge the view presented here is to their great credit.

The tapes were not transcribed verbatim. Rather, each topic was summarized in some detail with poignant quotes capitalized. These topic summaries were then coded similarly to the news stories and copied into other files. Thus an excerpt from an interview with Michael Keating concerning the robbery of a credit union by a person on home confinement, in which Mike speculates how the impact of such incident would be different in Texas, was coded into "alternative sanctions" and "size of state."

In addition to the documents and interviews, I also toured the prisons on a regular basis, sat in on staff meetings, focus groups, discipline and classification boards and attended a two-day retreat and team-building session for senior administrators. However, I was not allowed the unfettered access to the prisons that I enjoyed 25 years ago. Then, I had been free to come and go as I pleased at any time of the day or night and was left to find my own way on the inside. This time my tours were always arranged and I was always accompanied by an officer. I was never denied access to a place I wished to go, however, or stopped from talking with an inmate. The tours, moreover, gave me an opportunity to observe mid- and lower-level staff on the job and to talk with them about what they do, to gain a sense of what figures on participation in programming meant in terms of actual inmate activity, and to observe unobtrusively conditions or incidents that confirmed or confounded expectations I had developed from other sources.

As I conclude writing this study, I realize that from it we learn more about the informal social organization among inmates as it was 20 years ago than as it exists today. In part, this is the result of limited time and energy. It is also reflective of the story I have sought to tell, the history of the prison during a period in which bureaucratic authority and formal controls have supplanted other forms of power and informal accommodations as the cornerstone of order. But as I contemplate this limitation, I realize that it is not specific to this study. While there has been an abundance of correctional research over the past decade, it is heavily weighted toward the operational and evaluative, toward research in the service of bureaucratic goals, and so-called pure research concerned with the formal organization.[3] As a result we know little about what inmate life is like in the newly emerged corporately managed prisons and how it may differ from what was reported 20 or 30 years ago. For example, although I find flattering the continued references in texts to my earlier work on race relations, I cannot help but think that race relations in the prison have changed substantially since that time when the civil rights movement was at its peak and the war on drugs had not yet been declared. Yet, apart from some research on gangs in the larger state systems, there has not been, to my knowledge, any systematic treatment of race relations in prisons over the past two decades. Similarly, to my knowledge there has been no field research on how inmates do their time in new high-tech maximum security prisons. Certainly, inmate social life and staff-inmate relations in prisons where inmates live in small modular units, remain in their cells for over 20 hours a day, are monitored by closed-circuit televisions, and where officers spend most of their time in enclosed control centers must differ from what was found in the "big house" of old. But, of the nature and extent of this difference, we know nothing.

John DiIulio's fundamental thesis—that good management matters and that "where higher custody prisons are concerned, those govern best who govern most and most formally"[4]—is a sound one. His attacks on sociology, however, seem to me misguided. However sociological research may have been received by correctional administrators, researchers such as Sykes[5] were not prescribing management by cooptation, but describing patterns of interaction, analyzing their importance of those patterns in maintaining order and drawing out the logical implications of their analysis. Rather than negate it entirely, a more balanced and useful posture, it seems to me, is to view that earlier research as a representation of the prison social order at an earlier point in time, a time prior to the emergence of bureaucratic rationality in corrections. Having charted the structure of the emergent formal organization, we need now to begin tracing the contours of the informal order that parallels it.

NOTES

1. Leo Carroll, *Hacks, Blacks and Cons: Race Relations in a Maximum Security Prison* (Lexington, MA: Lexington Books, 1974; Chicago: Waveland Press, 1988).

2. Robert Harrall, *Section 1983 Prison Cases: A Study of 'Palmigiano v. Garrahy'* (Ph. D. Dissertation, University of Connecticut, 1988).

3. An exception is Mark S. Fleisher, *Warehousing Violence* (Newbury Park, CA: Sage Publications, 1989).

4. John J. DiIulio, Jr., *Governing Prisons: A Comparative Study of Correctional Management* (New York: The Free Press, 1987), p. 237.

5. Gresham M. Sykes, *The Society of Captives: A Study of a Maximum Security Prison* (Princeton: Princeton University Press, 1958).

Acknowledgments

In a very real sense, I wrote this book in collaboration with a number of people, those upon whose experiences it draws and those upon whose support and assistance I depended during the research and writing. It is with a deep sense of pleasure that I acknowledge my gratitude to them.

Judge Raymond J. Pettine and J. Michael Keating, Jr., Esq., went to great lengths to provide me with access to the extensive files of the *Palmigiano* case, many of which had been buried and forgotten long before I began the research. They also spent untold hours helping me make sense of it all and giving me the benefit of their observations and thoughts. Likewise, Corrections Director George Vose gave me entree to the Department of Corrections, opened its records to me and gave generously of his time over several years. Special thanks are due to Assistant Director A. T. Wall, upon whom fell most of my requests for reports and statistics, and to Lieutenant Ken Rivard, who also aided in my quest for documents and who patiently explained the union's position on the many complex labor-management issues that have faced the department over the years.

The research benefitted immensely by virtue of the fact that most of the key administrators over the past quarter-century remain in the state and consented to be interviewed. Former directors John Moran and Anthony Travisono were particularly gracious in welcoming me into their homes. In the past, I have been critical of some of their judgments and decisions, and still am at various points in the text, but have no question of their integrity, dedication to public service and commitment to improving the corrections system.

Several colleagues were kind enough to read portions of the manuscript and provide me with the benefit of constructive critiques. Their suggestions, as often as not at cross-purposes, sharpened my thinking while leaving me no choice but to find my own way and to take full responsibility for it. To Ben Crouch, Frank Cullen, Jim Marquart and Michael Vaughn: Thanks.

Marie Beaumont and her staff at the University of Rhode Island Library responded graciously to my requests for source materials and were zealous in their pursuit of them. Karen Feinberg, as usual, did exceptionally fine work editing an early draft of the manuscript and helping me reorganize it. Analyzing and organizing this amount of material was a prodigious task. My ability to handle it is no small measure due to the excellent training I received years ago from Sister Mary Andrius Douglas, CSJ, cousin of my father and one of my high school English teachers.

Financial assistance at various points in the research and writing was provided by various agencies of the University of Rhode Island: the URI Alumni Foundation, the URI Research Council and the URI Center for the Humanities. Without this assistance, the research would never have been attempted, let alone completed.

I was invited to be the George Beto Professor in the College of Criminal Justice at Sam Houston State University in Huntsville, Texas during the Spring 1993 semester. My stay there provided me with the opportunity to see at first-hand the changes wrought by judicial intervention in Texas prisons and to discuss the course of that controversial case with both prison managers and academic colleagues. My thanks to all those who made this sojourn possible and enjoyable, and especially to Rolando del Carmen.

At home, I have had the enormous good fortune of being able to draw deeply from the love, strength and wisdom of my wife, Jeanne, my partner in life. Words alone can never fully express my gratitude to her. And finally, Simon, my dog, has been a constant source of support, at my feet through every word whether written in the heat of a summer's afternoon or the dead of a winter's night.

Series Editors' Foreword

This series is dedicated to readable and thoughtful scholarly analysis. Leo Carroll exhibits both qualities in this volume. In the tradition of Sheldon Ekland-Olsen and Steve Martin's *Texas Prisons—The Walls Came Tumbling Down*, Carroll skillfully guides us through the maze of a major prison lawsuit where actors play out the timeless saga of regulating the keepers and the kept. While those close to the courtroom drama seem to enjoy pointing fingers and placing blame, moaning about judicial interference and neglect, the objective reader sees a pattern. In analyzing cases such as *Holt v. Sarver, Gates v. Collier, Ruiz v. Estelle,* and *Baxter v. Palmigiano,* we can discern common causes, themes and factors that lead to prolonged litigation and successful resolutions.

Prison reform literature offers the reader an opportunity for an in-depth look at the micro and macro features of the often-secretive world of prisons and the slow and complicated process by which they change. Unlike the narrower perspective of the litigation that precedes them, these narratives provide historical background as well as political and sociological insights into the people and the places that incur the "monster" lawsuits. Perhaps because these epic cases serve as lessons, we can actually prevent more of them from occurring—something like using a vaccine or immunization against a disease. On the other hand, maybe these cases are more like earthquakes, they just build up and happen and there is nothing anyone can do to stop them. Carroll provides the information and insight, it is up to the reader to decide the true nature of prison litigation.

Marilyn D. McShane
Frank P. Williams III

Lawful Order

CHAPTER 1

Introduction

On August 10, 1977, in what was the first major "totality of conditions" case outside the South (*Palmigiano v. Garrahy*), the Honorable Raymond J. Pettine, then Chief Judge of the Federal District Court for Rhode Island, found that the conditions in Rhode Island's prisons "do not provide [a] tolerable living environment" and "would shock the conscience of any reasonable citizen who had a first hand opportunity to view them."[1] Judge Pettine ordered remedial action in virtually all aspects of the prison system's facilities and operations including the closure of the state's only maximum security prison and appointed a special master to monitor the implementation of the decree. Eighteen years later the case was finally dismissed and the court terminated its jurisdiction. In that time conditions in the prisons had undergone such a remarkable transformation that Alvin Bronstein, then director of the ACLU's National Prison Project which has handled much of the nation's prison litigation including this case, considered it the Project's biggest success.[2]

This book began as a narrowly defined attempt to assess the impact of *Palmigiano* on Rhode Island's prisons. It soon became clear, however, that the intervention and its impacts could be neither understood nor assessed apart from a full consideration of the many features of the organizational environment influencing the course of the prison system's development. Among the more obvious and important of these influences are the attempt to implement the rehabilitative ideal in the 1950s and 1960s and the abandonment of that attempt in the subsequent decades, the unionization of correctional staff, the changing demographic composition of both the prisoner population and its keepers, the rapid growth in the number of prisoners brought on by successive wars on drugs, and the development of highly sophisticated carceral technologies. What follows, then, is an analysis of the evolution of a prison system as it has adapted to the myriad influences impinging upon it in the latter half of the twentieth century.

THE COURSE OF JUDICIAL INTERVENTION

Historically, courts refused to interfere with prison administration. The "hands-off" doctrine, as it is known, was initially justified by the view that prisoners had sacrificed their constitutional rights, that they were in fact "slaves of the state"[3] and later in terms of federalism, the separation of powers or the lack of sufficient penological expertise on the part of judges. By ordering an end to *de jure* racial segregation in the nation's public schools in *Brown v. Board of Education* the U.S. Supreme Court demonstrated its willingness to reform social institutions to guarantee the civil rights of disadvantaged minorities. In the years following that historic decision marginalized groups—blacks, women, gays and lesbians, the poor, the mentally ill and the learning disabled, etc.—successfully pressed their claims for both equal treatment and special entitlements through the federal courts. It was in the context of this "fundamental democratization" of American society that prison conditions were first seen as falling within the purview of the courts.[4] The close connection of the reversal of the "hands-off" doctrine to the civil rights movement is clearly evident in the first case in the which the Supreme Court took notice of prisoners' claims. In *Cooper v. Pate*[5] the Court recognized the standing of Black Muslim prisoners to challenge regulations which denied them any opportunity to worship. The law under which the prisoners were found to have standing was Section 1983 of the United States Code which was originally passed in 1871 to protect former slaves from abuses of their civil rights by persons "acting under the color of law." Despite the availability of other remedies, Section 1983 suits have remained the primary vehicle for prisoner rights litigation.

Once drawn to look over the prison's walls by such fundamental constitutional issues as freedom of religion and racial segregation, judges were appalled by what else they saw. In an explosion of litigation over a relatively few years, courts recognized that while prisoners' rights were unavoidably diminished by their incarceration, "there is no iron curtain drawn between the Constitution and the prisons of this country."[6] That the state had a duty to protect from harm those it confines and to provide adequate medical care for their serious needs was made clear. Corporal punishment was abolished and prisoners were afforded minimal due process rights in disciplinary hearings. Arbitrary censorship of mail and publications was prohibited and prison officials were required to insure that inmates had meaningful access to the courts. [7]

Until 1970 prisoners' rights litigation had been framed in terms of specific practices or conditions but in that year a new principle was established. Inmates at Arkansas' two major prisons challenged the constitutionality of a number of administrative practices and institutional conditions. In making its determination the court examined the totality of conditions on the assumption that prison conditions and practices which might not be unconstitutional when viewed separately could, when taken as a whole, constitute cruel and unusual punishment in violation of the Eighth Amendment.[8] This totality of conditions principle subsequently became the basis for some of the most important challenges to the constitutionality of prison conditions and the rationale for some of the most wide-sweeping remedial decrees such as those in Alabama, Texas and Rhode Island.[9]

In challenging virtually every detail of institutional life, these cases implicitly attack the organizational culture and administrative structure of the prison. As might be expected, these decisions came under sharp attack from state officials who viewed such intrusion as beyond the proper scope of judicial authority. Ironically, as lower courts found themselves becoming involved in reforming prisons, the Supreme Court, made more conservative through appointments by President Richard Nixon, was coming to share the views expressed by the critics. Thus, the Court began advocating what some have termed a "one hand-on and one hand-off" doctrine. Continuing to proclaim the need

to provide safe and humane conditions of confinement, it nonetheless began to adopt standards that pay greater deference to correctional administrators. This position was clearly stated in *Bell v. Wolfish* in which the Court chided lower court judges who become "enmeshed in the minutiae of prison operations" in the mistaken belief that their solutions to prison problems are better or more workable than those of administrators and admonished them that:

> . . . the first question to be answered is not whose plan is best, but in what branch of government is lodged the authority to initially devise the plan. This does not mean that constitutional rights are not to be scrupulously observed. It does mean, however, that the inquiry of federal courts into prison management must be limited to the issue of whether a particular system violates any prohibition of the Constitution. . . . [10]

Bell concerned the constitutionality of a host of conditions and practices in a modern federal jail. The lower courts had found these deprivations to be unconstitutional on the grounds that detainees should be subjected only to those restrictions and privations that are inherent in confinement itself or are "justified by the compelling necessities of jail administration." The Supreme Court, however, rejected the argument that the presumption of innocence should have any bearing on the rights of a pre-trial detainee during confinement and held that the conditions and practices were permissible in that they were reasonably related to the legitimate government objective of maintaining security and order.

Two years later, in *Rhodes v. Chapman*[11] the Court reinforced the admonitions of *Bell* in advising that courts cannot assume that state legislatures and prison officials are insensitive to the requirements of the Constitution. In this case, the lower courts had ruled in favor of the plaintiffs who were long-term inmates who spent most of their time in their cells and who, because of overcrowding, were forced to share that space—space scarcely sufficient for one—with another prisoner. The Supreme Court, however, using the totality of conditions principle, emphasized the other conditions of confinement—that the prison was new and "unquestionably a top-flight, first-class facility"—in holding that double-celling under these circumstances does not inflict unnecessary or wanton pain.

Before *Rhodes* lower courts considering cases in which the physical conditions of confinement were alleged to be cruel and unusual punishment held to the view that conditions which inflict unnecessary or wanton pain such as depriving prisoners of the basic necessities of life violate the Eighth Amendment regardless of the intent of prison officials. Nothing in *Rhodes* changed that view as the Court looked only to objective conditions in that case. In *Wilson v. Seiter*,[12] however, the Court explicitly rejected the traditional standard holding that to prevail in such cases, even where the conditions are systemic in nature, plaintiffs must prove not only that the conditions inflict unnecessary or wanton pain but that officials were deliberately indifferent to the situation. What is meant by deliberate indifference was made clear recently in *Farmer v. Brennan* where it was defined as meaning that an official is "aware of the facts from which the inference could be drawn that a substantial risk of serious harm exists, and . . . also draw[ing] the inference."[13] Such a narrowly drawn standard seemingly offers substantial protection from liability to high-level administrators and elected officials.

The Court has sought to narrow the scope of intervention in First and Fourth Amendment cases as well. The "reasonableness" standard articulated in *Bell* has subsequently been applied to infringements on freedom of speech and religious expression.[14] Where previously, prison officials had to be able to demonstrate that such infringements were essential to secure a legitimate penological interest, in effect plaintiffs must now show that the connection of such infringements to legitimate penological objectives is so remote as to be irrational. Similarly, while *Wolff v. McDonnell* extended minimum due process projections in disciplinary proceedings to inmates facing charges of serious misconduct, subsequent decisions have greatly restricted the types of situations in which such projections apply. Most recently, for example, the Court ruled that confinement in disciplinary segregation for 30 days "did not present the kind of atypical, significant deprivation in which a state might create a liberty interest" requiring due process projections.[15]

In spite of the attempt by the Supreme Court to discourage the involvement of courts in prison operations, judicial intervention has continued to grow over the past 15 years. In 1980, for example, there were 13,000 civil rights petitions filed by prisoners in federal district courts. This number increased steadily through 1994 when it reached 39,065.[16] Only a very small percentage of these cases survive screening, to be sure, but inmates continue to prevail in those cases going to trial. One analysis of lower court treatment of prison and jail overcrowding cases found that from 1979 through 1986 the plaintiffs prevailed in 80% of the trials and two-thirds of the appellate decisions,[17] and a recent review of published decisions concludes that lower court judges continue to rule in favor of inmates when confronted with evidence of grossly inadequate or unsafe conditions.[18] As of January 1995, prisons in 39 states plus the District of Columbia, Puerto Rico and the Virgin Islands were operating under court orders or consent decrees to limit population and/or improve conditions; in nine jurisdictions the orders covered the entire system. In all, more than 275 prisons were operating under court supervision and in some 150 conditions were being monitored by a court-appointed master.[19]

THE IMPACT OF JUDICIAL INTERVENTION

Although still small in comparison to the hundreds of interventions, there is a growing body of research on its effects. Two careful reviews of the available evidence—one by Malcolm Feeley and Roger Hanson and another by Susan Sturm[20]—suggest that while the impact of court-ordered reforms on prison conditions and practices has varied considerably, overall intervention has been a qualified success. Despite widespread resistance, intervention has been successful in eliminating the most flagrant abuses in targeted institutions and in improving physical conditions and basic services such as medical care to a tolerable level. In other areas of institutional life such as programming, however, courts seem to have less impact. Thus, even where conditions have been considerably improved, the quality of life generally remains far below what might be considered good. Moreover, there is considerable evidence of backsliding when active involvement of the court ceases.

More generally, judicial demands for performance standards and accountability have contributed to the bureaucratization of correctional systems. Whether well run or poorly run, the management of prisons in the pre-litigation era tended to be informal and personalized. By definition court intervention entails accountability, however, and this in turn requires written rules and regulations, clear delegation of responsibilities, explicit systems of monitoring and supervision, documentation and formalized decision-making according to rational criteria. Although not ordered by courts, these secondary or indirect consequences are quite possibly the most important effects of intervention. Where such organizational changes have taken root, court-ordered reforms have been sustained while in their absence of such systemic changes court-ordered reforms, if implemented at all, tend to be short lived.

Not all indirect consequences of intervention are positive, however. Indeed, one of the most persistently noted consequences is an upsurge in violence and disorder. Both the reviews conclude that the causal connection between litigation and violence has not been clearly drawn, however. They see no reason that court intervention would be any more likely to produce violence than would pressure for institutional change from any source. Moreover, they note that not all interventions are accompanied by violence and suggest that the connection between the two is drawn from "a skewed sample that overemphasizes resistance to change," and that in any event it appears to be a short-term effect rather than a permanent consequence.[21]

While the number of studies of court intervention into prisons and jails is growing, most of our impressions of the process and its impacts remain based upon a few comprehensive case studies. Because of the importance of these few studies, and because like the present study most focus on cases involving the totality-of-conditions, I summarize them here in some detail.

Stateville

One of the first studies to call attention to the impact of court-ordered reforms on prisons was James B. Jacobs's landmark study, *Stateville:*

The Penitentiary in Mass Society.[22] As the subtitle indicates, Jacobs draws upon Edward Shils's interpretation of American society as a "mass society," one in which the masses are being progressively incorporated into central institutions, treated with enhanced dignity, and coming to share the same values as the elites. From this perspective, Jacobs traces the history of Stateville as it moves from a position on the periphery of society into ever-closer integration with institutions at the core, and shows how in the process the extension of citizenship rights to inmates and demands for accountability from external groups disrupted the authoritarian regime that had developed under the charismatic Joe Ragen and his more traditional successor, Frank Pate. Stateville, once widely regarded as the world's toughest prison, spun out of control as the demoralized correctional officers retreated to the perimeter in the face of the challenge posed by street gangs.

Judicial intervention was only one of many forces disrupting traditional patterns of authority, but it was key. Following a review of several cases involving Stateville, Jacobs finds that the holdings of the courts were quite modest and indeed paid considerable deference to administrators. Certainly, in his opinion, there was nothing about the decisions that made prison administration impossible. But administrators and staff viewed the intrusions of the court as illegitimate and resisted. Virtually every decision was appealed, then implemented in the most narrow terms, prompting further litigation. Structurally, the organization was unable to meet demands for documentation, and officials were more often than not unable to articulate a rational basis for their decisions. Jacobs concludes that it was the legal process itself and the symbolic importance of the decisions, not their substance, that destabilized the traditional regime. The recognition that inmates may have legitimate grievances and the provision of a forum in which they might seek redress altered the status of inmates, while demands for accountability and formal rationality exposed the limitations and weaknesses of administrators and undermined their claims to authority.

As Jacobs was concluding his fieldwork in 1975, a "corporate"-style management based on principles of organizational rationality was emerging under a newly appointed warden. Jacobs saw in this new model of management the capacity to integrate the reforms of the previous years with aspects of authoritarian control and thereby restore order. He also recognized, however, that the new order was precarious and that the movement toward rational-legal forms of authority is not preordained. These concerns foretold the future: the new order was short lived and the institution remained in crisis for another decade.

Judicial Intervention in Texas Prisons

The most thoroughly researched intervention is that in the Texas prisons. In 1980, Judge William Wayne Justice in *Ruiz v.Estelle* found conditions in the Texas prison system to be unconstitutional and issued a comprehensive and detailed remedial decree and appointed a special master with extensive powers to monitor compliance.[23] In *Texas Prisons: The Walls Came Tumbling Down*, lawyer Steve J. Martin and sociologist Sheldon Ekland-Olson focus their attention on the litigation, the legal resistance to the court's orders and the involvement of the case with state politics.[24] Prior to the litigation, Texas prisons were run along the lines of old-style plantations. The central values of this system were order and economic self-sufficiency and its success in achieving them had led many correctional experts, both in and outside of Texas, to regard the system as among the very best in the country. Thus there had developed a separate, isolated and largely autonomous moral order, almost immune to criticism and relatively untouched by evolving legal standards. When the system was finally attacked, officials fiercely defended it in a trial that consumed 161 trial days over nearly a year. Then for 15 months after the order was entered, corrections officials outrightly defied it, publicly denigrated the judge and threatened to file suit to dismiss the special master and have his staff investigated for criminal charges.

At the heart of this resistance was the steadfast claim by officials that inmates used as "building tenders" were no more than porters with no supervisory powers over other inmates. As incontrovertible evidence to the contrary mounted, however, these officials lost credibility and political support, and in 1982 the state agreed to abolish the building tender system. Further evidence of brutality and mismanagement of

funds and a wave of unprecedented violence forced the resignation of
Director W. J. Estelle and a large number of high-level officials in
1983 and 1984. Estelle was replaced by Raymond Procunier, who had
previously headed four systems including California. Procunier brought
in a cadre of officials from outside the state and set about imposing a
number of administrative controls and negotiating a settlement
agreement on outstanding issues. Centralization and micromanagement
further alienated staff, however, and the agreement was not supported
by Governor Mark White. Procunier resigned in 1985 and was
succeeded by Lane McCotter, a retired military officer, who had been
Governor White's choice to succeed Estelle but who, for political
reasons, had been appointed Procunier's deputy.

In 1986 prison issues once again were a major issue in the
gubernatorial campaign. This time Bill Clements, who had been
governor when the building tender system had been dismantled and who
was defeated shortly thereafter by Mark White, was elected to another
term. The month after the election Judge Justice found the state in
contempt of court for failing to implement major provisions of
agreements going back to 1981 and threatened to fine the state $24
million per month. Governor Clements immediately promised to bring
the prison system into compliance with constitutional standards and
secured legislative approval for a $500 million bond issue to accomplish
that task. He also secured the resignation of McCotter and replaced him
with James Lynaugh, the department's finance director, who viewed the
operation as a $400 million per year business. At the conclusion of
their study in 1987, Martin and Ekland-Olson foresaw the Texas
Department of Corrections becoming a stable bureaucracy administered
by professional managers who possessed a very different vision of what
the system should be like than had their predecessors. The process,
however, was far from complete.

Sociologists Ben Crouch and James Marquart had been conducting
research in Texas prisons for several years prior to the *Ruiz* decision
and were able to continue that research through 1987. In *An Appeal To
Justice: Litigated Reform of Texas Prisons*,[25] they examine the impact
of *Ruiz* on the internal control structure of several prisons to which they
had access. Crouch and Marquart see the system as developing in three

stages which parallel those found by Jacobs at Stateville: from a "repressive order" through a "legalistic order" to a "bureaucratic order." The repressive order developed under the regimes of legendary leaders O.B. Ellis and George Beto who headed the system from 1947 through 1972 and remained intact under Estelle, Beto's less colorful and more traditional successor. The primary goals of the system were economic self-sufficiency and the total control of inmates. Staff were bound closely together and to administrators by a subculture emphasizing paternalism and personal loyalty and were granted enormous discretion to both reward and punish inmates. Much of this discretionary power was used to reward selected inmate elites, the building tenders, who, in turn, controlled the mass of inmates. Although there was much violence under this system, it was brutality in the service of totalitarian control; from the outside, the system seemed safe and secure.

In attacking the building tenders, the court was thus attacking the very cornerstone of the system's control structure. What Crouch and Marquart term a legalistic system came to replace the system of personalized control. The operant goal of this system was constitution-ality. Under Procunier, decision-making was highly centralized and discretion severely limited by a proliferation of formal regulations and reporting systems. Suspicion came to replace trust, and loyalty gave way to alienation. Veteran staff became disillusioned and turnover increased dramatically. Many of those who remained on the job became apathetic. Hundreds of new officers hired to replace the building tenders received little in the way of leadership and by themselves lacked the experience to maintain control. Predatory inmate gangs emerged, and a tide of violence and disorder rose in the vacuum created by the dismantlement of the building tender system.

By the late '80s gang violence had been brought under control by frequent lock-downs and extensive use of administrative segregation. As conditions improved, court intervention became more passive, and Crouch and Marquart could see an emerging bureaucratic order. Once again, the aim became the control of inmates, but now control was to be achieved within judicially approved parameters. Authority, though still centralized, was being delegated more and discretion at lower levels was being increased. With experience, staff had become skilled in using the new rules and procedures to maintain order, and inmates reported feeling safer than they had during the transition period and even prior to the intervention under the repressive system of control.

A quite different view from those above is presented by political scientist John DiIulio in *Governing Prisons: A Comparative Study of Correctional Management.*[26] DiIulio's primary concern is not court intervention but correctional administration. Convinced that good prisons are possible, he seeks to identify the administrative conditions under which they may be developed and maintained. At the outset he defines a good prison as "one that provides as much order, amenity and service as possible given its human and financial resources."[27] He then proceeds to compare and contrast prisons exhibiting markedly different management styles in three states: California, Michigan and Texas. Following this analysis, DiIulio concludes that the best prisons are those which are managed by administrations organized as paramilitary bureaucracies and operated strictly by the book.

The exemplar of good prison administration, according to DiIulio, was the Texas "control model." This is not the bureaucratic order seen to be emerging in Texas prisons in the post-*Ruiz* era but that of the pre-Ruiz order under Beto and Estelle. The key elements of this model as described by DiIulio were the sense of mission on the part of staff and their high *esprit de corps,* the organization of staff into a clear and simple chain of command with military titles and trappings, the treatment of all inmates as maximum security risks, the constant monitoring of inmate movement and rigorous enforcement of rules, certain and swift punishment for rule infractions together with generous rewards for compliance, and productive activity in the form of both work and treatment. The use of building tenders, according to DiIulio, was "never a major systemic feature of Texas prison management" and thus not an integral part of the control model. It was a "latent defect," a "rotten crutch" employed in some prisons but of far less importance than tight formal controls.[28]

DiIulio thus argues that the disorder and violence which swept the Texas prisons in the aftermath of the *Ruiz* decision was not due to the dismantlement of a well-nigh totalitarian system of repression but to the administrative instability and abandonment of the formal system of controls. Although the court was not directly responsible for what happened, in DiIulio's opinion, it nonetheless played a key role. Events might well have taken a different turn had Judge Justice been

> ... more judicious, his information better, his appreciation for what TDC had achieved in the past less unkind, and his preoccupation with its sores less total, or if he and his aides had troubled themselves to consider the possible unintended consequences of their sweeping actions, there can be no doubt that things would not have degenerated as they did. The new legal framework imposed on TDC was not ... a "straitjacket"; rather it was more nearly a poorly designed and ill-fitting suit which the agency was rushed into wearing and which eventually, and predictably, burst at the seams.[29]

Contradictions and internal inconsistencies, not to mention its one-sided nature, make DiIulio's account of events suspect. He seems to have been captivated by the personality of the legendary George Beto to whom he attributes development of the control model and from whom he gathered much of his information about its operation. In characterizing the pre-*Ruiz* regime as bureaucratic, thus by implication lawful, he fails to see that in fact management under Beto and then Estelle typified Weber's description of pre-bureaucratic forms of domination which combine "a sphere of strict traditionalism and . . . a sphere of free arbitrariness and lordly grace."[30] A high degree of order achieved through rigorous enforcement of rules upon a captive population by officials organized in a paramilitary hierarchy, traits emphasized by DiIulio, are not the defining marks of bureaucracy. Rather, bureaucracy requires rules which govern the behavior of officials in the conduct of their office— that not only prescribe what they do but that also define the scope of their authority, limit their discretion, provide a standard to which they can be held accountable and that are justified by their rational relation to some larger legitimate purpose. The behavior of Texas prison officials in the pre-*Ruiz* era, especially those at the top, was nearly the antithesis of rational-legal authority so defined. In particular, the management style of the charismatic and free-wheeling George Beto so much admired by DiIulio seems to have been more typical of a benevolent despot than of the head of a public bureaucracy.

DiIulio's conceptual confusion over the meaning of bureaucracy also relates to his treatment of the building tenders. Feeley and Rubin, in an incisive review, see it as a classic case of cognitive dissonance.[31] Having concluded that the pre-*Ruiz* administration should serve as a model for others and having bestowed upon it the mantle of legality, DiIulio must explain away facts at variance with the image he has constructed. To do so he resorts to a variety of familiar and time-worn devices: arguing that it was tightly controlled, denying its universality and importance and minimizing the effects of its abandonment. Nowhere, however, does he explain why such forceful administrators as Beto and Estelle never rid the system of this "latent defect" nor why officials risked their credibility and careers to defend to the death a system that was merely a "rotten crutch."

Alabama and Georgia

Intervention appears to have been only a partial success in Alabama, hence the title of law professor Larry Yackle's analysis—*Reform and Regret*.[32] Despite sharing the premises that prisons should be self-sufficient, prior to litigation Alabama's prisons were quite unlike those in Texas. They were managed by political appointees with little or no correctional experience and staffed, or more accurately woefully understaffed, by poorly educated whites drawn from the immediately surrounding rural areas. Physical conditions were unfit for human habitation, idleness was pervasive, and violence was rampant. Thus, there was little for officials to defend and in a brief trial before Judge Frank Johnson, they did little more than blame the legislature for inadequate funding. Judge Johnson found conditions to be in violation of the Eighth Amendment and issued a detailed and specific remedial order. He did not, however, appoint a special master, preferring instead to establish a Human Rights Committee composed of both local leaders and nationally recognized corrections experts to monitor compliance. As Yackle makes clear, the judge expected resistance and hoped that this committee would assist in implementation of the decree by galvanizing public support for change, lobbying the legislature and working directly with the Board of Corrections.

As expected, the order was greeted with a storm of protest. Governor George Wallace, Judge Johnson's longtime nemesis, was gearing up to run for the presidency and seized upon the order as a rallying point for his campaign, proof that "thugs and federal judges have just about taken over our society,"[33] and retained private counsel to appeal. Not to be outdone the state's attorney-general, who had signalled his intention not to appeal, reversed direction and joined forces with the governor. The lieutenant governor, who also wished to establish himself as a credible successor to Wallace, used his position to influence the recommendations of a legislative task force established to review the provisions of the order. The panel was sharply critical of prison management—characterizing it as a "family affair"—and endorsed most provisions of the order, but rather than increase appropriations, the panel recommended that management exploit prisoner labor more effectively and use the profits to pay for the needed improvements.

Except for the development of a classification system which he saw as essential to controlling violence, Judge Johnson did not press for immediate implementation. On the one hand, he was concerned that the order might be reversed on appeal. On the other hand, he hoped that officials would eventually implement the reforms voluntarily. Over a two-year period, not much progress was made, and changes that were made, as in classification, were quickly abandoned. Nonetheless, the impetus for change grew. Despite its recommendation on funding, the legislative task force's report had legitimated the order to some degree. This was reinforced by periodic reports from the Human Rights Committee, and by court hearings in which even experts retained by the state would not defend existing conditions. In 1978, the order was largely upheld on appeal, though the Human Rights Committee was not and was replaced by a Prison Implementation Committee composed of four experts whose role was solely to monitor compliance and advise the court, and a newly elected Governor, Forrest H. "Fob" James, pledged to implement it.

Judge Johnson placed the prison system in receivership, naming Governor James as receiver and thereby stripping the Board of Corrections of its power. James in turn appointed Robert Britton as Commissioner of Corrections, the first corrections professional from outside the system to hold that position. Overcrowding was relieved through emergency releases and construction of a new prison and planning for three others was begun. But the promise of implementation went unfulfilled for several reasons. First, despite his pledge, Governor James's fiscal conservatism led him to cut the corrections budget, and his tough stance on crime kept admissions high. Second, those named as Britton's deputies were political appointments and undercut his authority; Britton left after two years. Third, Judge Johnson left to take a seat on the Fifth Circuit Court shortly after he had appointed Governor James as receiver.

The case was inherited by Judge Robert Varner, who, although willing to use the power of the court to enforce existing orders, was a conservative on civil rights. The number of sentenced prisoners held in local jails climbed dramatically and Judge Varner ordered early releases but was reversed on appeal and advised to find officials in contempt of court and fine them. When the new prison designed for 1000 finally opened in 1984, it was filled with 1600 inmates. Judge Varner found the state in contempt but again was reversed on appeal in light of the Supreme Court's holdings in *Rhodes v. Chapman*.

In the meantime, George Wallace had been re-elected governor in 1982. Confronted with the high cost of prison construction, he moderated his stance on compliance and charged his commissioner, Fred Smith, to improve conditions and to develop alternatives to incarceration. Over the next two years, Smith managed to make significant improvements in physical conditions, especially with respect to health care, and to reduce overcrowding somewhat through a restitution program for nonviolent offenders. Following the reversal of Judge Varner's finding of contempt, the Implementation Committee advised the judge, now looking for ways to extricate the court, that the system was in sufficient compliance to permit the case to be dismissed, which it was in November 1984.

Yackle returned to Alabama two years later and in an epilogue he recounts standing in the yard of one of the prisons and recalling all the changes that had taken place. Although improvements had been substantial, Yackle "could not share state officials' view that the Alabama prison system was now affirmatively good as opposed to merely better," and already he could see signs of deterioration.[34] It is not clear from his account, given its focus on the legal process, to what extent the premises on which the system was based had changed nor to what extent management had become professionalized and accepting of constitutional standards. Alabama's recent experiment with chain gangs, however, suggests that such normative change as occurred was not deeply internalized.

Court intervention into conditions and practices at the Georgia State Penitentiary (GSP) in Reidsville followed a very different course than that in either Texas or Alabama. That course of this case, *Guthrie,* is charted by political scientist Bradley S. Chilton in *Prisons Under the Gavel: The Federal Court Takeover of Georgia Prisons.*[35] Located in an isolated rural area, the prison prior to litigation was insulated from external controls by both its economic self-sufficiency and the political connections of its wardens. Its profitability, however, derived as much, if not more, from the poor conditions in which the prisoners were kept as from the quantity or quality of its agricultural products. These conditions were challenged in 1972 when some 50 black inmates filed suit alleging racial segregation, racial discrimination in hiring, inadequate medical care, unsafe and unsanitary environmental conditions, lack of due process in disciplinary proceedings, arbitrary and unduly severe punishments, undue restrictions on mail and visitation. Ultimately these seven issues grew into a list of over 2500 items for compliance.

Guthrie never went to trial but was settled through a complex process of mediation and negotiation. At the time the suit was filed, correctional reform was already underway in Georgia. Governor Jimmy Carter had appointed the nationally known and highly regarded Ellis MacDougall as commissioner of corrections and he and his staff were reorganizing the department and seeking to gain control over GSP. Rather than defend the institution at trial, MacDougall met with Judge

Anthony Alaimo and agreed to attempt to mediate the issues. This effort failed, however, and was abandoned after several months. As preparations for trial began, Judge Alaimo appointed a special master, Marvin Pipkin, to conduct fact-finding for the court and to hold pre-trial hearings in an attempt to narrow the issues to be litigated. These proceedings dragged on for a number of years amidst a backdrop of racial violence in the prison which remained essentially unchanged.

One issue that had been resolved through mediation had been the need to desegregate the living and dining facilities. This was done in 1974. Almost immediately violence erupted and escalated continuously for four years as roving gangs of blacks and whites preyed upon each other and sought vengeance for past injuries. A good number of inmates were killed and scores more injured seriously. The prison was frequently locked down and at one point temporarily re-segregated by court order. Finally, in 1978 public outrage after a correctional officer was killed in a disturbance moved Governor George Busbee to release over a $1 million from his emergency fund for immediate improvements to security at the prison and to seek nearly $7 million for more long-term renovations and expansion.

Governor Busbee's actions were in response to the violence, not the court. At this time, however, Judge Alaimo approached the governor and his attorney-general to "'do what's right by cleaning up GSP'" and settling *Guthrie*.[36] Both officials pledged their cooperation and these pledges were honored by their successors. Thus the case changed direction once again, moving from trial preparation to negotiated settlements. Over the next several years, the special master presented the judge with a series of reports summarizing the facts on an issue. These reports then became the basis for negotiating consent decrees. In all some 61 consent decrees were entered between 1978 and 1984.

In 1979, Judge Alaimo appointed law professor Vince Nathan to monitor compliance. As he was to do later in Texas, Nathan kept a close watch at GSP and was seemingly uncompromising in his insistence that the provisions of the decrees be implemented. Administrators whose political connections in the legislature had heretofore ensured their survival resigned in the face of this close scrutiny and were replaced by others from outside the state, many with years of experience in the federal prison system. The prison administration was re-organized along the lines of unit management, resistance of lower staff slowly overcome and reforms gradually implemented. By 1985, the improvements were sufficient for Judge Alaimo to dismiss the case.

THIS STUDY: ITS PURPOSES, PLACE IN THE LITERATURE AND AN OVERVIEW

The foregoing review leads to the conclusion that judicial intervention into prisons has been a qualified success. Although it generally encounters significant resistance and is often accompanied by an upsurge in violence, in the end conditions improve to some degree, violence decreases and management practices become more rational. However, this conclusion is drawn from a comparatively small number of studies, many of which concern atypical cases selected for their high drama. With one exception, the most detailed case studies have all been done on systems in the old South. Until intervention these systems existed as separate and isolated social orders with the result that intervention took on something of the character of a moral crusade and, to the extent it was successful, resulted in the replacement of one social order with another founded on fundamentally different premises. Just as conclusions regarding the process and impact of school desegregation would be distorted if based solely on the experience in the South so also may conclusions regarding the parallel phenomenon of court-ordered prison reform.

A second limitation of the available evidence is that most of the research has concerned short-term consequences. Feeley and Hanson[37] speculate that innovations which initially encounter much resistance may, as in the case of the *Miranda* warnings and the police, become merely another aspect of the operational environment over the long haul. Equally true, of course, is Sturm's observation[38] that reforms are sometimes quickly abandoned once active monitoring ceases. Even the longitudinal case studies summarized above are, in some sense, subject to this limitation. Stateville, as we noted, slid back into crisis after

Jacobs completed his fieldwork. The studies of *Ruiz* were completed
and published before the case was dismissed. At the time the system
was still heavily reliant upon administrative segregation, and it was not
entirely clear how well rooted the bureaucratic transformation was. In
Alabama, the intervention itself was ended prematurely by a judge who
seemingly had little will for it, and the same may have been true in
Georgia where, Chilton notes, the judge grew tired of the process and
ended it rather abruptly.[39]

A third limitation derives from the focus of most of the research
on compliance with the provisions of court orders and how the courts
have sought to secure that compliance. There has been comparatively
less attention to the impact of intervention on the social organization of
the prison. Of the five case studies summarized above, for example,
only two offer detailed analyses and one of these was published twenty
years ago; the others provide only glimpses of the prisons seen through
the window of the courthouse.

Scholars continue to point to additional case studies of litigated
prison reform to provide a more representative body of knowledge
upon which to base conclusions about its processes and impact.[40] This
study addresses that need by providing an in-depth analysis of a major
court intervention into a prison system outside the South. No claim is
made that Rhode Island is in any way a representative state, only that
it is significantly different, culturally and socially, from those in the
South so as to provide an informative comparison. To take but one
example, Rhode Island traditionally has had a very different cultural
orientation toward crime than have southern states. It is one of only
twelve states to not have a capital punishment statute on the books, and
its correctional leaders firmly endorsed the rehabilitative ideal and the
new penology of the 1950s and 1960s. Another difference is the state's
strong labor tradition. Its correctional officers were among the first in
the country to unionize. Indeed, if the cultural prototype of the Texas
correctional officer might be said to be the lonesome cowboy on the
prairie, that of the Rhode Island correctional officer has been the
worker standing in solidarity with his fellow union members outside the
factory gate. A third difference is the small size of the state and its
prison system. Rhode Island is one of a handful of states in which the

jail system is operated by the state, thereby making it impossible for the state to diffuse the problem of prison overcrowding by foisting it onto county jails as typically happens in larger states. Moreover, Rhode Island's small size increases the importance of the media. Prison events that go unnoticed in larger states where prisons are spread through remote rural areas receive extensive coverage in Rhode Island, which has a newspaper with statewide circulation and three network-affiliated television stations that reach across the entire state. The central purpose of this study is to examine how these and other features of the prison's environment may have been related to the deterioration of conditions within the institution to the point where they were deemed to constitute cruel and unusual punishment, how they may have affected the response of officials to intervention, shaped its course and conditioned its impact.

A second aim of the study is to follow the course of a major intervention over its full history, from its starting point to its dismissal. Although the focus is on the case of *Palmigiano v. Garrahy,* I also consider several prior interventions. In addition to being essential to understanding the genesis and impact of *Palmigiano*, examination of these other cases permits a comparison of intervention on issues within the same system and thus serves to enrich our understanding of the process itself. Moreover, unlike the cases in Alabama and Georgia, termination of the court's jurisdiction in *Palmigiano* was carefully planned and scripted and accomplished to the satisfaction of all parties. Thus, this study is able to present a picture of a prison system after it has experienced prolonged litigation that all parties agree has been successful. To my knowledge, this stage in the process has not been treated previously, and it is my hope that its treatment here will prove useful in other cases as the parties attempt to develop exit scenarios.

Intervention in this case, as will become clear, became institution-building, and a third goal of this study is to trace the link between actions of the court and changes in the prison's formal and informal social organization. Unlike states such as Texas, Alabama or Georgia, whose sheer size may dictate that the researcher choose between a focus on the court or the prison, Rhode Island's small size and compact nature allow treatment of the court, the correctional system and the relationship between them. It thus affords an excellent opportunity to examine precisely how, if at all, court intervention fosters a more professionalized and bureaucratic organization and to weigh intervention against other influences that may be promoting or retarding such changes.

Related to this third goal is a fourth. There is a rich tradition of sociological research on the prison. Beginning with Clemmer's pioneering study of the Menard prison in Illinois during the Depression of the 1930s, two generations of scholars have charted the social organization of the American prison.[41] In the past this research was conducted in northern prisons. Today, however, in an interesting turn of events, the only recent studies of prison social organization by sociologists have been in the south.[42] Indeed, the last major study of a northern prison was that by Jacobs published nearly twenty years ago. With this study, I hope to extend and enrich the body of sociological research on which it is built and to update the social history of prisons in the north.

In keeping with this sociological tradition, the prison is here viewed as an organization in action, a natural system in dynamic interaction with its environment.[43] At a minimum organizations produce outputs valued by some sectors of their environments and are dependent upon their environments for the resources necessary to achieve their goals. Changes in the organizational environments—cultural, social, political, economic, technological—create pressures that may produce adaptive responses, disrupt internal structures or both. In turn, organizations react back upon their environments in ways that may disrupt features of it and/ or evoke adaptive changes.

Organizations have many and varied goals, stated and unstated. Moreover, organizational participants have their own goals: some of these they bring with them to the organization, while others are developed in the course of their participation within it. Effective attainment of organizational goals may be impeded by conflict among those goals or with other goals of participants. The situation is complicated further by virtue of the fact that, in acting to achieve goals, participants act with limited or bounded rationality: perceptions of the situation are clouded by past experiences; full information is never available; not all alternative courses of action are considered; the effects of a course of action are complex and never fully known. Greater clarity about goals, more information, better communication and improved division of labor expands the limits of rationality but never eliminates them.

Finally, organizations are about power. They are instruments designed to attain goals. Those in charge are endowed with authority and have access to a wide range of resources with which to mobilize and direct activity toward goal attainment. But claims to authority may not be recognized and even challenged; decisions may have quite unintended consequences; other participants may have different agendas and access to resources as well. Coalitions with others, both inside and outside the organization, form and dissolve; bargaining, negotiation and conflict are as much a part of organizational life as is hierarchical control.

Although the interpretative framework outlined above informs the following account, it has not been imposed upon it. Indeed part of its attraction is that it forces the observer to attend to the nuances of specific contexts and the importance of concrete detail. What is presented in the following chapters is thus,to the extent that such is possible, a natural history. The first two chapters deal with events prior to the *Palmigiano* decision. Chapter 2 begins with the formal adoption of the rehabilitative ideal in Rhode Island in 1956. Of major concern in this chapter is how this goal came to be defined and implemented amid the rapidly changing political climate of the 1960s, and the effects both of this goal and the political climate on the internal structure of authority and control. The chapter concludes with an examination of the first major court intervention and its immediate aftermath. Chapter 3 looks at the responses of the various groups within the prison system to the turmoil triggered by the foregoing events. It traces the emergence of unions among both the prisoners and the officers, the creation of a centralized department of corrections and analyzes how factors within and outside the prison system influenced the power struggle among these three groups.

The next four chapters deal with the intervention in *Palmigiano*. Chapter 4 details the trial, the order and the reaction of state officials to it. It documents the role of the court in restoring order to the troubled institution by bringing professional correctional leadership to the department and supporting that leadership as it struggled to reduce disorder and tension. Chapter 5 turns to the less dramatic issue of implementing the wide-sweeping decree between 1977 and 1985. Even with popular support and professional leadership, as we shall see, other features of the system's environment made implementation problematic. By 1985, however, the department was in substantial compliance with much of the order and had itself undergone significant change. Chapter 6 analyzes the threat posed to these gains by the rapidly increasing population of prisoners taken in the war on drugs. It focuses on the inability of the department, due to political constraints, to cope with the expanding population and the actions taken by the court to relieve population pressures. New facilities opened and population growth slowed in 1991. Chapter 7 charts the emergence and development of a highly rational and decentralized corporate management structure in the wake of the crisis. It concludes with a treatment of the dismissal of the *Palmigiano* case and the termination of court jurisdiction.

NOTES

1. *Palmigiano v. Garrahy,* 443 F. Supp. 956 (D. R.I. 1977), at 979.

2. Telephone interview, August 21, 1996.

3. *Ruffin v. Commonwealth,* 62 Va. 790 (1871).

4. James B. Jacobs, *New Perspectives on Prisons and Imprisonment* (Ithaca, NY: Cornell University Press, 1983), p. 35.

5. *Cooper v. Pate,* 378 U.S. 546 (1964).

6. *Wolff v. McDonnell,* 418 U.S. 539 (1974) at 555-56; 94 S. Ct. 2963 at 2974.

7. On corporal punishment and harm, see *Jackson v. Bishop*, 286 F. Supp. 804 (E.D. Ark., 1967), *aff'd,* 404 F.2d 571 (8th Cir. 1968); on medical care, see *Estelle v. Gamble,* 429 U.S. 97 (1976); on due process, see *Wolff v. McDonnell,* 418 U.S. 539 (1974); on censorship, see *Procunier v. Martinez,* 416 U.S. 396 (1974); on access to courts, see *Johnson v. Avery,* 393 U.S. 483 (1969), *Bounds v. Smith,* 430 U.S. 817 (1977).

8. *Holt v. Sarver,* 309 F. Supp. 362 (E.D. Ark. 1970); *Hutto v. Finney,* 437 U.S. 678 (1978).

9. *Pugh v. Locke*, 406 F. Supp 318 (M.D. Ala., 1976); *Palmigiano v. Garrahy*, 443 F. Supp. 956 (D. R.I. 1977); *Ruiz v. Estelle*, 503 F. Supp. 1265 (S.D. Tex., 1980).

10. *Bell v. Wolfish*, 441 U.S. 520 (1979) at 531.

11. *Rhodes v. Chapman*, 452 U.S. 337 (1981).

12. *Wilson v. Seiter*, 111 S.Ct. 2321 (1991).

13. *Farmer v. Brennan*, 114 S. Ct. 1970 (1994) at 1973.

14. *Turner v. Safley*, 482 U.S. 78 (1987); *O'Lone v. Shabbaz*, 482 U.S. 342 (1987).

15. *Sandin v. Conner*, 115 S. Ct. 2293 (1995) at 2299; on the lack of necessity of due process, absent a state-created liberty interest, in intrastate transfers to other facilities which are more aversive, see *Meachum v. Fano*, 427 U.S. 215 (1976).

16. Kathleen Maguire and Ann L. Pastore, eds., *Sourcebook of Criminal Justice Statistics 1994* (U.S. Dept of Justice, Bureau of Justice Statistics, Washington, D.C.: USGPO, 1995), Table 5.69, p. 489.

17. Jack E. Call, "Lower Court Treatment of Jail and Prison Overcrowding Cases: A Second Look," *Federal Probation* (June 1988): 34-41.

18. Susan P. Sturm, "The Legacy and Future of Corrections Litigation," *University of Pennsylvania Law Review* 142 (1993): 705 and fn. 316.

19. "Status Report: State Prisons and the Courts," (Washington, DC: National Prison Project of the ACLU Foundation, January 1995); George and Camille G. Camp, "Adult Corrections," *The Corrections Yearbook 1995* (South Salem, NY: Criminal Justice Institute, 1995), pp. 6-7.

20. Sturm; Malcolm M. Feeley and Roger A. Hanson, "The Impact of Judicial Intervention on Prisons: A Framework for Analysis and a Review of the Literature," in *Courts, Corrections and the Constitution*, ed. John J. DiIulio (New York: Oxford University Press, 1990), pp. 1-46.

21. Feeley and Hanson, pp. 19-21; Sturm, pp. 668-69; Others, however, disagree to some degree. Useem and Kimball, for example, following their detailed study of prison riots from 1971 through 1986—a study not cited in either of the two reviews—conclude that courts played a singular role in the process of administrative breakdown, the key factor they see as causing riots. Only courts can declare conditions unconstitutional and in so doing, especially in situations that were no worse than they had been for decades, they delegitimated prisons, stripping authorities of ideological support and setting in motion a chain of events that made conditions worse and eroded security. Nonetheless, they see court intervention as the well-nigh inevitable result of a broader social movement that has benefitted the majority of citizens and note

that any social, economic or political upheaval is likely to have a destablizing effect on administration. Good administration, by which they mean one capable of ensuring that prison conditions and practices are legitimate according to prevailing standards, is thus always problematic but is crucial in preventing violence and disorder. Bert Useem and Peter Kimball, *States of Siege: U.S. Prison Riots, 1971-1986* (New York: Oxford University Press, 1991), pp. 227-231.

22. James B. Jacobs, *Stateville: The Penitentiary in Mass Society* (Chicago, University of Chicago Press, 1977).

23. *Ruiz v. Estelle*, 503 F. Supp.

24. Steve J. Martin and Sheldon Ekland-Olson, *Texas Prisons: The Walls Came Tumbling Down* (Austin, TX: Texas Monthly Press, 1987).

25. Ben M. Crouch and James M. Marquart, *An Appeal to Justice: Litigated Reform of Texas Prisons* (Austin: University of Texas Press, 1989).

26. John J. DiIulio, *Governing Prisons: A Comparative Study of Correctional Management* (New York: The Free Press, 1987).

27. *Ibid.*, p. 12.

28. *Ibid.*, pp. 11-12, 209.

29. *Ibid.*, p. 229.

30. Max Weber, "Bureaucracy," in *From Max Weber: Essays in Sociology*, trans. H. H. Gerth and C. Wright Mills, 2d ed. (New York: Oxford University Press, 1946), p. 217.

31. Malcolm M. Feeley and Edward Rubin, "Prison Litigation and Bureaucratic Development," *Law and Social Inquiry* 17 (No.1, 1992): 141.

32. Lawrence W. Yackle, *Reform and Regret: The Story of Federal Judicial Involvement in the Alabama Prison System* (New York: Oxford University Press, 1989).

33. *Ibid.*, p. 105.

34. *Ibid.*, p. 259.

35. Bradley S. Chilton, *Prisons Under the Gavel: The Federal Court Takeover of Georgia Prisons* (Columbus, OH: Ohio State University Press, 1991).

36. *Ibid.*, p. 47.

37. Feeley and Hanson, pp. 22-23.

38. Sturm, pp. 673-74, 681.

39. Chilton, p. 71.

40. Feeley and Hanson, p. 42; James B. Jacobs, "Judicial Impact on Prison Reform," in *Punishment and Social Control: Essays in Honor of Sheldon*

L. Messinger, ed. Thomas G. Blomberg and Stanley Cohen (New York: Aldine De Gruyter, 1995), pp. 66-67.

41. Donald Clemmer, *The Prison Community*, 2 ed. (New York: Holt, Rinehart and Winston, 1958). The following are some of the major studies in this tradition up to 1975: Gresham M. Sykes, *The Society of Captives: A Study of a Maximum Security Prison* (Princeton, NJ: Princeton University Press, 1958); Rose Giallombardo, *Society of Women: A Study of a Women's Prison* (New York: John Wiley & Sons, 1966); David Street, Robert Vintner and Charles Perrow, *Organization for Treatment: A Comparative Study of Institutions for Juveniles* (New York: The Free Press, 1966); Leo Carroll, *Hacks, Blacks and Cons: Race Relations in a Maximum Security Prison* (Lexington, MA: Lexington Books, 1974).

42. Mark Colvin has recently published an illuminating study of the social organization of the New Mexico Penitentiary, but that study is restricted to events leading up to and including the 1980 riot. It does not treat the subsequent court intervention nor contemporary conditions. *The Penitentiary in Crisis: From Accommodation to Riot in New Mexico* (Albany, NY: SUNY Press, 1992).

43. For a more extended treatment of this model and a discussion of its limitations, see Charles Perrow, *Complex Organizations: A Critical Essay*, 3d ed. (New York: McGraw-Hill, Inc., 1986), chs 4, 5 and 8; W. Richard Scott, *Organizations: Rational, Natural and Open Systems*, 2 ed. (Englewood Cliffs, NJ: Prentice-Hall, Inc., 1987), chs. 2-5.

CHAPTER 2
Disruption

Reforming offenders has been a primary goal of incarceration at least since the invention of the penitentiary. The means by which reformers have sought to attain this goal, however, has changed dramatically since then. Early reformers emphasized isolation from the community, silence, religious exhortation and a strict regimen of hard work and severe discipline. But as the nineteenth century shaded into the twentieth religious exhortation gave way to therapeutic intervention. Strongly influenced by the then-emerging social sciences, a new penology was constructed on the assumption that criminality was the product of natural causes. These causes, it was asserted, could be discovered by applying the scientific method to the study of crime, and the knowledge thereby gained could be used to develop treatment programs. Each offender was to be diagnosed through detailed study and subjected to the appropriate prescribed treatment.[1]

This rehabilitative ideal, as it has been termed by Francis A. Allen,[2] was reflected in virtually every criminal justice innovation of the first half of the twentieth century: presentence reports, probation, indeterminate sentences, the classification of inmates, parole and a separate system of juvenile justice. Rothman's brilliant analysis makes clear,[3] however, that such widespread acceptance of the rehabilitative ideal was due more to the increased discretionary power it accorded officials and their capacity to use that discretion for their own mundane purposes than to any heartfelt commitment to rehabilitating offenders. Thus, while the framework of a therapeutic state had been created in the first two decades of the twentieth century, by mid-century that framework remained virtually devoid of substance.[4]

Failure to more fully implement rehabilitative programs was ascribed to the Great Depression of the 1930s and the two world wars which had sapped much of the nation's resources, and the rehabilitative ideal continued to dominate reformist thinking and action at mid-century. Indeed, the optimism and confidence generated by victory in World War II and post-war prosperity strengthened commitment to it. A wave of prison riots in the early 1950s—40 occurring over 18 months beginning in 1952—were used to buttress arguments for more treatment-oriented programs. To emphasize its commitment to rehabilitation, the American Prison Association in 1954 changed its name to the American Correctional Association and advocated that prisons be redesignated "correctional institutions."[5]

In line with this renewed emphasis on rehabilitation, the Rhode Island State Prison became the Adult Correctional Institutions (ACI) in 1956. As we shall see, measured by the state's commitment of resources, this change was more symbol than substance. Nonetheless, it dramatically altered the nature of the institution, providing greater freedoms, privileges and power to inmates, disrupting the old order, and igniting a wave of violence.

IMPLEMENTATION OF THE REHABILITATIVE IDEAL

In many respects, Rhode Island was fertile soil in which to plant the seeds of the rehabilitative ideal in the mid-1950s. From the time of its foundation with the religious dissent of Roger Williams and Anne Hutchinson from the orthodoxy of Massachusetts Puritanism, it had developed and maintained a strong tradition of political and economic liberalism. Since the 1930s depression, state government had been dominated by New Deal Democrats. Moreover, its rate of common crime was low by national standards; the homicide rate for 1955, for example, was 0.7 per 100,000—15 percent of the national rate.[6] The prison population was small, numbering less than 500 in a typical year (see Table 1, Appendix), and unlike most states, the prison was not in a remote area but only a short drive from the state's major population center.

Rhode Island's correctional institutions are situated in a single complex in Cranston about seven miles south of the capital city,

Providence. Sitting on a hill, so close to an interstate highway that commuters can see the guards in the towers at each corner of the double barbed-wire fence surrounding the yard, is what has recently become the Special Needs Unit. The main facility of this unit is a long and narrow red brick building, three stories high, in which inmates are housed in dormitories. Constructed in the early 1930s to accommodate the burgeoning population resulting from the enforcement of prohibition laws, it was originally called the Men's Reformatory and intended to house youthful offenders.

Visible in the distance from the highway, about one-half mile west of the reformatory, is a cupola atop the cell blocks which form the front wall of "Old Max," what was formerly the R. I. State Prison. This Auburn-style facility, constructed between 1874 and 1878[7] with massive slabs of gray granite, resembles a decaying medieval castle. The original structure contained four interior cell blocks of three tiers each. Three of these blocks were reserved for sentenced felons while the northernmost block was the Providence County Jail. A fifth cell block, containing 198 cells, was added on the south side in 1924. A 20 foot wall extending 600 feet back from the cell blocks on either side encloses within the yard an industrial building and several shops.[8]

Today the correctional complex includes six other facilities, all in close proximity to the old state prison and men's reformatory, none of which existed in 1956 when the Adult Correctional Institutions was created. No new institutions were authorized at the time. The act of creation was strictly administrative; the legislation simply decreed that the State Prison, the Men's Reformatory and the state's county jails were henceforth to be the Adult Correctional Institutions charged with the "most efficient possible rehabilitation of individual prisoners" consistent with public safety.[9] The jails, which had been the object of sharp criticism for years, were thereby removed from the control of the county sheriffs. Shortly after passage of the bill, three of the state's five county jails were closed and their functions centralized at the ACI.[10]

To effect the rehabilitation of prisoners, the law mandated the establishment of a receiving and orientation unit in which all new prisoners were to be segregated while undergoing a battery of tests to assess their needs, a classification unit to collect and record the data, a classification board to review the data and establish a rehabilitation program for each prisoner and an educational and vocational training unit. Inmates regarded as high risk were to be assigned to the old state prison, now designated Maximum Security, while those seen to be lesser risks were to be assigned to the old reformatory, now Medium/Minimum security. And guards became correctional officers.

Companion legislation appropriated over $500,000 for a variety of improvements and renovations. Two new buildings were to be constructed in Maximum Security, a new infirmary and a combination classroom/indoor recreation building. Security was to be upgraded by the installation of a new control center in Maximum Security, the construction of an additional guard tower and a perimeter fence.[11]

The legislation creating the ACI reflected recommendations made by James V. Bennett, legendary director of the Federal Bureau of Prisons and a native Rhode Islander, following a study he made of the state's institutions in 1955. Bennett was also instrumental in finding a warden for the newly-designated correctional institutions, Thomas J. Gough. Gough had been a member of the first class in the federal prison officers school in 1930 and served eleven years as a correctional officer. For the 15 years prior to his retirement from the federal service he had been an associate warden of the Federal Penitentiary at Atlanta. A diminutive man with flowing white hair and an easy smile, Gough was described in a press release from Atlanta at the time of his appointment as "a devoutly religious man who believes there would be no need for prisons if the people in them lived according to their professed faith."[12]

Within two weeks of his arrival, Gough had begun writing policy and procedures along the lines of those in the Federal Bureau and had established a 13-week retraining course for all correctional officers with much of the instruction being given by himself. Attendance was required of all officers but made palatable by the prospect of higher pay upon completion.[13] Later that year a director of classification was appointed and procedures developed to implement the classification program. A supervisor of education was also hired, and a night school using part-time teachers was established and made compulsory for all inmates with less than a fifth grade education. Bids were let and construction started on the education/recreation building and some of the enhancements to security which had been recommended by Bennett.

Prison reform in Rhode Island seemed to be off to a good start. Unfortunately, Warden Gough did not live to see it through. On the morning of April 26, 1957 he suffered a cerebral hemorrhage while working at his desk and died shortly thereafter. Gough's superior, Harold V. Langlois, who had been the assistant director for correctional services in the Department of Social Welfare since 1951, assumed the position of warden. Prior to being appointed assistant director, Langlois had served as an FBI agent for 10 years. Langlois also had a master's degree in psychiatric social work and advocated a rehabilitative approach to corrections. Tall, handsome, and articulate he had "a mystique about him" which he cultivated and used to good advantage.[14] He was an active member of the American Correctional Association (ACA), and in 1964 he was elected President of the ACA succeeding the renowned Donald Clemmer.[15]

In the year following Langlois's appointment, the number of civilian employees at the ACI grew by over two-thirds (see Figure 2.1)[16] and a number of new programs were instituted. A psychiatrist and a clinical psychologist were retained on a part-time basis to assist in the classification process and to conduct group therapy. Classification counselors and teachers were hired, and with the completion of the education/recreation building in Old Max at the end of 1957—the first new construction in the unit in 50 years—the education program was expanded to include high school as well as elementary school. Classes were conducted in the evening, and the work day was shortened. Inmates who chose not to attend school were no longer confined to their cells after dinner. A television was placed in each cell block and dormitory unit. Pool, ping-pong, handball and weight-lifting were available in the basement gym of the education/recreation building during the winter. Basketball, softball and baseball could be played outdoors on regulation courts and fields in the summer. Uniforms and marching in lines were abolished.

These changes were widely publicized by Langlois in speeches to

Figure 2.1 Number of Uniformed and Civilian Staff, 1956-1965

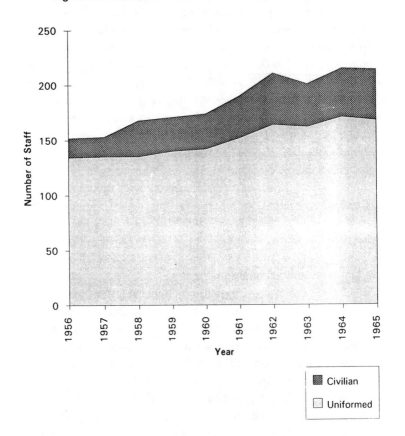

community groups, radio interviews and in a series of newspaper articles. One reporter invited to tour Old Max early in the summer of 1958 described the yard as "look[ing] like a public park" on a Saturday or Sunday afternoon.

> At one corner a game of baseball goes on; in another a game of boccie [an Italian game like horseshoes but played with balls]. Some inmates toss horseshoes. Others sit on benches along the grassy sections, basking in the sun to darken the prison pallor, playing checkers, or just talking about whatever men talk about when locked inside the high, gray walls.[17]

Following the outbreak of a severe riot at the nearby Concord (MA) Reformatory in April 1959, Langlois was asked about the possibility of a riot at the ACI. He "did not want to tempt fate by ruling it out altogether," Langlois replied, but he saw it "as only a remote possibility . . . because the climate [at the ACI] is not right for trouble."[18]

In truth, the change in climate brought about by increased recreation was more dramatic than were the changes in substantive rehabilitation programs. As can be seen in Figure 2.1, following the two-thirds increase in the number of civilian positions in 1957-58, the civilian staff grew at about the same rate as the uniformed staff. From 1958 to 1965, only about one-quarter of the increase in staff positions were civilian positions. Moreover, as can be seen in Table 1 of the Appendix, more than half of the civilian positions added during this period were managerial or clerical support, having little if any relation to treatment. Data on expenditures during this period tell essentially the same story. As shown in Figure 2.2 expenditures for salaries and benefits doubled from 1956 through 1965, going from about $2.6 million to about $5.3 million in 1990 dollars. However, the operating budget changed virtually not all, hovering at about $1 million. Thus, while a small number of treatment staff were added, about 10 in all, there appears to have been little, if any, increase in funding for treatment programs.

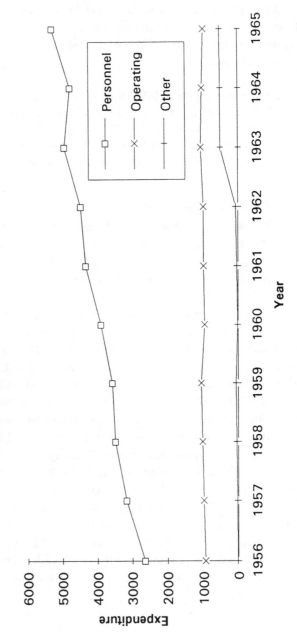

Figure 2.2 ACI Expenditures, 1956-1965 (in 1990 dollars)

Impact of Reforms on Security

Many of the changes made by Langlois were introduced with neither planning nor sensitivity to the difficulties they might pose for officers. Where Gough had moved slowly and deliberately, consulting with the deputy wardens and putting all changes in writing, Langlois implemented changes abruptly and swiftly and often by word of mouth. In a 1971 interview, a "lifer" sentenced in 1954, vividly recalled the following incident.

> We used to line up to march back and forth to work and the dining hall and to our "rooms." When we lined up, there was no smoking, no talking and you had to have your jacket on, buttoned to the neck, and your hat square on your head. I remember he [Langlois] came in the yard one day with two civilians and a captain. He yelled to us "Do you guys want to wear those hats?", and we all yelled "No." "Then throw them out in the yard," he said, and we all did. That was the end of the hats.[19]

In similar fashion over the next few years, Warden Langlois did away with buttoning jackets to the neck, formations in the yard, marching in lines and, eventually, even uniforms.

Three months after Warden Langlois's statement that a riot at the ACI was only a remote possibility, trouble came in another form. Near midnight on July 31, 1959, three extremely dangerous inmates, using homemade keys, let themselves out of their cells in the hospital's segregation unit where they were being held for psychiatric observation and used a grappling hook and rope taken from the machine shop to escape over the wall. It was a week before they were recaptured following the largest manhunt in Rhode Island's history.[20]

In response to public criticism, Henry Davis, an official of the Federal Bureau of Prisons, was brought in to study the institution and made a number of recommendations to improve security, including the reinstitution of a training program for correctional officers, the one begun under Gough having apparently lapsed. However, Davis was most impressed with the "progressive character of the program," and inclined to see the obvious lapses in security as the result of complacency which sometimes develops when programs are well run.[21]

Two years later questions about security rose again. In March 1961 two medium-security inmates, using 18-inch needles from the upholstery shop to overcome a guard and take his keys, escaped with handguns and ammunition taken from the prison's arsenal.[22] Later that same year, an escape from Maximum Security was foiled when a window bar was found to have been sawn. Initial reports praised guards for their diligence and alertness, but, as the full story became known, it seemed that diligence and alertness had only narrowly prevented what carelessness and laxity had encouraged.[23] The deputy warden in charge of Maximum Security was dismissed for failure to properly supervise his subordinates; two officers were officially reprimanded and assigned to new duties, and Warden Langlois was forced to admit publicly that elementary measures basic to competent prison administration had to be "reaffirmed" at the ACI.[24]

A grand jury returning indictments against the foiled escapists recommended a legislative investigation of conditions at the institution. Once again the state requested the assistance of the Federal Bureau of Prisons. Noah L. Alldrege, a deputy director of the Bureau, conducted a week-long study and made a number of recommendations to improve physical security. As Davis had done two years earlier, however, Alldrege went out of his way to praise Langlois as a "progressive, well-informed administrator" and to suggest that Rhode Island's officials had a tendency to exaggerate weaknesses in the system.[25] The physical improvements Alldrege recommended, outside lighting and the reconstruction of three guard towers, were made with funds from a bond issue in 1962. For several years thereafter, the ACI was again calm.

THE COLLABORATIVE INSTITUTION

As cities were swept by civil disorder in the early 1960s, "crime in the streets" emerged as a major political issue. In 1965 President Lyndon Johnson, established the President's Commission on Law Enforcement and the Administration of Justice, charging it to study all aspects of the crime problem and to report its findings and recommendations the following year. In its report the Commission made the following observation about past models of corrections and what it saw to be the future.

> Correction of offenders has also labored under what is coming to be seen as a fundamental deficiency in approach. All of the past phases in the evolution of corrections accounted for criminal and delinquent behavior primarily on the basis of some form of defect within the individual offender. . . . Until recently reformers have tended to ignore that crime and delinquency are symptoms of disorganization of the community as well as of individual personalities. . . . [26]

Within this new conception of rehabilitation, the salient feature of offenders was their social disadvantage, not their psychological disability. The Commission recommended that emphasis be placed on community-based corrections. Probation should be greatly expanded, probation workers trained in mobilizing and coordinating community resources for their clients and much greater use made of half-way houses. New institutions should be small, designed to approximate a normal residential facility and located close to or within the community from which its residents are drawn.[27] Even close custody institutions should contribute to the reintegration of offenders into the community by "the establishment of a collaborative regime in which staff and inmates work together toward rehabilitative goals, and unnecessary conflict between the two is avoided."[28]

The Task Force on Corrections went into some detail about what it meant by a collaborative institution. In addition to the standard fare of education, vocational training and counseling, the Task Force recommended that correctional officers be trained in counseling and function as part of unit teams along with social workers; that mass treatment be ended and life in the institution be kept as close as possible to life outside the walls with inmates given considerable autonomy and discretion in such matters as waking, sleeping, food, clothing; that rules be kept to the absolute minimum essential for security and order; that inmates be involved in limited ways in the administration of the institution; that community organizations be invited to establish rehabilitative programs in institutions; and that isolation from the community be further decreased through extensive use of furloughs and work/study release.[29]

As President of the American Correctional Association in 1965-66, Warden Langlois was well acquainted with the new orthodoxy. Indeed, many of the President's Commission's recommendations for a collaborative institution might have been taken out of a book written by Langlois himself. Returning from a tour of European prisons in 1965, he began advocating the establishment of a pre-release center to house inmates who would be allowed to work in the community and furloughs for those eligible for parole. The following year a work release bill was enacted and a work release program for inmates who had completed one-sixth of their sentences was begun in June 1966.[30] That same year, he revised the ACI's *Inmate Guide*, and in its "Preface" wrote of the institution as a "'home away from home'" which has a "'way of doing things' . . . that exists for the common good of the greatest number" but noting that "we purposefully . . . refrained from listing a series of 'do's' and 'don'ts' because . . . no one answer covers all situations or circumstances."[31]

Visits were increased from one a week to one per day, and inmates were permitted to have comforts such as televisions in their cells. An arts guild was initiated under the tutelage of a local volunteer artist, and a grant from a local foundation permitted expansion of the recreation program. Concerts spanning the range of music from classical through jazz and rock—the latter sometimes featuring "go-go" girls—were held several times each summer in the yard. Groups such as Alcoholics Anonymous were invited to set up chapters in the prison, and inmates were encouraged to take charge of their rehabilitation themselves. For example, a prisoner who had attended Daytop Village in New York was allowed to conduct weekly group sessions with inmates who had substance abuse problems. Education classes at all levels were now scheduled in the day so that an inmate could choose to go to school instead of work, and students from nearby universities were enlisted to tutor inmates in the evening.[32]

Although he had staunchly refused to consider any form of inmate self-government in the past, Langlois now permitted the formation of several inmate voluntary associations. Prominent among these organizations was a chapter of the state Junior Chamber of Commerce established in 1966 with the help of a chapter in a nearby town. The idea behind the JayCees was to facilitate the rehabilitation of inmates by involving them in activities of benefit to their community— the prison—and providing them with legitimate role models who might also assist them upon their release. The chapter soon embarked on a campaign to secure books for the prison library and to construct a new visiting room. Funds were raised through a canteen they were permitted to operate in one cell block. These funds also subsidized Christmas parties, family days, functions for retarded and handicapped children and an early version of "scared straight"[33] in which inmates provided guidance to juveniles on probation. At the conclusion of its first year, the prison chapter was recognized at the annual awards dinner as "the most successful first year chapter" in the history of the state organization.[34]

A bi-monthly prisoner newspaper, *The Challenge*, was started in August 1967.[35] Although there had been several prisoner papers in the past, these had circulated only among the prisoners and had been short lived due to conflicts over censorship. *The Challenge*, however, was operated under the supervision of a member of the Governor's Advisory Committee on Social Welfare and was to be censored by the administration only for patently slanderous or inflammatory statements. The paper had 2200 subscribers around the state. Its staff worked full-time researching legal and penal developments around the country, reporting on these and editorializing on needed changes in the state's laws and correctional establishment.

Seeds of Conflict

The organizations provided means for articulating inmate discontent and pressuring for change. Together the JayCees and *The Challenge* in 1968 initiated a Legislative Forum, a dinner to which state legislators were invited and at which prisoners presented proposals for legislative enactment. In addition to annual forums, the inmates were able to call upon the influence of their sponsors to arrange periodic private meetings to lobby members of the governor's staff and legislators. At the first forum, they proposed that time served awaiting trial be subtracted from the time to be served on the sentence and that inmates convicted of violent crimes be eligible for work release. Both measures were passed the following year. In 1970, they were successful in having the time to be served before "lifers" could be paroled reduced from 20 to 10 years.[36]

In February 1969, an entire issue of the *Providence Journal's* Sunday Magazine was devoted to the prison, featuring articles highly critical of prison conditions written by *The Challenge* staff.[37] The inmate authors complained of poor food but even more of inadequate services and programs. Newly admitted prisoners in admission and orientation, they claimed, spent nearly thirty days in their cells but saw a classification counselor for only an hour during that time and met the classification board for only several minutes. A large part of every day, for most inmates, was spent merely "hanging out" in the shops, the wings, the gym or the yard. The most active part of the day, especially in good weather, was the late afternoon or early evening when they could participate in the extensive recreation program. Indeed, they asserted that more was spent on referees and umpires than on educational and psychological services.

As shown in Figure 2.3, the number of civilian positions increased from 46 to 52 between 1965 and 1969. However, only some 16 of these were professional positions (cf. Table 2, Appendix) and at any given time several of these were vacant. In 1966 the Rhode Island Medical Society had investigated complaints of inadequate medical care and found them to be baseless but warned of serious understaffing.[38] Two years later, nonetheless, the ACI was without the services of a full-time physician, psychiatrist or psychologist, and three of the five authorized positions for nurses remained unfilled.[39] Understaffing was true in other areas as well. In the fiscal year ending in June 1969, several positions for classification counselors and teachers were unfilled. Moreover, operating losses had forced the closing of several prison industries in the mid-1960s, aggravating an already serious unemployment problem.[40]

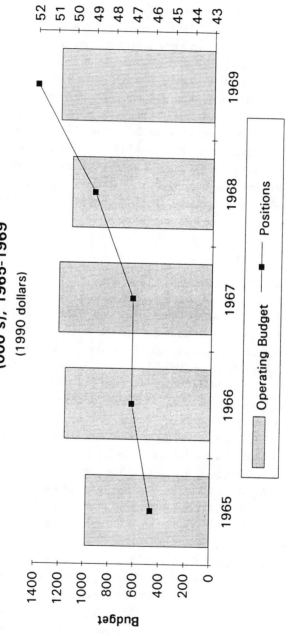

Figure 2.3 Number of Civilian Positions and Operating Budget (000's), 1965-1969

(1990 dollars)

In an effort to find funds to divert to more therapeutic uses, Warden Langlois in 1968 proposed to close the medium security facility.[41] With the declining population, the facility housed only 39 prisoners. Nearly half of these, the warden believed, could safely be placed in a new work release cottage to be built with part of the savings realized from the closing, and the remainder would be transferred to the maximum security facility but housed in a separate cell block. Some of the 32 officers employed in the unit would be reassigned to fill 13 existing vacancies; the rest would be let go. He estimated that the move would save about $250,000 a year which could be used to hire a psychologist, social workers and teachers and generally improve rehabilitative programs. The plan, however, encountered bitter opposition from the officers' union.

Unionization

Rhode Island's correctional officers are, for the most part, the children and grandchildren of European immigrants who had come to the state to work in its factories and textile mills where they labored under conditions so oppressive that it was said that a worker in the presence of an overseer "scarcely dared say that his soul was his own."[42] Throughout the latter half of the nineteenth century and the first half of the twentieth, Rhode Island had been a hotbed of labor conflict as workers organized to secure higher wages, safer conditions and greater control over the workplace. The unions achieved notable success during World War II, but over the next two decades the mills and factories moved south. Rather than follow their jobs south, many workers chose to enter employment in the expanding public sector where they sought to employ the same tactics that had been successful in the mills and factories. Rhode Island was in the vanguard of public employee unionism. State employees gained the right to organize in 1958 and the right to bargain collectively in 1966.[43]

The correctional officers at the ACI formed Local 114 within Council 70 of the American Federation of State, County and Municipal Employees (AFSCME). In their first round of collective bargaining in 1966, the officers had been able to win a pay raise considerably greater than that accorded other state employees.[44] Faced with the elimination of jobs by the closing of Medium Security in 1968, they again displayed their strength. Although unable to prevent the closing, they were able to put the issue off for at least a year through separate legislation, enacted over the governor's veto, to establish a commission to study its feasibility.[45] Before the commission reported its findings, an upsurge in the inmate population and major disturbances at the ACI made the matter moot. But it was clear that the officers' union was a political force of considerable power.

Racial Conflict

Prior to 1965, the black inmates at the ACI appear to have been a docile group, constituting only some 15 percent of the population. But while the inmate population as a whole declined through the 1960s, the percentage who were African American increased dramatically, to almost 25 percent in 1969.[46] Moreover, they became a more solidary group as the civil rights and black power movements, not to mention the violence which swept America's cities in the middle of the decade, sparked an awareness of their heritage and triggered their sense of injustice. Racial conflict first emerged in the inmate organization during the summer of 1968. Editors of *The Challenge* thought articles written by black staff inflammatory and refused to publish them, and the black vice-president of the "JayCees" was impeached soon after he succeeded to the presidency following the parole of a popular white leader.

Following the latter incident, black inmates received permission from the warden to form their own organization to study black history and culture. It was named the Bag of Solid Souls, or BOSS, which in the vernacular of the 1960s meant first class or first rate. Almost immediately, the organization began to petition to wear African-style haircuts, clothing and jewelry, to have "soul" food included on the prison menu, and to change somewhat the complexion of the all-white prison administration and parole board. Langlois appears to have been unresponsive to these requests but when the organization requested to have a dance at which they would be allowed to wear African clothing and the guards would be in civilian suits, he called a meeting to discuss with them the direction the organization was taking.

Arriving late for the meeting, Warden Langlois took exception to the seating arrangements which had him in the center of a horseshoe formed by the organization's leaders and a sergeant-at-arms standing behind him. Protesting that "this is not Nazi Germany," he told those standing next to him to sit down and demanded to sit next to the president at the head table. At this, all the inmates walked out of the room with Warden Langlois yelling after them that the organization was disbanded.

Later that day, the organization held another meeting in the library of the education building. When informed of it, Langlois interpreted their action as mutiny and ordered the gate to the building be locked and all other prisoners be placed in their cells immediately. Hearing the buzzers announcing the lockup, finding themselves locked in the building and armed officers at the gates, the inmates began breaking up furniture to arm themselves and to build a barricade. When the warden tried to convince them to give up before the situation got too out of hand, he was spit upon and struck with a billiard cue. He thereupon summoned the state police who surrounded the building and filled it and the connecting cell block with tear gas until the inmates surrendered.

Intense racial conflict among inmates continued for the next six months. In retaliation for what was perceived as a "bullshit beef," white inmates set fire to the cells of five BOSS leaders who were in segregation, destroying their belongings. These inmates were placed in segregation along with those who had been involved in the riot. Tension built as racial epithets were hurled back and forth twenty-four hours a day. On April 4, about 15 white inmates returning from outside recreation stormed across the cell block and assaulted four black inmates doing maintenance work. Several prisoners and officers were injured, and one white prisoner was hospitalized in critical condition.

The April incident ended overt conflict of a specifically racial nature. Black inmate leaders were transferred to a segregation unit in Medium Security while several white leaders were transferred out of state. The race war in segregation, however, triggered disorder throughout the prison. From mid-April through the end of May 1969, the *Journal* contained at least one story a week reporting a sit-down strike, a fight or a fire. Then, on May 23, three inmates set fire to the roof of one of the cell blocks in Maximum Security. The blaze raged for several hours before being brought under control, causing over $1.5 million (in 1969 dollars) in damage and necessitating the transfer of 115 prisoners, most of whom were moved to the underutilized medium security building. Within two weeks of the fire, six of the transferred inmates, all serving long sentences, escaped.

Warden Langlois Resigns

Frank Licht, a Democrat who had been labor lawyer and then a judge of the Superior Court, had been sworn in as governor just two weeks before the BOSS riot in January 1969. Faced with what was clearly a major racial problem in an institution which each day seemed to grow more out of control, he appointed a panel of inquiry. The panel was chaired by the recently retired senior partner of a prominent Providence law firm, William H. Edwards and composed mainly of university and social service administrators. Governor Licht charged the commission with investigating the causes of the riot and "all other matters connected therewith."[47]

In its report, the Edwards Commission commended Warden Langlois for permitting the formation of BOSS and recommended that it be continued, but it chided the warden for not monitoring it adequately. Further, in what was the first general criticism of Langlois, the Commission found that "administratively . . . the ACI at the present time is in serious difficulty." Not only are treatment and education programs not what they should be, the Commission reported, but "every echelon of officials seems dissatisfied . . . rules may be capriciously changed without notice. . . . and disseminated only by the grapevine" and relations among the higher level officials are characterized by "competitive hostility . . . infighting and dissension." As a result of administrative confusion and conflict "the atmosphere of the ACI . . . in respect to inmates is too often one of do-nothing lethargy."[48]

The Edwards' Commission had only two months to complete its work and was almost apologetic for what it saw as its superficial treatment of very deep and complex problems. It recommended further study by someone with greater expertise. Once again James V. Bennett, now retired from his position as director of the Federal Bureau of Prisons, was called upon to investigate prison conditions in his native state.

Bennett's findings agreed in the main with those of the Edwards' Commission, but he went further. In addition to inadequate programs, he expressed concern about political patronage in the hiring and promotion of personnel, undue union influence in managerial decisions, the need for better pay and pension benefits to attract more qualified personnel, a proliferation of unnecessary posts for guards but inadequate attention to basic elements of security and a deteriorating physical plant.[49] His criticism of Warden Langlois was only thinly veiled.

> Many of the problems . . . that now beset the institution are the
> result of a policy of indecision and drift. They have not been dealt
> with constructively over a considerable period of time.[50]

On the day the Bennett report was released to the press, the new administration asked for and received Warden Langlois's resignation.

THE FIRST COURT INTERVENTION

Among the major weapons in President Lyndon Johnson's "war on poverty" in the mid-1960s were local community-action programs. Intended to coordinate and channel all available resources to strike at poverty in the streets of the inner city, these programs were set up outside established state and local political structures to ensure the resources reached the target populations. The programs were also designed to enable the urban poor to pressure local governments into providing more services and to challenge laws and policies affecting the poor. To effect the latter objective, a Legal Services Division was established within the Office of Economic Opportunity to institute and coordinate neighborhood legal services projects. By 1968, some 250 legal services projects operated about 850 offices staffed by approximately 1800 attorneys around the country.[51] One of these was in Rhode Island, and it was to this organization that a group of ACI inmates turned in 1969 to challenge living conditions in the segregation unit to which they were confined.

The fire on May 23, 1969 had destroyed nearly two-thirds of the roof of Old Max making one whole cell block—some 122 cells—uninhabitable. Due to problems in letting the bids and labor problems once they were let, repairs did not begin until August and were not completed until late in the fall. In the interim, living conditions in the facility deteriorated, sparking a number of protests by inmates. Most of these disruptions were non-violent sit-down strikes of short duration and provoked little response from authorities. Then on September 24, about two-thirds of the 200 inmates remaining in the maximum unit refused to go to work. The shops were closed for several days, and all 200 were locked in their cells.[52]

Although the work stoppage seems to have been little different from other prisoner demonstrations over the past several months, three months of organized protest was too much disruption for interim warden, John F. Sharkey, who had publicly declared the restoration of order and the rebuilding of staff morale to be his highest priorities.[53] In consultation with his superior officers, Sharkey selected 23 inmates whom he believed were leading the demonstrations and placed them in segregation. Within a few days the prison returned to a normal routine, but the conflict had merely been moved backstage. Those placed in the segregation unit protested what they regarded as arbitrary and capricious punishment by throwing food and excrement out of their cells. In response, officers refused to let the inmates out of their cells to exercise or shower. Neither guards nor inmates would clean the mess and shortly the unit posed a serious health hazard to the entire prison population.

On a Saturday evening on Columbus Day weekend, Ira Schreiber, legal counsel for the Department of Social Welfare, and John Donahue of R.I. Legal Services telephoned U. S. District Court Judge Raymond J. Pettine at his home to inform him of the situation at the prison, a situation they saw as requiring immediate action. Judge Pettine, upon hearing their description, agreed with their assessment and scheduled a hearing for Monday afternoon. Thinking that the appearance of the prisoners was "perhaps the best evidence of what was going on down there," he directed that the petitioners appear at the hearing in exactly the condition they were presently in their cells.[54] Having served 13 years as an assistant attorney general for the state and 5 years as U. S. Attorney before being appointed to the bench by President Johnson in 1966, Judge Pettine was familiar with the prison. But he was unprepared for what greeted him in the courtroom on that Columbus Day afternoon. "It was shocking, absolutely appalling. It made me sick." Indeed, so filthy were the prisoners, that Judge Pettine felt compelled to order the entire courtroom—tables, microphones and benches— thoroughly cleaned with disinfectant before its next use.[55]

Judge Pettine immediately entered a temporary order requiring prison officials to provide the plaintiff prisoners with showers and clean clothing, to permit them outdoor exercise and access to religious services. Then he began several days of hearings and negotiations during which it became clear that the suit involved serious questions of due process of law in addition to the Eighth Amendment claims raised initially. Given the court's assurance that it would consider the procedural issue, the plaintiffs agreed to clean up the food and excrement and a continuance was granted so that plaintiff's attorneys could prepare the broader challenge to the ACI's disciplinary and classification procedures.[56]

Courts at the time were just beginning to investigate abuses of prison disciplinary process. Sensing the importance of the case, William Bennett Turner of the NAACP Legal Defense Fund and a renowned prisoners' rights attorney entered the case as chief counsel for the plaintiffs. An amended complaint alleging a class action on behalf of all prisoners at the ACI was filed in mid-December and a trial date set for January. However, Judge Pettine directed the parties to attempt to negotiate a consent decree prior to trial. Early in January the parties submitted a draft of proposed disciplinary and classification procedures for the court's review. Following modifications in light of both expert and inmate reaction, the rules were entered as an interim order with the court retaining jurisdiction for 18 months in order to revise the rules as experience with them might dictate. A final decree incorporating substantial modifications to the regulations was entered in April 1972.[57]

The "Morris Rules," as they are known, define four categories into which inmates are classified and specify in some detail the privileges and constraints of each category.[58] Reclassification hearings are to be held at periodic intervals, the length of time permitted being in inverse relation to the deprivations imposed. The rules detail how classification hearings are to be conducted and what written records are to be maintained. With respect to disciplinary action, the rules set forth five mandatory steps: a written charge, investigation and review by a superior officer, a hearing before a disciplinary board, administrative review, and maintenance of a written record. Each of these steps is defined in detail, and the rules also contain a listing of inmate conduct subject to disciplinary action and the actions which may be taken by a disciplinary board.

Judge Pettine arranged for the implementation of the "Morris Rules" to be evaluated by a team of researchers from the Harvard Law School's Center for Criminal Justice. These researchers concluded that, at least during the first six months of implementation, "the effectiveness of the procedural due process model at the ACI was critically limited" and "did not meet the expectations of the court."[59] In the researchers' view, the flawed implementation was due, for the most part, to an almost inherent incompatibility of a due process model with the multiple purposes of imprisonment and the closed nature of the prison setting. It was also in part due, they believed, to staff resentment at not being involved in the development of the decree, the absence of any training of the staff in its provisions and staff objections to certain provisions.[60]

If anything, the researchers underestimated the level of staff resentment. It was not only the custodial staff who were resentful but also the top administrators. Sharkey and his superior, Anthony Travisono, felt the decree had been forced upon them. Sharkey saw the decree as an undue infringement on the discretionary power he needed to maintain discipline; Travisono thought it unduly restricted staff authority to make individualized decisions regarding treatment. Thus, for different reasons both men were convinced that they would be "giving away the ship" by accepting any agreement extending rights of due process to inmates and wanted to go to trial. However, they were

ordered to settle the case by Governor Licht who, as a former judge
and political liberal, felt personally embarrassed by it. Both because of
their strong feelings against what was being negotiated and because they
felt their participation unwelcome, neither Sharkey nor Travisono
participated to any great extent in the negotiations which were
conducted by almost solely by the state's and the plaintiffs' attorneys.[61]

In an effort to gain staff cooperation, Judge Pettine directed the
Department of Social Welfare's legal counsel to conduct staff training
sessions and went himself to the prison to meet with the correctional
officers. Judge Pettine, who has the manner and bearing of an Old
World gentleman and whose dress and grooming are such that, as a
journalist recently observed, he "looks less formal with his robe on,"[62]
was ill at ease as he addressed the angry men in gray. He told them of
his childhood on America Street in the heart of Providence's Italian
American ghetto, of his years as a prosecutor, of how these experiences
made him sympathetic to the difficult job with which they, the officers,
were faced. He spoke of the evolution of prison law and the importance
of this particular case, calling for their cooperation in a challenging
experiment. All he asked from them, he emphasized, was a good faith
effort; they need not worry about legal technicalities as he was not
interested in refereeing a contest over who knows the procedures best.
And he invited them to submit comments on specific rules to be
incorporated in future modifications of the rules and agreed to meet
with a delegation to discuss the comments.[63]

When the judge had finished his presentation, an unidentified
officer yelled "We find it impossible to run this damn place . . . with
these fantastic rules." Another interrupted the judge's attempt to
respond, shouting "This is a lot of fucking bullshit," a comment which
was repeated like a chant throughout the rest of the session. It was
obvious the officers had not the slightest intention of making any effort
to apply the rules. Ronald Brule, who later became the warden of
Medium Security, was promoted to lieutenant shortly after the rules
went into effect. He remembers having to sit on countless disciplinary
boards because the deputy warden of Maximum Security at the time
"didn't accept the 'Morris Rules' and wouldn't do anything that had
anything to do with them."[64] Arnold Anderson, now a captain in the

High Security Center, came to work at the ACI while the rules were being developed. He recalls that

> when these Rules came in, it was total chaos. Officers used to say "these courts ain't gonna tell us how to run this place. If they wanna run it, let 'em come down and run it. We'll go out in the street."[65]

In a sense, the officers did "go out to the street." Feeling betrayed by the court, sold out by their superiors who—in their view—had negotiated a settlement rather than defend what was right and intimidated by inmates who seemingly knew the rules better than they did, the officers abandoned any effort to maintain order through rule enforcement. Instead they sought to maintain control while minimizing their personal trouble through cultivating close personal ties with inmates. The result was a pervasive corruption of authority, on the one hand, and a rebellion against the courts and the administration, on the other.[66]

COMMUNITY CORRECTIONS INSIDE THE WALLS

On August 17, 1970, just two weeks after the meeting between Judge Pettine and the correctional officers, about 40 angry officers stormed into the warden's office screaming "we've reached the breaking point" and demanding that "things better change around here." After raging about for ten minutes, the officers left abruptly, leaving the new warden, Frank A. Howard, baffled about specifically what it was they wanted changed.[67] In point of fact, they probably could not articulate a precise list of grievances; in their view everything was wrong, their world was on the verge of collapse.

Howard, who had been appointed warden in March, held a law degree and had twenty years experience in corrections, most of it in parole. None of his prior experience had been administrative, however, a fact of which he was very conscious. Nonetheless, he hoped that it would earn him credibility and support with the guards. Moreover, although white, he had worked in inner-city areas and hoped his sympathy with the plight of blacks would aid in reducing racial tensions. His philosophy of corrections reflected the prevailing sentiment which, despite public concern over lawlessness and demands for stricter law enforcement, remained strongly in favor of rehabilitation.[68] If anything, Howard's view of how offenders might be rehabilitated was even more liberal than that of Langlois. Inmates, in Howard's view, "have been sinned against as much they have sinned," and the mission of the prison is to provide them with opportunities so that they return to the community as "better citizens rather than as better criminals."[69] This mission could be best accomplished, he believed, by keeping life inside the prison as close as possible to that outside and encouraging members of the outside community, including ex-inmates, to participate in planning and running programs.

Despite public endorsement of rehabilitation and Warden Howard's repeated warning that without additional funds, the ACI would have to revert to a "repressive Alcatraz-type facility,"[70] the legislature was not inclined to approve substantial increases in spending for corrections. Economic growth had slowed; the state's coffers were low, and the biggest issue in the upcoming 1970 general election was a state income tax. Voters the previous year had rejected five bond issues by a resounding margin; one of them would have provided $5 million to the ACI to renovate buildings.[71] Federal money for corrections, however, was just becoming available to the states through the new Law Enforcement Assistance Administration (LEAA) and other agencies. Just after Howard's arrival, the ACI had started a small vocational training program in machine operations with a grant from the Department of Labor under the Manpower Development and Training Act (MDTA). A year later, the basic education program was expanded using vocational rehabilitation funds received through the state's Department of Education. And in 1972, additional funds were secured from LEAA for further vocational training programs and to establish a treatment team of social workers and counselors. Thus, operating and other expenditures, most of which were capital, nearly doubled between 1969 and 1972 after having been remained virtually stable for the preceding decade (cf. Table 3, Appendix A).

Little of this funding was available in 1970, however, and Warden Howard had no intention of turning the ACI into Alcatraz. The cost of rehabilitation, he believed, could be decreased by tapping resources available in the community. One of his top priorities was to decrease the number of inmates in close custody, thereby decreasing the costs of security and making community resources more accessible. Shortly after his arrival, he was able to secure an abandoned building on the grounds of the nearby state Institute for Mental Health and, using inmate labor, renovated it for use as a work release facility. Acquisition of this unit more than doubled the number of prisoners who could be placed on work release, from 20 to about 50, and permitted linkage between completion of vocational training and immediate placement on work release.

He also sought to bring the community into the prison. Within a month or so of his arrival, he permitted the black inmates to form an Afro-American Society with the understanding that the emphasis was to be on education and that all meetings were to be attended by a black officer who was assigned as liaison. An external board of directors was established to encourage community participation and within a few weeks courses in math, science, English, Swahili and African history and culture were being taught by volunteers. About 500 people from the community attended a charter night banquet in November 1970 at which soul food was served. Warden Howard sat at the head table in a business suit side by side with inmates dressed in dashikis. Guards remained along the walls of the dining hall as inmates speaking of being political prisoners in a racist society were frequently interrupted by those in the audience jumping to their feet, raising clenched fists and shouting "right on, brother!"[72]

Other organizations were encouraged to expand their programs. Students at local universities formed The Friends of Challenge, affiliated with the prisoner newspaper, to provide individual tutors for inmates in subjects ranging from English composition to guitar playing. In the fall of 1970 this group launched a drive to found a halfway house for ex-felons. In July 1970 about 600 people attended the first Family Day sponsored by the JayCees in the yard of Maximum Security. The six-hour celebration featured a rock band for the inmates and clowns for the kids. The following month the JayCees sponsored a Field Day for mentally retarded children from all over the state in what was sort of an early version of the Special Olympics.

New organizations were started—an art guild, a drama club, a yoga society, a lifers' association. But the most radical of Howard's experiments was the Wing of Hope, an off-shoot of a federally funded residential drug treatment program. Located in a third-floor dormitory in Medium Security which had been renovated by the 20 or so residents, the program was based on the treatment employed in Synanon and Daytop Village.[73] Central to the concept is the principle that the residents are a family with authority to create rules and discipline its members. Thus, while residents of the Wing remained subject to staff supervision outside their dormitory, the maintenance of order and security within it was the responsibility of the residents. No staff were to enter the Wing except by invitation or in an emergency.[74]

Continuing Disorder

The early 1970s were a tumultuous period in the nation's prisons. The number of prison riots, for example, increased from five in 1967, to 27 in 1970, 37 in 1971 and to 48 in 1972.[75] At Rhode Island's ACI, as can be seen in Figure 2.4 (cf. Table 4, Appendix for definitions), the disorder which had begun in the latter half of the 1960s continued into the 1970s. As discussed above, 1969 had begun with a riot and several other serious disturbances followed in its wake. The number of disturbances declined in 1970-71, but other forms of disorder increased. Whereas there had been no homicides in the 14 years since 1956, two inmates were killed in 1970-71, and the number of escapes increased. In December 1970, it was reported that police statistics placed the number of escapes in the past twelve months at 30, more than twice the number reported in any previous year. Warden Howard replied that he would classify most of these as "walkaways" rather than escapes as they involved inmates from minimum security and work release.[76] True though it was, Howard's defense glossed over several incidents which were at the root of growing public concern about the prison's security.

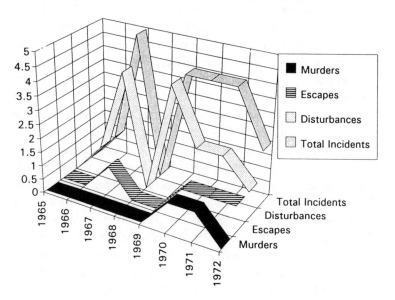

Figure 2.4 Indices of Disorder, 1965-1972

Late in October 1970 three inmates escaped from Maximum Security, using tools from the machine shop to break out of a cell block through a utility tunnel and scaling the wall, eluding five guards in the process. The three were implicated in a number of robberies over the next several days. A week after the escape, one was found executed gangland-style. Two days later, another was captured after being wounded in a gun battle by police. The third was captured a week later but not until after he had murdered a prominent physician.[77] In another incident in December, a long-term inmate who had escaped from minimum security committed 22 holdups before being captured after a shoot-out with police. And in still another escape, a walkaway from work release was charged with kidnapping and rape.[78] Eight months later, in August 1971, the two inmate coordinators of the Wing of Hope escaped from the Medium Security dormitory having sawn through the window bars in the bathroom and climbed to the ground using a rope made of burlap bags.[79] This seemingly inexplicable escape—one of them was on work release and could have walked away from his job at anytime—put an end to the experiment.

Although there were fewer serious disturbances, disorder appeared on the increase inside the prison as well. Family Days, holiday banquets, meetings between inmates and community groups, tutorial sessions and the like multiplied opportunities to convey contraband into the institution, and relaxed regulations concerning what an inmate could have in his cell made it more difficult to detect. Drugs and alcohol were so readily available through visitors, inmates claimed, that it was not worth either the price or the risk to bribe an officer.[80] No statistics are available, but both officers and inmates at the time were in agreement that assaults on officers, virtually unknown until the late 1960s, were on the increase.

Much of the tension was racial. Members of the Afro-American Society developed a strong solidarity as they studied the works of Malcolm X, Eldridge Cleaver and George Jackson[81]—themselves revolutionaries who had developed in the concrete and steel womb of the prison. The leaders saw the organization as a vehicle to "transform the black criminal mentality into a revolutionary mentality,"[82] but the vast majority of the members lacked such commitment. For them the posters and slogans were a psychological release, not a redemption; the meetings and classes were more for socializing than self-improvement, more to secure contraband than to coordinate activities; and solidarity was geared not to future revolution on the outside but to "keeping the white man off our backs" today on the inside.[83]

Almost against the will of its leadership the Afro-American Society was, from late 1970 through the summer of 1971, drawn into increasing confrontation with the guards. Officers, even lieutenants and captains, attempting to write disciplinary reports on black inmates were often surrounded by black prisoners demanding an explanation or protesting the charges. Threatened, most officers became more vigilant, thus seeing more offenses by black inmates, but being less likely to action because they were also intimidated. Whatever lawful authority the officers had, began to erode.[84]

The Formation of RIBCO and the NPRA

When the guards stormed into Warden Howard's office in August 1970 demanding that "things better change around here" the things they wanted changed had as much to do with his programs and lack of attention to security as with the "Morris Rules." Foremost among the concerns identified by the union leaders following meetings with Howard and John Sharkey, who was now the assistant director of social welfare for correctional services, were understaffing, post designations and the lack of training. The small number of new recruits made a continual training program difficult to maintain and training programs had been started and stopped throughout the '60s. Officers who began working at the ACI at about this time remember working posts in Maximum the first day on the job without even the benefit of written post orders. All instruction was by word of mouth from older officers and dependent upon the quality of the senior officer himself and how he felt about the recruit.[85] Moreover, the many changes instituted by Warden Howard had made the post assignments obsolete.

Howard and Sharkey agreed to continue to meet with the union leaders to resolve these and other problems, but no action followed. Officers, many of whom continued to work nearly 60 hours per week, in the face of mounting problems of control, retreated even further from performance of their duties, thereby contributing to the very problem about which they were so angry.

At least part of the reason that the officers were unable to pressure the administration into making concessions was that the state-wide union with which they were affiliated refused to support them in matters that were so specific to the prison and publicly disavowed some of their actions. In October 1970, 184 of the 240 members of the bargaining unit petitioned the state labor relations board to hold a new election on prison employee representation. In the subsequent election, the majority voted to form an independent union, the Rhode Island Brotherhood of Correctional Officers (RIBCO).[86]

Within a few days of its inception, the new union organized a work stoppage after a JayCees dinner at which liquor and drugs were apparently in ample supply and an officer was assaulted by an intoxicated inmate. Declaring that "the inmates have gotten so far out of hand now they are almost uncontrollable," John Galligan, the President of RIBCO, forced Warden Howard into agreeing to transfer several inmates, to impose a partial lockup until the entire prison was searched for contraband and weapons and to ban inmate parties temporarily.[87] Throughout the rest of 1971 RIBCO aggressively brought its case to public attention. Reporters were invited to spend a day on the job with guards, and their stories contrasted the comforts and rights extended to prisoners with the tension and stress to which officers, portrayed as doing "life on the installment plan," are subject. Work stoppages with impromptu press conferences set against the gray granite walls of Old Max and amid a chorus of obscenities from within were used to protest disciplinary action against officers as well as the absence of discipline for inmates.[88]

Meanwhile, the inmates were also organizing. As part of the program to reduce racial tension following the riot in 1969, the administration had initiated a series of meetings between black and white inmate leaders. These meetings continued informally after the administrators had achieved their purposes, and from them arose a shared understanding among the leaders that racial conflict among inmates benefitted only the officers. The inmates also agreed upon an arrangement to prevent future disagreements from erupting into overt conflict.[89] Although severely tested on more than one occasion, the arrangements between black and white leaders did manage to contain racial conflict over the following 18 months.

Following the establishment of RIBCO early in 1971, the inmate leaders, in one of their regular meetings with Warden Howard, requested the formation of a formal elected inmate advisory council. Howard agreed to consider it and gave his permission for a steering committee, composed of the various organization leaders, to develop plans for it and to prepare a report recommending changes they would like to see implemented. Throughout the rest of the year, the steering committee began investigating conditions in the prison, occasionally meeting with the warden and members of the community. Charles Fortes, a labor leader, and Larry Schwartz, head of the Providence Corporation, an antipoverty agency in the capital city, took a particular interest in working with the prisoners, and together they developed the idea to incorporate an organization of inmates and outsiders and to seek their own funding for programs and projects of benefit to prisoners. Early in 1972, what had been the steering committee became the internal board of directors of the legally incorporated National Prisoners Reform Association (NPRA). Although strictly local at first, the members intended to form alliances with other similar organizations then developing around the country, hence the "national" in their name.[90]

The first formal meeting of the new organization, to discuss its goals and to begin development of a constitution and by-laws, was held at the ACI early in April 1972 and was attended by Warden Howard. A second meeting was planned for April 13. On that day however, John Sharkey, now Howard's superior,[91] summoned Larry Schwartz to his office to tell him that the meeting was cancelled, that he would not allow the inmate members to meet and that Schwartz and the other community members of the group were henceforth "persona non grata" at the ACI.

Within two weeks of this action, Sharkey had to defend it before Judge Pettine. What Sharkey feared was that a united inmate body allied with influential people outside the prison, running its own programs with its own funds, would demand participation in the administration of the prison. His testimony, however, dealt only with the security problems created by inmate organizations and the financial impact of the resultant escalation in overtime pay to provide supervision. As other organizations existed in the prison, all of which ran evening programs in conjunction with people from the community, Sharkey's expressed concerns seemed weak to Judge Pettine, and he granted the NPRA an injunction which enjoined Sharkey from "banning, preventing, interfering or otherwise impeding, except by reasonable pre-existing regulation, meeting of the association within the prison. . . . "[92]

The Impact of Attica

In what was up to that time the largest prison riot in the United States, and which today remains the most famous, some 1300 inmates seized control of a portion of the Attica Correctional Facility in upstate New York on September 9, 1971. Holding some 40 officers hostage, the inmates negotiated with the state for four days over a series of demands ranging from better food and medical care through minimum-wage salaries for their labor to the reconstruction of the prison. Convinced that no acceptable compromise could be reached, authorities ordered an assault to retake the prison on September 13. In the assault 29 inmates and ten hostages were killed, all by the untrained and ill-disciplined state police who conducted it.[93]

In the wake of Attica, fear and panic spread among Rhode Island's correctional authorities like a forest fire, and fuel was added to these flames by a number of local incidents.[94] Black inmates, as noted above, were becoming more aggressive in their confrontations with staff, and early in October the makings of a home-made bomb were found in the cell of a black inmate. Meanwhile, the bi-racial steering committee formed earlier in the year was going about its investigations of prison conditions in preparation for its report recommending changes. On the other side of the fence, RIBCO was demanding the formation of a joint administration-union committee to develop a written code of conduct for inmates. On October 30, following a confrontation between a large number of black inmates and a captain in which the besieged officer was forced to discard a disciplinary report alleging an assault, the officers refused to work until the administration agreed to their demands.

The various tensions and pressures at the ACI came to a head in mid-November. Late in the evening of November 18, 11 inmates were taken from their cells, stripped and shackled, placed in state police cars and driven through the night to federal penitentiaries around the country. Four of those transferred were leaders of the Afro-American Society; the other seven were whites whom the administration viewed as troublemakers and escape artists. At a press conference, Governor Licht explained that the action had been taken to avert an insurrection. The scenario sketched by the governor was remarkably similar to what had happened at Attica two months before. From a variety of sources, according to the governor, prison officials had learned that the Afro-American Society was planning to take hostages and use them to force the administration to concede to a set of "unreasonable" and "impossible" demands. At the same time, white inmates planned to use the disorder to escape. Whether this was part of a bi-racial conspiracy or sheer opportunism on the part of the whites was never made clear.

Although he publicly endorsed the transfer, Warden Howard was skeptical of the rationale for it. Indeed, he had learned of the impending action only a day or two before it transpired and had wanted a more thorough investigation. By now, however, the warden and his superior, John Sharkey, were barely on speaking terms, and the decision was Sharkey's to make. While holding a graduate degree in social work and styling himself a reformer, Sharkey clung to the traditional view of inmates as dangerous psychopaths. Moreover, he was by nature a dour man, more inclined to see obstacles than opportunities and to micro-manage Rhode Island's small Division of Correctional Services. Never in support of Howard's programs, he encouraged Howard's subordinates, with whom he had worked closely for years, to bring operational matters to his immediate attention and frequently issued memos countermanding Howard's directives. The information concerning a planned uprising had been brought to Sharkey's attention, not Howard's, and as he had a year before, Sharkey moved quickly to restore order. In consultation with Howard's assistant, Bob Houle, a list of inmates to be transferred was drawn up and arrangements for the transfer made with the Bureau of Prisons and the state police before the warden even learned of the plan. Howard went along with it despite his reservations because he "was caught in the momentum of the thing."[95]

The transfer had the desired chilling effect on the ACI. For nearly a year the institution was relatively calm and orderly. That was to prove to be only a temporary respite, however. Late in 1972, another dramatic escape from Maximum Security triggered a wave of unparalleled disorder which, as we shall see in the next chapter, was to last for nearly five years.

The transfer also resulted in further curbs on the administration's discretionary powers. Within days of the transfer, attorneys for Rhode Island Legal Services, acting on behalf of the inmates, filed suit challenging its constitutionality, contending that the action, accomplished without notice or opportunity for a hearing, violated the due process and equal protection clauses of the Fourteenth Amendment.[96] At the subsequent trial, it was shown that the transferees were subjected to considerable privations as a result of their move: loss of contact with family and friends, problems with state court proceeding and parole hearings, extended segregation and a low priority in access to work and rehabilitation programs at the receiving institutions. The nature and degree of these deprivations, in Judge Pettine's eyes, were "sufficient to warrant that there be some procedural safeguards followed in imposing [them]."[97] Thus, he not only ordered the transferees returned to the ACI but also extended the "Morris Rules" governing disciplinary proceedings to cover involuntary interstate transfers.[98]

NOTES

1. David J. Rothman, *Conscience and Convenience: The Asylum and Its Alternatives in Progressive America* (Boston: Little, Brown and Co., 1980), especially ch. 2.

2. Francis A. Allen, *The Decline of the Rehabilitative Ideal* (New Haven: Yale University Press, 1981), p. 6.

3. Rothman, ch. 2.

4. Francis T. Cullen and Karen E. Gilbert, *Reaffirming Rehabilitation* (Cincinnati: Anderson Publishing Co., 1982).

5. Bert Useem and Peter Kimball, *States of Siege: U.S. Prison Riots, 1971-1986* (New York: Oxford University Press, 1990), p. 6.

6. Federal Bureau of Investigation, *Uniform Crime Reports, 1955* (Washington, DC: U. S. Government Printing Office, 1956), Table 31.

7. James Nutting, "The Poor, The Defective and the Criminal," in *State of Rhode Island and Providence Plantations at the End of the Century: A History*, ed. Edward Field (Boston: Mason Publishing Co.,1902), pp. 457-75. The original state prison was located in Providence. Built between 1837 and 1838, it was situated on swampy land and so poorly constructed that it was chilly and cold in the winter, hot and steamy in the summer and inundated with mud slides in the spring. As the prisoner population grew after the Civil War, the decision was made to construct a new prison outside the city and to abandon the original. For details on the original prison and early jails in Rhode Island, see Richard A. Greene, *Rhode Island Prisons,1638-1848* (Master's thesis, University of Rhode Island, 1963).

8. These internal buildings were razed following a riot in 1991 and replaced by three buildings outside the walls and enclosed by security fencing and barbed wire. Cuts were made in the walls to provide entry from the prison and electronic gates installed to bar access during a disturbance.

9. R.I.G.L. Chapter 55 (1938) as amended in 1956.

10. *Providence Journal,* April 27, 1956, p. 21. Hereinafter this newspaper will be referred to simply as the *Journal* and its companion paper, the *Providence Evening Bulletin*, as the *Bulletin*.

11. *Journal*, April 28, 1956, p. 12.

12. *Ibid.*, December 18, 1955, p. 40.

13. *Ibid.*, May 11, 1956, p. 16.

14. Personal interview with Anthony Travisono, June 24, 1993. Mr. Travisono was director of social welfare from 1969 to 1972 and then director of corrections from 1972 to 1974.

15. *Journal*, December 8, 1964, p. 39.

16. The actual numbers from which these figures are developed are in the Appendix.

17. *Journal*, June 19, 1958, p. 16.

18. *Journal*, April 23, 1959, p. 15.

19. Personal interview, April 26, 1971.

20. *Journal*, August 5, 1959, p. 1.

21. *Sunday Journal*, September 13, 1959, p. N18.

22. *Journal*, March 23, 1961, p. 1; March 31, 1961, p. 26.

23. *Journal*, November 15, 1961, p. 1. Initial accounts proclaimed that the conspirators planned to kill the warden and kidnap his wife and children. But later reports dropped reference to this, and no such charges were entered against the frustrated escapists.

24. *Journal*, November 28, 1961, p. 1; *Sunday Journal*, December 31, 1961, p. N9.

25. *Journal*, March 2, 1962, p. 20.

26. President's Commission on Law Enforcement and the Administration of Justice, *The Challenge of Crime in a Free Society* (New York: Avon Books, 1968), pp. 395-96.

27. *Ibid.*, pp. 398-415.

28. *Ibid.*, p. 415.

29. Task Force on Corrections, President's Commission on Law Enforcement and the Administration of Justice, *Task Force Report: Corrections* (Washington: U.S. Government Printing Office, 1967), ch. 5.

30. *Sunday Journal*, March 7, 1965, p. N26; *Bulletin*, June 28, 1966, p. 27. Inmates convicted of violent and/or sex offenses were not eligible for the program.

31. Adult Correctional Institutions, *Inmate Guide,* March 1, 1967.

32. For a view of these programs and their impact, based on first-hand observation of their operation, see Leo Carroll, *Hacks, Blacks and Cons: Race Relations in a Maximum Security Prison* (Lexington, MA: Lexington Books, 1974; Prospect Heights, IL: Waveland Press, 1988 reissue), especially ch. 2.

33. "Scared straight" was a program developed in New Jersey in which prospective delinquents were brought into the prison and an attempt was made by inmates to scare them straight. Much ballyhooed in the media at the time, later evaluations show it had little or no effect on the juvenile's subsequent behavior. See James O. Finckenauer, *Scared Straight! and the Panacea Phenomenon* (Englewood Cliffs, NJ: Prentice Hall, Inc,1982).

34. *Journal*, May 27, 1968, p. 29.

35. *Bulletin*, September 15, 1967, p. 27.

36. *Journal*, May 10, 1968, p. 36; *Bulletin*, April 29, 1970, p. 37. The time to be served by lifers to be eligible for parole was subsequently raised to 15 years.

37. "The Rhode Islander in Prison," *Rhode Islander Magazine (Providence Sunday Journal)*, February 16, 1969.

38. *Bulletin*, October 25, 1966, p. 1.

39. *Journal*, February 10, 1968, p.1.

40. State of Rhode Island and Providence Plantations, *Personnel Supplement to the State Budget: 1969*, pp. 41-42; *State Budget: 1969*, pp. 74-75.

41. *Journal*, February 1, 1968.

42. "No Longer Afraid," *The People*, March 20, 1896, as quoted in Paul M. Buhle, ed., *Working Lives: An Oral History of Rhode Island Labor* (Providence, RI: Rhode Island Historical Society, 1987), p. 8.

43. "An Act Recognizing the Right of State Employees to Organize," *Public Laws of the State of Rhode Island* (1958), Ch. 178.; Title 36, Ch. 11, R. I. G. L. (1966). For a general history of AFSCME, see Leo Kramer, *Labor's Paradox: The American Federation of State, County, and Municipal Employees (AFL-CIO)* (New York: John Wiley and Sons, 1962). More specific information on the origins of unionism among correctional employees can be found in John M. Wynne, Jr., *Prison Employee Unionism: The Impact on Correctional Administration and Programs* (Washington, DC: U.S. Government Printing Office, National Institute of Law Enforcement and Criminal Justice, 1978), ch. 3.

44. *Journal*, September 7, 1966, p. 1.

45. *Journal*, June 12, 1968, p. 15; June 18, 1968, p. 3.

46. Carroll, pp. 39-40. Unless otherwise noted the following accounts are based on this report and that of the investigatory commission cited below.

47. "Report of the Panel of Inquiry Appointed by Governor Frank Licht to Inquire into Certain Problems at the Adult Correctional Institutions"(University of Rhode Island Library, March 14, 1969).

48. *Ibid.*, pp.10-11.

49. James V. Bennett, "Report on Rhode Island Adult Correctional Institutions" (University of Rhode Island Library, June 1969).

50. *Ibid.*, p.2.

51. Frances Fox Piven and Richard A. Cloward, *Regulating the Poor: The Functions of Public Welfare* (New York: Vintage Books, 1971), ch. 9; Sar Levitan, *The Great Society's Poor Law: A New Approach to Poverty* (Baltimore: Johns Hopkins Press, 1969), p. 179.

52. *Sunday Journal*, June 29, 1969, p. N6; *Journal*, July 10, 1969, p. 3; July 16, 1969, p. 25; September 25, 1969, p. 1; *Bulletin*, July 30, 1969, p. 31.

53. *Journal*, June 6, 1969, p. 1.

54. Personal interview, Judge Raymond J. Pettine, October 12, 1992.

55. *Ibid.*

56. *Morris v. Travisono*, 310 F. Supp. 857 (D. R.I. 1970) at 858.

57. *Morris v. Travisono*, 499 F. Supp. 149 (D. R. I. 1980).

58. This summary is a description of the rules as amended and modified up through 1980. *Ibid.*, pp. 161-173.

59. Harvard Center for Criminal Justice, "Judicial Intervention in Prison Discipline," *Journal of Criminal Law, Criminology and Police Science* 63 (June 1972): 222.

60. *Ibid.*, pp. 223-27.

61. Travisono interview, June 24, 1993.

62. Doug Riggs, "The Verdict on the Judge," *The Rhode Islander Magazine (Providence Sunday Journal)*, February 2, 1993, p. 8.

63. I was present at this meeting, having just started fieldwork at the ACI. This summary is taken from notes made at the time. The training sessions that legal counsel was instructed by the judge to provide apparently were never held, at least none of the officers I talked to who were there at the time remember any training.

64. Personal interview, Warden Ronald Brule, October 16, 1992.

65. Personal interview, Captain Arnold Anderson, October 7, 1992.

66. See Carroll, especially chs. 3 and 6.

67. *Journal,* August 18, 1970, p. 45. A reporter's presence had been requested in advance by the officers.

68. Harris polls conducted in 1968 showed that 81 percent of the American public believed that law and order had broken down, but 72 percent believed that rehabilitation should be the primary goal of prisons. Louis Harris, *The Public Looks at Crime and Corrections* (Washington, D.C.: Joint Commission on Correctional Manpower and Training, 1968).

69. Robert Baldwin, "Some Wardens Are Prisoners Too," *The Rhode Islander Magazine (Providence Sunday Journal)*, September 12, 1971, p. 31.

70. *Sunday Journal*, August 23, 1970, p. N1.

71. *Journal,* June 25, 1969, p. 1. A state income tax was enacted in 1971.

72. This account and much of what follows are based on personal observation recorded in fieldnotes at the time.

73. For an excellent ethnographic account of a program utilizing these concepts, see Barry Sugarman, *Daytop Village: A Therapeutic Community* (New York: Holt, Rinehart and Winston, 1974).

74. *Bulletin*, November 20, 1970, p. 2.

75. Useem and Kimball, p. 18.

76. *Bulletin*, December 24, 1970, p. 1.

77. *Sunday Journal*, November 8, 1970, p. N1; *Journal*, October 26, 1970, p. 1; November 10, 1970, p. 1; *Bulletin*, November 18, 1970, p. 1.

78. *Bulletin*, December 24, 1970, p. 1.

79. *Bulletin*, August 31, 1971, p. 1.

80. Carroll, p. 174.

81. Eldridge Cleaver, *Soul on Ice* (New York: Dell Books, 1968); George Jackson, *Soledad Brother: The Prison Letters of George Jackson* (New York: Bantam Books, 1970); Malcolm X , *The Autobiography of Malcolm X* (New York: Grove Press, 1966).

82. Jackson, p. 21.

83. Carroll, pp. 101-108.

84. *Ibid.*, pp. 132-37.

85. Anderson interview, October 7, 1992; Personal interviews with Lt. James Yakey, October 7, 1992, and Lt. Kenneth Rivard, August 4, 1992. This was not an uncommon pattern at the time. For example, Lombardo found the same to be true at New York's Auburn Prison prior to 1972. As a result much of the training at Auburn was done by long-term inmates. Lucien X. Lombardo, *Guards Imprisoned: Correctional Officers at Work* 2d ed. (Cincinnati: Anderson Publishing Co., 1989), pp. 35-41.

86. *Bulletin*, December 18, 1970, p. 29.

87. *Journal*, January 18, 1971, p. 1.

88. *Sunday Journal*, October 17, 1971; p. A1.

89. Carroll, pp. 187-90.

90. Prisoners unions also developed in California and North Carolina at about this same time. See John Irwin, *Prisons in Turmoil* (Boston: Little Brown and Company, 1980), pp. 92-98.; Eric Cummins, *The Rise and Fall of California's Radical Prison Movement* (Stanford, CA: Stanford University Press, 1994), ch. 8. Chapters of the NPRA were also established at Walpole Prison in Massachusetts and at the state prison in Maine.

91. Sharkey was the Assistant Director for Correctional Services in the Department of Social Welfare.

92. *National Prisoners' Reform Association v. Sharkey*, 347 F. Supp. 1234 (D.R.I. 1972).

93. Useem and Kimball, ch. 3. For the most complete account of the Attica riot, see New York State Special Commission on Attica, *Attica: The Official Report of the New York State Special Commission on Attica* (New York: Bantam Books, 1972).

94. For a more detailed account of these events, see Carroll, pp. 198-212.

95. Personal interview with Warden Frank Howard, December 20, 1971.

96. *Gomes v. Travisono*, 353 F. Supp 457 (D.R.I. 1973). Interstate transfers of prisoners are not uncommon in small states such as Rhode Island,

and in fact an interstate compact exists providing for such transfers among the New England states. Previously transferred inmates were also named as plaintiffs, and the suit was certified as a class action on behalf of all male prisoners in Rhode Island.

I must note that I was subpoenaed as a witness in this case to testify about conversations and interviews I had with Warden Howard soon after the transfer, the substance of which is given above. Faced with a difficult ethical decision, I consulted with the Ethics Committee of the American Sociological Association and received conflicting advice from its members. To protect the profession, I retained an attorney to file a motion to quash the subpoena on the grounds that the conversations and interviews occurred as part of my research, that a promise of confidentiality had been made and that they should thus be treated as privileged communication. The motion failed, as we knew it would, and I testified as I thought I should.

97. *Ibid.*, p. 465.

98. As *Gomes* was being argued, the historic prison due process case, *Wolff v. McDonnell,* was finding its way to the U.S. Supreme Court. Having rendered its historic decision in *Wolff,* the Court vacated the judgement in *Gomes* and remanded it to the First Circuit for reconsideration in light of *Wolff.* On reconsideration, the First Circuit determined that the safeguards established by Judge Pettine in *Gomes* exceeded those of *Wolff* in only two respects: administrative review of the board decision and the provision of a lay advocate whenever requested. In a subsequent order, Judge Pettine eliminated the requirement of administrative review of involuntary transfer decisions but retained the right to assistance from a staff member in the hearing as in *Morris* the state had already agreed to such a condition in disciplinary proceedings. See *Wolff v. McDonnell,* 418 U.S. 539; *Gomes v. Travisono,* 510 F.2d 537 (1st Cir. 1974); *Gomes v. Travisono,* C. A. No. 4794, (D.R.I, February 18, 1975).

CHAPTER 3

Anarchy

Among the many recommendations made by the 1967 President's Commission on Law Enforcement and the Administration of Justice had been the development of strong, centralized administration in corrections.[1] Although the idea for a separate department had periodically surfaced in Rhode Island, it had received no political support, and corrections had remained a small division within the state's Department of Social Welfare. However, in the aftermath of Attica and the belief that an Attica-like tragedy had been narrowly averted at the ACI, the state's political leaders decided that corrections should be accorded a higher priority. Early in 1972, Governor Licht summoned Anthony Travisono, the director of social welfare, to his office and charged him with drafting legislation to create a new department which he would head. Working with the governor's legal counsel, Travisono developed the bill which, in an effort to remove political considerations from the department, gave the director a five-year term. Despite this unprecedented provision, the bill was approved, almost without debate, on the last day of the 1972 legislative session.[2]

A Rhode Island native and graduate of Brown University, Travisono earned a master's degree in social work at Boston University and had headed juvenile institutions both in Rhode Island and Iowa for a decade before being named director of social welfare by Governor Licht in 1969. In the three years he had been back in Rhode Island, he had become a popular and respected administrator with a reputation as "an uncommon bureaucrat who is far more interested in people and ideas than in titles or tables of organization,"[3] and, indeed, the new department of which he took charge in July 1972 was rather haphazard, more an aggregation of existing agencies than a planned organization.[4]

A month after the inmate transfers in November 1971, Governor Licht appointed a 17-member Citizens' Action Council (CAC) charged with making a comprehensive study of the ACI and recommending a program of improvements. The report of the Council was released to the press on the same day that Travisono became the first director of corrections. The rambling report criticized almost every aspect of the prison. However, in the eyes of the Council, whose members were for the most part academicians and human service providers with little or no exposure to prisons, the fundamental problem was that "custody has become an obsession" which thwarts any effort at "human repair and renewal."[5]

Director Travisono was largely in agreement with the criticisms and recommendations made by the CAC and accepted the report as a blueprint for change. Of both immediate and long-range concern to the new director was an upcoming bond issue in November 1972 requesting $7.5 million for the construction of new prison facilities. A capital development plan had been prepared by Sharkey in anticipation that the bond issue would be matched with federal funds, but the federal legislation had not been approved, leaving Rhode Island with a plan that was far too ambitious. Moreover, Travisono, who had not participated in the preparation of the plan, thought it planned for more secure space than was needed and, correlatively, allocated insufficient space for community facilities.[6] An architect was retained to prepare a short-term plan to renovate existing space and a grant sought to retain the recently formed National Clearinghouse for Criminal Justice Planning and Architecture to develop a more comprehensive long-range plan.

The short-term plan, completed in September 1972, was quite innovative. Rather than designing space in terms of security needs, and then fitting programs to it, the architect had adopted the programmatic needs identified by the CAC and re-designed existing space to meet those needs, dividing each facility into a number of service areas.[7] Even a business-oriented government expenditure watchdog group was sufficiently impressed with the plan, even more with the new capacity to plan being displayed by the department, to endorse it despite what it saw as a "curious lack of concern for prison security" and its "prisoner-advocate frame of reference."[8] The voters apparently agreed as the bond issue was approved by a large margin in November. Thus, as 1972 drew to a close, correctional reform in Rhode Island seemed to be back on track once again. It was, however, to be derailed by a worsening economy and a conservative swing in public sentiment.

The 1960s had been one of the most tumultuous periods in American history.[9] The decade had begun with peaceful protests in pursuit of civil rights for African Americans. Met with brutal attempts at repression on the part of state and local authorities in the South, the movement itself degenerated into riots and violent crime as it spread across the country. In mid-decade, what was ostensibly a military assistance mission in Viet Nam grew into the nation's longest war, albeit undeclared, claiming over 50,000 American lives before it was ignominiously lost. College campuses were paralyzed by anti-war demonstrations. Heroic figures were assassinated; innocent citizens killed. In an arrogant display of power, government agencies were ordered to violate their charters and the U.S. Constitution in their efforts to maintain order, and finally, in 1974, a President of the United States was, for the first time, forced to resign the office under threat of impeachment.

In the 1970s the fear of economic collapse was added to the threat of widespread social disorder. The rate of unemployment rose from 4.9 percent in 1973 to 5.6 percent the following year and to 8.5 in 1975, the biggest increase in unemployment since the Great Depression of the 1930s. Moreover, and made all the more frightening because it defied conventional economic wisdom, increasing unemployment in the mid-70s was accompanied by inflation which skyrocketed to double digits and remained there throughout the rest of the decade. To many observers, 1974 looked very much like 1929, and in fact, the recession of 1974-75 ended America's golden age of economic expansion.[10]

Thus by the mid-1970s, faith in government and optimism about its capacities to do good had been replaced by pervasive fear, anxiety and cynicism. In this new climate, scholarly research on correctional rehabilitation, research already well known among scholars but largely ignored, allegedly showing that "nothing works" drew widespread attention and became part of the conventional wisdom.[11] Liberals, now seeing the root of the problem as an inequitable social order protected by a repressive state, abandoned the rehabilitative ideal and began advocating a "justice model" of corrections which promised to protect offenders by greatly reducing the discretionary powers of state officials. Conservatives, meanwhile, defining the problem as one of moral decay, sought a return to "law and order," and advocated longer sentences, mandatory sentences and the selective incapacitation of repeat offenders.[12] The conservative crime control agenda offered more readily understood and appealing answers to the public's fears, and throughout the 1970s support for rehabilitation declined markedly while demands for social protection increased.[13]

Though sudden, the demise of the rehabilitative ideal was not instantaneous. Even as state legislatures were passing mandatory sentence laws and abolishing parole, departments of correction were receiving large grants from the Law Enforcement Assistance Administration (LEAA) to finance rehabilitation programs and develop standards which promoted rehabilitation as the major correctional goal. Thus, with respect to correctional philosophy and policy, the mid-70s were a period of intense debate, conflict and uncertainty. In Rhode Island the conflict and uncertainty undermined the authority of the new director and plunged the department into an unparalleled period of disorder and violence.

LOSS OF LEGITIMACY

During the recreation period on the night of September 20, 1972, four prisoners described as "extremely dangerous" and "hardened criminals" escaped from Maximum Security.[14] The deputy warden in charge of the unit, Roland Remillard, had learned of the planned escape and the identities of three of the inmates earlier that day and informed the warden. Warden Howard, however, after consulting with several other senior staff, decided to maintain a normal routine, keeping the identified escapees under "loose surveillance" while developing a plan with the state police to catch them as soon as they broke out onto the roof of the south state wing. Coordination and communication broke down, however. Officers in the wing were not informed of the expected escape because the administration feared they would tell the inmates. In consequence, the escapees were missing from the wing for nearly 20 minutes before the captain charged with keeping tabs on them knew they were gone. Moreover, they had not broken out onto the south state roof as planned but to a lower roof in an area which was covered by only a floating patrol.

An investigating committee appointed by Governor Licht was highly critical of the astonishingly lax security measures which had made the escape possible and called into question Warden Howard's judgement in not locking the inmates in their cells and searching for the escape route when he first learned of the plot. One member went so far as to call for his replacement.[15] Howard and Travisono, however, successfully countered the criticisms, using the escape to dramatize the need for a new and more secure prison complex. Thus, the escape was perhaps a factor in the voters' approval of the bond issue for new construction in November 1972. But winning the bond issue did nothing to stem the tide of disorder.

Three weeks after the election, two inmates in segregation managed to take a guard hostage and demanded to meet with Travisono and Howard to negotiate changes in conditions in the segregation unit. Arriving at the unit, Travisono began talking through a window to the inmates who were holding the bound guard with a pair of scissors to his throat when he was approached by an influential inmate reputed to be an enforcer for the New England organized crime family. Travisono recalls the inmate telling him "I can work with this" and the director told him to "go ahead." Within ten minutes, the guard was released in exchange for a promise of no reprisals and a pledge to consider the demands.[16]

The pledge of immunity touched off a political furor. The state's Attorney General, Republican Richard J. Israel, refused to honor it, claiming Travisono had no legal authority to grant immunity from prosecution for a felony. Travisono received strong support from a coalition of labor, social service and prison reform groups who saw the issue as one of morality rather than law and, somewhat ironically, emphasized the danger of undermining administrative authority. But

Governor Licht, in the last months of his tenure, offered little support and incoming Governor Philip W. Noel, although a Democrat, supported the attorney general.[17] The two inmates were convicted of kidnapping, assault and extortion,[18] and the two administrators lost both the political support of powerful state officials and credibility with the inmates.

The two incidents set off a wave of disorder which, as can be seen in Figure 3.1, was to engulf the institution over the next five years. In the four months from December 1972 through March 1973, at least four guards were assaulted and suffered injuries sufficiently serious to require medical attention. Assaults among the 500 or so inmates were even more numerous; in the last 10 days of March alone, there were five inmates stabbed .[19] At noon on April 2 some 150 to 200 maximum security inmates rioted. Taking six guards hostage, the rioters spilled out of the south state wing, where the riot had begun and surged into the industrial building. There they set fires and smashed equipment, causing nearly $1 million damage and virtually destroying the building which housed most of the industrial and vocational programs.[20]

The rampage, however, was over in about thirty minutes. When the state police arrived on the scene, the hostages—who had been protected by powerful inmates from harm at the hands of others—were immediately released. As firefighters set about their work, reporters moved freely about the yard interviewing staff and inmates. Director Travisono was also walking around the yard, shaking hands and talking with inmates. He gave his permission for inmate leaders to hold a press conference in the dining hall, after which all the rioters quietly returned to their cells.

Fragmentation

The riot threw into relief the tension which had been building within the institution for more than a year. An investigation ordered by the governor highlighted poor security, conflict among administrators, racial tensions and the growing power of both the NPRA and RIBCO as contributing to the outbreak. Upon taking office Travisono had discontinued departmental opposition to the NPRA and given sanction

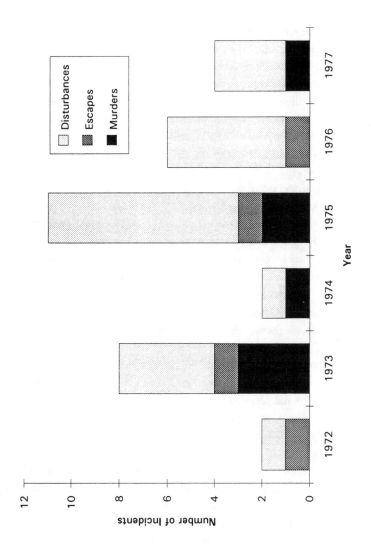

Figure 3.1 Indices of Disorder, 1972-1977

to the organization by inviting its participation in long-range planning. Granted its own office and an uncensored telephone line, the NPRA set out to increase both its base of support and the scope of its operations. Among other things, the organization began a program to provide inmate counsel to prisoners appearing before the disciplinary board, and in March 1973 its external board incorporated an organization to provide job training to ex-inmates.[21]

Not all inmates supported the NPRA, however. In particular, there was conflict within the Afro-American Society about the degree to which it should participate in the predominantly white organization.[22] The Afro-American leadership, by and large older and serving longer sentences, favored participation in NPRA and its program of self-help, grievance negotiation and legal action. Younger members, however, viewed such cooperation as cooptation and were demanding increased confrontation with the administration as a means of gaining redress and promoting change. It was in this conflict that the riot of April 2 had its immediate causes. The day before the riot a number of young black inmates, angered that the organization had not protested their punishment for fighting the week before, confronted the organization's leaders. A fight broke out and two inmates were stabbed. Just before noon on the day of the riot, one of those suspected of the stabbings was let out of his cell due to a breakdown in communication between the wing officer and his lunchtime replacement. Armed with a broom handle, he ran around the cell block rallying support. When Deputy Warden Remillard and six officers entered the wing in response to the officer's call for assistance, they were confronted by the inmate who by now had some 30 others with him. The inmate struck the deputy on the side of the head, knocking him unconscious. Two of the officers accompanying the deputy carried him back out of the wing while the other four fought a rear guard action against the now rioting inmates.

At the press conference which ended the disturbance, inmate spokesmen expressed strong support for Warden Howard and made only one demand: the removal of Remillard from his post as deputy warden. Conflict between the two administrators had been intense from the beginning of Howard's tenure. While John Sharkey had been Howard's superior, Remillard was frequently able to keep the warden in check, but this was no longer possible with Sharkey on the shelf and Travisono at the helm. In recent months, Remillard had been incensed by the NPRA's role in selecting lay advocates for inmates appearing before the disciplinary board, which he chaired despite his clearly stated opposition to the "Morris Rules." Where Howard had the support of the NPRA and most inmates, Remillard had the support of RIBCO and most officers. The officers saw him as "the last stronghold of order in this institution,"[23] and when, in January, Howard had moved to replace his chief subordinate, he had been forced to back down by "sick-out" orchestrated by RIBCO in Remillard's support.[24]

Following his failed attempt at replacing Remillard in mid-January, Howard became even more removed from his staff; while he continued to meet frequently with inmate groups his last staff conference before the April 2 riot had been on January 19. And the strong support he received from the inmates in the aftermath of the riot was, in the emerging political climate, actually a condemnation. Reluctantly, he resigned his position two weeks after the disturbance.

Control by Any Means

Prison riots in the 1950s had prompted calls for more and better treatment programs. In the climate of fear and cynicism of the early 1970s, however, riots were blamed on "country-club" prisons and ignited demands for tighter security and stricter discipline. The style of Rhode Island's new Governor, Philip W. Noel, was in tune with the changing climate. One observer described him as being "as much the guardian of public morality as the protector of public safety."[25] Burly, blunt, and outspoken, he liked to meet problems head-on and preferred the wisdom of the common man to the musings of experts and intellectuals. Soon after his election, as we have seen, he had publicly joined the Republican attorney general in attacking Travisono's grant of immunity to the prisoners holding a guard hostage. Privately the governor told Travisono that he would prefer that he resign, but the director, guaranteed a five-year term by the legislation creating the department, chose to remain in office.[26] Howard's resignation, however, gave Governor Noel the opportunity to appoint his own warden, and he chose a man whose views were similar to his own, James W. Mullen.

Though only 44 at the time of his appointment, Mullen had retired in 1971 after 20 years with the R. I. State Police. For the last several of these years he had held the rank of Captain and had been head of the detective division. Since his retirement he had been a regional supervisor for the Department of Justice's Organized Crime Intelligence System. Although he had no experience in corrections, the governor thought him ideally suited for the post which he saw as, more than anything else, requiring "a strong man who can command the attention and respect of those who work for him."[27] And, indeed, Mullen made it immediately clear that he intended to run the prison along strict paramilitary lines. In a series of memos he ordered staff to maintain a spit-and-polish appearance, prohibited casual conversations between officers and inmates and directed the two groups to address each other as "Mister" and "Officer." He himself toured the prison frequently, sometimes with a .45 strapped to his side.[28]

The situation in the prison had spun too far out of control to be remedied by such measures, however, and the disorder and violence continued unabated. Much of the facility had been gutted during the riot and there were no programs operating. Inmates spent the entire day hanging out in the wings or the yard. Assaults and stabbings became almost everyday events. On just one weekend near the end of May 1973 two officers were assaulted with a pipe, and another suffered a fractured foot when he was pushed down a flight of stairs; two inmates were likewise assaulted with pipes, and two others were stabbed, all requiring hospitalization. And on Saturday afternoon of the following weekend, an inmate was stabbed over 100 times, his body stuffed in a trash can and set on fire.[29]

Officers were intimidated by the prospect of being taken hostage, never far from consciousness under the best of circumstances but made an imminent threat by the riot and reinforced by the daily disorder. A good number of officers quit and recruits were hard to find leaving the guard force severely understaffed. The riot had disrupted the informal control structure as well. It had been initiated by young black inmates in opposition to the leadership of the Afro-American Society and specifically in opposition to the cooperation of these leaders with the predominantly white NPRA. Leaders of the NPRA, for the most part older and associated with organized crime, had lost face by going to their cells rather than participate in the riot and now found themselves opposed by a loose organization of young whites, a "wild bunch."[30]

For the past year, the officers had become increasingly aggrieved as Director Travisono and Warden Howard had consulted inmates on policy issues but not the union. Indeed correctional officers often learned of policy changes from the members of the NPRA. Now, with the safety of its members on the line, RIBCO took action. On the morning of May 31, the officers refused to let the maximum security inmates out of their cells and held a press conference at which union president, John Galligan, declared the institution "totally out of control" and demanded a general lockup until policies and procedures necessary to maintain order were developed and put in place.[31] Several days later, Governor Noel called a special press conference to discuss the situation at the prison. In an impassioned outburst, he let it be known that he had ordered corrections officials to use "whatever means are necessary," including the taking of life, to restore order. "If prisoners are going to act like animals, they will be treated like animals . . . . They should have no Bill of Rights," he asserted and revealed that he had told the warden and director not to feel constrained in any way by decisions of the federal court. "If the federal court wants to hold anybody in contempt, they can hold me in contempt because those are my orders."[32]

The governor's tough talk struck a responsive chord with the general public.[33] It did not, unfortunately, have a deterrent effect on inmates. Ten days later, for only the second time in the state's history, a Rhode Island correctional officer, Donald Price—who had started work at the ACI only three weeks before—was killed in a seemingly senseless and brutal attack.[34] Reaction to the killing was swift and severe. Governor Noel called the legislature into special session. Rhode Island, which had abolished capital punishment in 1852, second only to Michigan, reinstated the death penalty, virtually without debate and with only four dissenting votes, five days after Officer Price was killed.[35] The prison was declared to be in a state of emergency. Some

30 inmates thought to be responsible for most of the violence were placed in administrative segregation; all others were locked in their cells; programs and visits were cancelled; and forty state police officers were ordered into the prison to augment the guard force until 100 newly created positions could be filled. Order, for a time, was restored, but the actions taken to restore it ensnared the department in a web of legal entanglements.

The "Morris Rules" Again

In November of 1971, an Inmate Legal Assistance Program (ILAP) had been established at the ACI with a grant from LEAA. Staffed by two attorneys and an office manager and utilizing the part-time services of law students from Boston College, the program was designed to provide a full range of legal services to indigent prisoners.[36] Following the April 1973 riot the ILAP attorneys had met with inmate leaders and commenced what they expected to be a broad class action suit against the Department of Corrections. Many of these inmate leaders, now in segregation after the killing of the correctional officer, claimed that they were being intimidated by the brutality directed against them and feared retaliation if they continued to participate in the suit. On these grounds the ILAP attorneys sought an injunction against any further abuse of their clients. Following three days of testimony in which the inmates related what Judge Pettine characterized as "wicked conduct inflicted upon them by prison guards and/or state police," all of which was flatly denied by officers, the judge issued the injunction while noting that it was not based on specific findings of fact.[37]

At a later hearing, Judge Pettine found that the department had not followed the agreed-upon procedures for suspending the "Morris Rules" in emergency situations. Director Travisono had suspended them in their entirety without even a notice to the court, and those in segregation had been placed there on the basis of information from unidentified informants, without a hearing or even an explanation. Moreover, the "Rules" had remained in suspension long after the emergency had ended. Given such "remarkable insouciance" to the court, Judge Pettine believed that mere reinstatement of the "Rules" offered insufficient assurance that they would not again be totally ignored at some future date; thus, he specifically prohibited the state from ever again taking such action.[38]

Travisono Resigns

The lockup instituted after the slaying of Officer Price lasted only two weeks. Early in July, Warden Mullen gave inmates a choice of remaining in their cells or working to clean the institutions and repair the damage done in the April riot. Most chose to work and spent the summer scrubbing floors and walls, scrapping and painting, repairing broken windows and fixing machinery.

Much of this work was accomplished under the watchful eyes of armed state police officers who remained in the prison, in support of the correctional officers, for nearly four months. The publicity caused by the disorder and violence had made the recruiting and retention of officers difficult even before Officer Price was stabbed to death; now it became next to impossible. Moreover, under pressure from RIBCO the administration had extended the preservice training program from two to six weeks and had developed a new curriculum putting greater emphasis on security and self-defense. Thus, it was not until mid-November that the first class of 30 new officers replaced the state police.[39]

Within a few weeks of beginning work, over a one-third of the new officers quit. What they confronted, once the state police were withdrawn, was a regression to the previous pattern of lax and inconsistent discipline. Despite the warden's orders that all inmates were to be either working or in their cells, the cell blocks in Maximum Security were routinely filled with idle inmates. Moreover, the warden himself could frequently be found engaging in friendly conversation with groups of loitering prisoners, sometimes under a sign which proclaimed in large letters that any inmate standing in the area was subject to disciplinary action.[40]

In December some 50 inmates were involved in a brawl in the Maximum Security dining hall. A month later an equal number of inmates awaiting trial, also in Maximum, refused to enter their cells at the evening lockup until Warden Mullen, summoned from his home, agreed to grant them more out-of-cell recreation time.[41] Early in the

morning of February 6, 1974 two convicted murderers and another
inmate overpowered two officers in minimum security, took their keys,
stole three handguns and ammunition from the arsenal, and drove off
in the car of one of the officers. Two were recaptured but one
committed suicide as police in Boston attempted to take him into
custody.[42] Two months to the day after this suicide, another escapee
from minimum security killed a door-to-door fish vendor in a failed
robbery attempt and subsequently became the first person in over a
century to receive the death sentence in Rhode Island.[43]

Already racked by guilt over the murder of Officer Price, Anthony
Travisono resigned within a week of this last killing. Although there
had been calls for his resignation following the recent escapes, it still
came as a surprise to some, mainly because his long-range planning
was just now beginning to bear fruit. LEAA funds had been secured to
expand and continue the treatment team and to establish an education
administration unit. In 1973, the education division received about
$250,000 in grants, and, despite the disorder, a number of programs
had been implemented including a large adult basic education program
and the first college-level program.[44]

Implementing changes proved more difficult than securing grants,
however. Every program required changes in schedules and posts for
officers and RIBCO, now locked in a sort of sibling rivalry with the
NPRA, took a tough stand on any and all changes.[45] Dependence on
overtime, already high, increased, and RIBCO early in 1974 had held
programs hostage by refusing overtime until the Governor himself
personally negotiated a new contract with the union which granted
officers a substantial pay increase.[46]

Travisono was also disheartened by the intense opposition which
greeted the long-term strategic plan he had commissioned and which
was now released amidst the heightened public concern over the
disorder, escapes and violence. The report listed a number of options
for future development but those given highest priority involved
constructing new facilities at the present complex. The consultants
recommended that Maximum Security be converted to a warehouse and
replaced by a small high-security center and a separate jail, that
Medium Security be renovated for use as a "community corrections

center," and that a network of partial release centers be established throughout the state.[47]

The mayor of Cranston, Republican James L. Taft, was outraged. Medium security stood on land recently marked by a state commission for industrial development. Retention of the land by the state would mean a substantial loss in tax revenue to the city not to mention the continued burden of providing the prison with services. Claiming that his city's fire and rescue squads had been called to the ACI some 220 times in the past year and that the police had responded to 138 calls for assistance, he called upon the state to reimburse the city nearly $300,000 annually, labelled the plan totally irresponsible in its lack of concern for public safety and launched a campaign to pressure the state to relocate the prison to a rural area.[48]

Throughout the spring, Travisono was forced by Mayor Taft's opposition to explain and defend the plan in meetings with groups of citizens, most of whom were angry and quite vocal in their opposition. In this, he received no support from Governor Noel. Relations between the two, never cordial, had become increasingly strained over the past year. Except for emergencies, Travisono's only means of communication with the governor was through one or more of his policy aides, most of whom were barely out of college and knew little, if anything, about corrections. Moreover, he found himself in the awkward position of having to support pronouncements and implement policies with which he personally disagreed and about which he had not been consulted.[49] Thus, when offered the position of executive director of the American Correctional Association, he left Rhode Island for Maryland.

ADMINISTRATIVE PARALYSIS

The Department of Corrections had been created rather quickly and without detailed study. In response to a crisis, Travisono had cobbled together an aggregation of agencies that were charged with the evaluation, custody and supervision of offenders but which had very dissimilar philosophies and practices. More interested in ideas than in tables of organization, he had involved himself in long-range planning and the establishment of treatment programs rather than the development of managerial processes by which the newly merged units might be coordinated. As new programs such as the treatment team were developed, they were put into operation with little or no planning about how to articulate them with other units. As late as 1975, two consultants from the American Justice Institute observed that the department lacked such elemental features as a "clear, generally understood budget process" or regularly scheduled staff meetings.[50] Predictably, staff continued to function and to see themselves as part of a particular unit or program rather than as part of a broader enterprise, to see all problems only from the vantage point of their unit, and to regard other staff with suspicion and hostility.[51]

All of these problems had been present during Travisono's tenure but became painfully evident in the vacuum created by his departure. Belying his campaign image, Governor Noel did not act decisively to replace Travisono. To the contrary, he appointed Travisono's deputy, Donald D. Taylor, as acting director and, despite growing pressure to name a permanent replacement, left Taylor in that position for nearly two years. Taylor, an African American, had worked with Travisono in juvenile corrections both in Rhode Island and Iowa. For the ten years prior to being appointed deputy director, he had worked in human services and anti-poverty programs. As deputy director, he had maintained a low profile but openly supported Travisono's programs and long-range plans and had the support of prison reform groups in the community.

Lacking a clear mandate from the governor, Taylor felt unable to exert aggressive leadership. Nor could he look to any of his chief subordinates for support. John Sharkey had been named assistant director for research and evaluation when the department was created. This had been done to mute the conflict between Sharkey and then-Warden Frank Howard. His duties were highly circumscribed and he was an embittered man, openly critical of others in the department; he and Taylor had only a tenuous relationship. Taylor's other assistant, Anthony Orabone, was in charge of youth services and had no experience in corrections. Orabone was, moreover, faced with a difficult task— implementing the provisions of a 1973 consent decree with respect to conditions at the state's training schools. That left

Taylor with only Warden Mullen to oversee adult corrections, and Mullen had direct access to the governor. Because of this tie and the size of the ACI relative to other units in the department, he operated with almost complete autonomy. He was, moreover, a "street cop," more given to undercover surveillance and cultivating informants than to the nuts-and-bolts of correctional administration.[52]

This weak and fragmented administration was unable to provide meaningful programs for inmates. In Medium Security, now used mostly as protective custody, there were no organized programs whatsoever, and the facility had in the eyes of two professional observers become far more repressive than was necessary for its relatively benign population.[53] In Maximum Security, damage to the industrial building caused in the riot of April 1973 had not been repaired. As late as April 1975 only one industry, the license plate shop, was operating in Maximum and it employed only 32 of the some 400 inmates in the facility. Another 70 inmates were officially employed in building maintenance but the perpetual filth and squalor of the facility was a testament to their ingenuity in avoiding hard labor. Yet, despite the fact that few inmates were employed, the inmate payroll account was overdrawn five months into fiscal year 1975. Investigation disclosed that almost all inmates in Maximum Security, whether working or not, for unexplained reasons were being paid at twice the maximum dollar a day rate allowable under state law.[54]

The few programs operating were funded by LEAA. Most notable among these were an adult education program through which inmates could earn a high school general equivalency diploma, a treatment team of social workers and counselors to assist inmates in coping with personal problems and a pre-service training program for correctional officers. While meeting with some success,[55] the impact of these programs was severely limited by the continuing disorder, frequent lockups, inadequate facilities, high rates of staff turnover and patronage. Counseling sessions were conducted in the barber shop during its hours of operation or on benches in the cell blocks or yard. Taylor recalls seeing a teacher sunning himself in the yard at Maximum on a warm spring day when he should have been teaching, and feeling powerless to do anything because of the teacher's well-known political connections. In similar fashion, the head of the classification unit publicly acknowledged that his counselors frequently came to work late, left early or did not show up at all, but there was little he could do about it. Between January and July 1975, 23 new officers graduated from the training program but an equal number quit. [56]

Even the existence of these federal programs was in jeopardy from 1975 through 1977. In June 1975, LEAA funds were suspended because the department did not meet a 1971 requirement that all corrections departments receiving funds provide drug and alcohol treatment programs for inmates. The department pledged to develop and implement the required programs within six months and funding was restored. Eight months later, however, the department's proposal for a drug program was rejected by LEAA because it did not provide for separate living quarters for those undergoing treatment as was required. It was another 18 months before a small drug treatment unit for 20 inmates was opened, and this was accomplished only after LEAA provided consultants to assist in the development of the plans. [57]

An Upsurge in Violence and Disorder

In the year following Travisono's resignation as director, from July 1, 1974 through June 30, 1975, scarcely a day passed without a major story in the newspapers concerning disorder in the prison. In a population averaging about 550 prisoners, two inmates were killed, three more died of drug overdoses and another committed suicide following an aborted attempt to escape from Maximum Security. At least an additional 15 inmates were treated at local hospitals for injuries suffered in assaults; in seven cases the injuries were serious enough to require hospitalization. No fewer than 12 officers also received medical treatment following assaults, though no officers were hospitalized. There was, moreover, a major escape from Maximum Security, and the assistance of local or state police was requested to assist in quelling six disturbances. [58]

Following several general lock-ups late in the spring of 1975, the violence tapered off only to peak again in the fall. During the last week of that month, there were four separate stabbings. On October 30, two inmates were severely beaten with baseball bats as some 10 officers watched helplessly, prevented from intervening by their fear of being assaulted by the 30 or so inmates surrounding the attackers. Following an extended lockup, the violence picked up where it had left off. Between January 20 and January 25, 1976, there were several more stabbings, and a hobby shop in the industries building was destroyed by fire.[59]

The continuing high level of disorder and violence resulted in an unusually large percentage of the population requesting and being granted protective custody. By mid-July 1975, close to 100 inmates, nearly 20 percent of the population, were in protective custody, and what had been Medium Security was now used mainly to house them. Moreover, there was space for only 95 inmates in minimum security and work release.[60] Thus, many inmates who might have been classified as medium or minimum security, for the most part young inmates with short sentences, were forced to remain in Maximum, a situation which fed the burgeoning violence.

There existed a good number of abandoned buildings at the nearby training school for boys and at the state psychiatric hospital. An architectural study commissioned by the department in 1972 had, as noted earlier, produced impressive plans for renovating some of these buildings for use as medium and minimum security facilities. Following the defeat of the bond issue in 1974, the funds from the 1972 bond issue might have been used for renovating these buildings and thus eased the pressures in Old Max. The department, however, reserved these funds for its long-term capital development program and determined to go to the voters once again for the additional funds necessary to complete the entire building program.

The only plan to break the logjam in Medium Security was developed by the NPRA and then adopted by the administration. It involved transferring the protective custody inmates to a secure area in Maximum. When this plan was revealed, however, the protective custody inmates went on a hunger strike and sought an injunction to block its implementation. There followed two months of hearings and negotiations, all of which proved moot when the administration found they lacked the funds to pay for the additional security that would be needed.[61]

At a time requiring strong and decisive leadership, Rhode Island's department of corrections was left in the hands of a caretaker administration that was both inexperienced in corrections and internally divided. This administration was unable to provide meaningful activities for the inmate population and incapable of maintaining security and order by any means short of a general lock-up. Thus, the prisons bounced from brief lock-up to disruption and back almost on a monthly basis. In part, the problem was one of inadequate facilities and underfunding, as officials were quick to point out. More centrally, however, the powerlessness resulted from a near-complete collapse of the administrative structure, and in the absence of authoritative leadership, the power struggle between the officers' union and the prisoners' reform association intensified.

Labor-Management Conflict

Correctional officers' unions forming at this time were as concerned for issues of safety and security as they were for the "bread and butter" issues of pay and benefits.[62] Almost by definition, the drive to protect their members involved the unions in conflict with management over matters of policy and operations. As we have seen, this was no less true in Rhode Island than elsewhere. Indeed, in the eyes of Ohmart and Nelson, the consultants from the American Justice Institute retained by Governor Noel to evaluate the department in 1975, one of the major factors weakening the administration was the "usurpation of traditional management prerogatives by organized labor."[63] This usurpation had gone so far, they believed, that, somewhat paradoxically, it was exacerbating dangerous conditions that endangered staff.

Ohmart and Nelson were referring especially to the seniority clause in the officers' contract. By this provision the administration "recognizes and accepts the principle of seniority within a class of position in all cases of shift preference, transfer, vacation time, days off, job and location assignment, holiday time, lay-offs and recall."[64] In practice, this clause means that the allocation of officers to the various institutions, shifts and posts as well as the distribution of several benefits was taken out of the hands of the administrators and determined by a complicated bidding system overseen by the union.

Rhode Island's administrators, like correctional administrators across the country, railed at such provisions which, in most cases, had been negotiated by the state labor relations office and which, corrections officials argued, hamstrung them in their attempts to maintain security.[65]

Throughout 1975, corrections officials publicly attributed their inability to stem the tide of disorder that had engulfed the prison since 1969 to the seniority clause. From their perspective, the bidding system set in motion a vicious circle. The most experienced officers bid out of those positions requiring the most contact with inmates. These positions, generally the most sensitive, were thus filled by the youngest and least experienced officers, who were both less knowledgeable and more easily intimidated. As a result, disorder increased, and the increasing disorder caused a high rate of turnover among the new officers.

Union leaders countered that senior employees should have the right to the more desirable assignments and that there was no solid evidence to support the administration's claims. In their view, the administrators were scapegoating the union rather than admit their own inadequacy. Selecting another point in the circle as a starting point, the union representatives argued that it was management's failure to develop and enforce clear policies and procedures that at once caused the disorder and senior officers to bid into safer positions.

Reported incidents offer support to both points of view. In July 1974, for example, a young officer working alone was assaulted by an inmate. Warden Mullen had circulated a memo stating that all inmates striking officers were to be placed in the segregation unit pending a hearing, but in this case Deputy Brule merely ordered the inmate locked in his cell. Mullen supported Brule's action. Outraged, the Maximum Security officers walked off the job and defied a direct order from the governor to return to work. Governor Noel promptly fired the guards and brought in the National Guard to run the unit, which they did for two days.[66]

Late in October 1975, as noted previously, four inmates brutally beat two others with baseball bats. Those beaten were hospitalized with severe injuries. This incident occurred in the presence of some ten officers who had stood by without intervening. The president of the Brotherhood explained that the officers had failed to intervene out of fear of being assaulted by the 30 or so inmates who were also watching the beating.[67]

Shortly after this incident, Deputy Warden Brule sent a letter to the governor. "It is impossible to discipline and control inmates until you can discipline and control employees," he wrote, and that is impossible because of the protection afforded officers by the union.[68] Brotherhood president, Gene Fagnant, threatened to bring Brule up on charges within the union for publicly criticizing it in ways that could subject it to legal action. No such action was taken, but the threat itself is indicative of the strength of the Brotherhood.

The deputy wardens in Rhode Island, while responsible for the operation of an entire facility were, nonetheless, at this time members of the same union as the lowest ranking officer.[69] The deputies were thus subject to severe role conflict. Brule's managerial orientation created intense conflict with the officers in Maximum and exposed him to the threat of both formal and informal sanctions from his fellow union members and subordinates. In contrast, Fred Chiarini, the deputy in charge of Medium Security, was one of the founders of the original union. Although heading a faction that was at odds with the current leadership on many issues, he remained a staunch union member. Most officers working in Medium had bid into the job to work for Chiarini and were intensely loyal to him. Together, they ran the unit with an iron hand. Indeed, in commenting on the dangers faced by officers working in Maximum, union officials frequently pointed to the absence of such dangers in Medium.

Others, however, held a different view of conditions in Medium. As noted above, Ohmart and Nelson thought the unit more repressive than necessary and there were continual allegations of brutality. In October 1974, a jury found in favor of three inmates who claimed they had been beaten and gassed in their cells and ordered Deputy Chiarini to pay $5000 in punitive damages.[70] Several months later, a subcommittee of the Governor's Advisory Commission on Corrections issued a report in which they characterized the Medium Security officers as "Caesar's legions" and likened the situation to a concentration camp.[71]

Finally, in December 1975, Judge Pettine found sufficient evidence of a pattern of brutality to issue a permanent injunction ordering the officers to desist from using unnecessary force against inmates. [72]

While the state's attorneys were unsuccessfully defending correctional officers against charges of brutality, the officers' union was in conflict with the state's chief executive on another front. In an austerity move, Governor Noel early in 1975 ordered a five percent reduction in pay for state employees and placed limits on the use of overtime. Specifically, he prohibited any employee from working overtime for 30 days following the use of a sick day. [73] This unusual edict seemed to be specifically directed at the correctional officers. Expenditures for overtime at the ACI were at the time running about twice the amount budgeted, a much higher overrun than in any other state agency. [74] The was due to many factors. An administrative error by Warden Mullen had led to the creation of more posts than could be staffed with the normal complement of officers, a situation which was aggravated by the high rate of turnover. Moreover, the continuing disorder meant more officers were taking sick time, and more had to be assigned to hospital details for inmates. It had long been rumored, however, that officers worked together to fatten their paychecks by manipulating sick time and overtime, calling in sick on a workday and being called in to work on their day off in place of another officer who called in sick. It was this alleged abuse that the governor's edict aimed to correct.

The Brotherhood immediately challenged the ban, referring it to the American Arbitration Association for binding arbitration as provided for in its contract. In August, 1975, the arbitrator found in favor of the Brotherhood and ordered the state to make restitution to officers who had been unfairly deprived of opportunities to work overtime. [75] Expenditures for overtime, meanwhile, continued to skyrocket.

For years the officers had felt besieged by inmates and their liberal allies and ignored by reformist administrators. Locked in conflict on all fronts, most officers developed an intense loyalty to the Brotherhood that contrasted sharply with the enmity and lack of respect they now publicly proclaimed for most administrators. The union's defiance of the governor and its ultimate victory on this issue gave them hope of achieving what was uppermost on their agenda—the imposition of a custodial regime and the restoration of their own status and power. These political goals could not be attained through collective bargaining, but disorder in the prison and larger social currents were making the voting public increasingly receptive to the officers' message.

A Mob-Controlled Prisoners' Union

During this period, the NPRA was also gaining power at the expense of the administration. As we have seen, the NPRA was a coalition of inmate organizations and outside groups with an interest in prison reform that had been formed in 1972. Initially opposed by John Sharkey, it had been granted legitimacy by Travisono and Howard who provided it with office space, a telephone and involved it in long-range planning.

Like its counterparts in several other states, the NPRA's ultimate goal was to reduce "the differences between the legal status and social circumstances of the prisoner and the free person."[76] More specifically, it sought to expand the constitutional rights of inmates, protect them from inhumane treatment, provide them with meaningful work at fair wages, improve the conditions of confinement, ease the transition from confinement to freedom, and secure the complete restoration of rights of citizenship upon release. In pursuit of these goals, the NPRA was extensively involved in litigation and political action. The action that resulted in a permanent injunction against brutality by guards was initiated in 1974 on behalf of all ACI inmates by the NPRA. Early in 1975, the organization filed several suits concerning medical treatment, classification, education and vocational training programs, and in April they challenged the unions' seniority clause claiming it was responsible for the violence in the institution.[77] Ultimately these and other complaints were combined and became an Eighth Amendment challenge to the totality of conditions. The litigation of this case and implementation of the resulting decree is the major topic of the balance of this book.

The organization was granted wide latitude to pursue its political agenda. With donations from church and community organizations, it established *The NPRA News*, a monthly newspaper virtually uncensored by the administration. The newspaper published stories on correctional developments around the country, articles critical of corrections in Rhode Island, reports of NPRA activities and proposals for reform. The public was also invited into the prison for NPRA-conducted tours, and once a year members of the legislature were invited to an NPRA sponsored forum at which members of the constituent inmate organizations presented legislative proposals. Many of these initiatives, such as a highly successful furlough program, were subsequently enacted. The NPRA office and telephones provided them almost unlimited access to the media. They issued press releases on their activities, held press conferences and campaigned for favored candidates for state office.[78]

Following the riot in 1973 the NPRA began moving into the void created by the absence of state-organized programs. In January 1974 the organization received permission from Warden Mullen and a $4000 loan from a local bank to start a "fast-food" service in Maximum Security. Rather than eat in the dining hall, inmates could now order food from the NPRA restaurant and have it delivered to their cells. Profits from the store were combined with grants, donations, and monies raised through a variety of activities from flea markets to banquets to fund other programs and services. A wood-working and craft shop was established in the old industries building and its products marketed in a trailer located in prison's parking lot. Bikers were put to work in a motorcycle repair shop. The laundry was refurbished and made operational so that once again inmates could have their clothing cleaned and pressed. By the end of 1975, the NPRA had as many inmates working for it—some 100—as did the state.[79]

The organization expanded its activities beyond the walls as well. In 1973 the Providence Corporation, the anti-poverty agency that had helped establish the NPRA, created a job training and placement program for ex-felons, Project Beginning, with a large federal grant. That summer the NPRA took control of Project Beginning. At a poorly attended meeting in the prison, the NPRA representatives on Project

Beginning's Board voted to form an Internal Board of inmates and to employ inmates to screen and refer others to the training and placement services outside. Over the next several months, the administration of the Project was moved inside the walls to the degree that the external staff had to come to the prison for their paychecks which were signed by the president of the NPRA. Jobs in the prison, such as those in the print shop where the *NPRA News* was produced were defined as vocational training and those occupying them were paid out of Project funds. In much the same way it screened inmates awaiting trial to determine their eligibility for assistance from the R. I. Bail Fund established by the State Council of Churches with a grant from a private foundation.[80]

The degree of autonomy permitted NPRA and the scope of its activities seems quite at odds with the views expressed by Warden Mullen and his mandate from the governor to take control by any means necessary. It seems all the more strange in view of Warden Mullen's treatment of other groups challenging his administration. He had, for example, evicted the Inmate Legal Assistance Program from its office space at the ACI following the riot in April 1973, and in 1975 Governor Noel became embroiled in a public feud with the Roman Catholic bishop of Providence after the warden barred the Catholic Chaplaincy Team from the ACI for its advocacy of inmate rights.[81] Why, then, did he so actively cooperate with the NPRA, a group which at the same time was engaging him in almost continual legal skirmishes?

Mullen had inherited an institution in which the traditional balance of forces had long ago been destroyed. The absence of a strong central administration, the demoralization of the correctional officers, his own lack of experience, the power of the inmates and the directives of the federal court made the simple restoration of a custodial regime impossible. This became clear early in 1974, when disorder and violence quickly escalated after the withdrawal of the state police who had been supporting the correctional officers for nearly six months following the killing of Officer Price. At that time, Mullen appears to have adopted a new strategy of control: accommodation with the NPRA.

The litigators and politicians were only one of the NPRA's faces. Equally involved in the organization, although only a few held formal leadership positions, were a number of "heavies," inmates known to have strong connections to organized crime. Tom DeFusco, an inmate member of the NPRA, described the organizational structure:

> We had a governing body. We had our own diplomatic corps, so to speak, guys who could meet the politicians or go to the administration, talk and put things in writing. And we had our own police force, behind the scenes, 10 to 15 guys who could do business. . . . If somebody stepped out of line, they got taken care of. If somebody needed to get their head broken, they got their head broken.[82]

Mullen's strategy was to cooperate with both the politicians and the "heavies" and thereby increase legitimate program opportunities, on the one hand, and gain control of the population, on the other. He accorded the NPRA leaders special privileges, turned a blind eye to their abuses and granted them immunity from punishment. In return, he demanded only two things: "Don't escape and don't assault my officers."[83] Otherwise the NPRA leaders could do as they pleased. They had the best cells in the most comfortable cell block, on the walls of which artists from a local college had painted an enormous mural. A number had phones installed in their cells. They received visits at all times of the day and night. Some of the visits, allegedly business, occurred in the suite of private offices they maintained on the top floor of the industries building, entry to which was forbidden to correctional officers. After passage of the furlough bill in 1975, even lifers, who were not eligible under the bill, went home regularly. Where most inmates were able to purchase an occasional hamburger from the store, NPRA leaders had steak and lobster whenever they wished, perhaps with a glass of wine. Inmates working in the craft shop purchased their materials at a substantial markup and kicked back a portion of their profits. Inmates referred to Project Beginning paid a kickback out of the salary the project provided while they were in training. Families of inmates being held awaiting trial paid to have the inmate declared eligible for the Bail Fund. If an officer, by mistake, "booked" one of the leadership for an infraction, Brule or Mullen overturned it or the "booking" was lost.

Mullen's strategy of accommodation, however, failed to restore order. In fact, it contributed to the violence. There were several reasons for this. First, NPRA activities increased the amount of contraband. Although drugs were opposed by the NPRA leadership, both drugs and alcohol flowed into the institution with the waves of visitors and materials, and fueled much conflict. Weapons such as knives and clubs were produced in the shops and a black market in weapons flourished as virtually every inmate sought to arm himself for protection.

Second, the treatment accorded the NPRA leaders and the "heavies" generated envy and intense hostility among those not so favored. In particular, it sent tremors along the fault lines of age and race for, although the Afro-American and Latin American Societies were represented on the Internal Board, the leadership of the NPRA were predominantly older white inmates. Many of the disturbances during the period, such as that in February 1975 described above, involved young black inmates demanding equal treatment. The rash of stabbings, the beating of two inmates with bats and the burning of the hobby shop resulted from the on-going conflict between the NPRA leaders and a band of younger white inmates heavily engaged in drug trafficking whom the leaders believed were bringing too much heat.

Third, the double standard demoralized the officers. New officers having been instructed in the importance of being "firm, fair and consistent" came on the job to find that there were two classes of inmates, one to whom the rules applied and one over whom they had no authority. If they attempted to exert authority where they were not expected to, they were overruled by their superiors. To exert it where it was expected to be applied frequently provoked resistance from inmates who, with good reason, protested that it was arbitrary. In the face of such pressure, many simply resigned, and those who remained retreated from any attempt to maintain order and merely bided their time until they had sufficient seniority to bid into another post.

In essence, the NPRA was a miniaturized version of a mob-controlled union. Mullen, like many businessmen, tried to keep peace by cooperating with it but in the end was victimized. Nothing more clearly symbolized his victimization than the name of the goat which one of the more notorious inmates kept in the cell next to his. The goat was named "Jimmy."[84]

"SUPERMAX"

Throughout 1974 and most of 1975, Governor Noel vacillated on setting correctional policy. On the one hand, he met crises with tough talk and quick action but, on the other hand, he did not take any sustained action to deal with the continual turmoil. Mounting criticism from his political opponents and the press eventually moved the governor to action, however. Late in 1975, he publicly admitted that his approach to the problems at the ACI had been a failure and promised to chart a new course of action.[85] When announced, that new course proved to be a sharp break from the long-range plan developed by Anthony Travisono and contrary to the recommendations of his own advisory commission and professional consultants.

The Governor's Advisory Commission on Correctional Services was established by statute in 1973. The 21-member commission was composed of representatives from the courts, law enforcement, local communities and prison reform groups. While containing some conservatives such as Mayor Taft of Cranston, it remained decidedly liberal and oriented to rehabilitation. The commission was charged with conducting investigations to evaluate correctional services and personnel and preparing plans in each of three areas: institutional services for adults, institutional services for juveniles and community programs.[86]

During the court hearings on brutality in 1974, the subcommittee on adult corrections decided to make its own investigation of conditions in Maximum and Medium. By April 1975, the subcommittee had prepared several reports containing a series of far-reaching recommendations. Its first report concerned leadership and contained the recommendation that Warden Mullen be fired immediately. Accepted by the full commission, the recommendation triggered a groundswell of support for the warden—from groups as diverse and at odds with each other as the Brotherhood of Correctional Officers and the NPRA—and was summarily rejected by Governor Noel. Mullen, however, announced his intention to resign as soon as a suitable replacement could be found.[87]

Governor Noel's rejection of the commission's recommendation on Warden Mullen forecast his response to their second recommendation concerning the implementation of the department's long-range plan. As we have seen, the voters had approved a $7.5 million bond issue in 1972 but their rejection of a second bond issue in 1974 left the state with the problem of what portion of the plan to implement first. That question had been referred to the advisory commission. The commission recommended that the state first build an intake service center to house inmates awaiting trial and to provide diagnostic and classification services to those recently sentenced.[88]

In June 1975 the state solicited bids from architects to design an intake center. However, three months later, following a narrowly averted escape by a number of dangerous inmates, one of the governor's staunchest allies, Senate Majority Leader Joseph Walsh, proposed that the funds be used instead to build a small "super maximum security" to house the estimated 80 to 100 "incorrigibles." Walsh argued that "Supermax," as it was dubbed, would not only relieve the tension in Maximum Security but, unlike the intake center, would also reduce the risk of escape by dangerous prisoners.[89] In mirror image of the reaction to the commission's recommendation to fire Warden Mullen, there was an immediate groundswell of support for "Supermax," and most of those with doubts eventually were moved to support the concept by the continuing violence in the prison.[90]

The only significant opposition to "Supermax" came from liberals such as acting Director Taylor, members of the subcommittee, and from the consultants from the American Justice Institute, Ohmart and Nelson, who had been retained by the governor to study management of the department. They pointed out that construction would take three or four years and that a more expedient solution was to transfer "incorrigibles" to the federal system. More importantly, in their view the "routine co-mingling of unconvicted accused (many of them youthful and with insignificant records . . .) with the state's most aggressive, most assaultive and sexually predatory criminals [as was occurring in Maximum Security], transgresses about every canon of modern corrections. "[91] Expressing surprise that the practice had not been the subject of litigation before this, they declared that the need to put an end to it made the intake center the highest priority.

"Supermax," however, was the perfect solution for a governor faced with a disaffected public clamoring for a restoration of order in the prison. Not only did it offer security but it satisfied the increasingly punitive sentiments of people threatened by high unemployment and runaway inflation, a citizenry that every day grew less interested in rehabilitation and more interested in incapacitation. Thus, in February 1976 the governor announced the appointment of a new director, a reorganization of the department along the lines recommended by Ohmart and Nelson, and a new long-range capital development plan for corrections with the construction of "Supermax" as the first step. That same day, Governor Noel announced his intention to seek election to the U.S. Senate in the upcoming elections.[92]

REORGANIZATION

The new director was a forty-year-old career civil servant, Bradford E. Southworth, whose college degree was in horticulture, who had no experience in corrections, and who, by his own admission, had been in a prison only once in his life and that had been just a month prior to his nomination. To many, like the editors of the *Journal-Bulletin*, the appointment appeared "misguided and not at all in the public interest."[93] In defending his nominee, however, Governor Noel pointed to Southworth's proven administrative and planning abilities and to his recent experience as the director of the Governor's Justice Commission which had responsibility for developing coordinated criminal justice plans in conjunction with LEAA funding.[94]

Southworth's top priority was to implement the reorganization recommended by the American Justice Institute. That report had observed that there were too many levels of management in the department and that responsibilities were only vaguely defined. It was thus "unclear at times who has the final authority" with the "practical result [being] that no one does."[95] In addition to the changes recommended by the consultants, the governor wanted to limit the term of the director to two years and make it concurrent with that of the state's chief executive, to remove all positions from deputy warden on up from the state's classified service and to define the position of deputy warden in such a way as to disqualify them from membership in the officers' union. He also wanted to make legislative approval unnecessary for future reorganizations.[96]

With all of these considerations in mind, Southworth set about devising the new structure and crafting the legislation to be submitted to the legislature, securing its approval and recruiting for the new positions. These tasks immediately snared him in politics and took several months to complete. Several people whose positions were to be eliminated or whom the consultants had informally suggested replacing had over 20 years of state service and were protected by a law that requires the state to reassign employees with that longevity to comparable positions at the same pay. Southworth thus had to find comparable positions in other agencies, alter the plan to create positions for them, or keep them in their current positions. At the same time, the deputy wardens brought considerable political pressure through key legislators to keep their positions within the classified service.[97]

When finally completed in July, the reorganization, as shown in Figure 3.2 divided the department into three major service divisions (adult, youth and field services) and two functional divisions (management services and support services). Each of the five divisions was headed by an assistant director, and a sixth assistant director was placed in charge of program development but with virtually no staff nor budget. Several new positions were created and the titles of others changed. Among the more prominent of the new positions were those of chief inspector, director of public relations and legal counsel, all of which were responsible to the director. The warden of the ACI under the new structure became the deputy assistant director for adult services, and the deputy wardens became associate directors, a title which removed them from the union but kept them within the state's civil service.

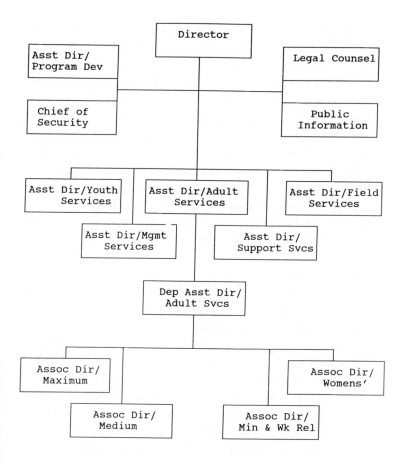

Figure 3.2 Table of Organization, 1976

Southworth appointed some promising new players to the major positions but had to retain most of the old cast in key supporting roles. William Laurie, a probation officer who had founded and directed a much-praised Youth Services Bureau, was appointed assistant director for adult services, and Linda D'Amario who had headed a foster placement program was named to head youth services. Both of these key aides were young, and neither had experience administering institutions. Likewise the director of management services was brought in from outside corrections. Warden Mullen, whom Laurie replaced, was named to the post of chief inspector. Donald Taylor was kept on as assistant director of support services and John Sharkey became the assistant director for program development. To accommodate Robert Houle, who had been Mullen's assistant warden and who, like Sharkey, was a veteran with over 20 years experience, a position was created between the assistant director of adult services and the associate wardens—the deputy assistant director for adult services or warden. In actuality, however, administrative responsibility for the institutions was placed directly in the hands of Laurie.

The reorganization had been influenced by political considerations and constraints as much, if not more, than by a clear sense of the department's mission and goals. In consequence, it did not reduce the number of administrative layers as the consultants had urged, and while areas of responsibility may have been clarified to some degree, the new and unfamiliar titles created even more confusion over lines of authority. Moreover, the neophyte director was surrounded by aides who were either young, inexperienced and naive or experienced but intensely bitter and cynical.

With his new staff on board, Director Southworth set about the task of convincing voters to approve yet another prison construction bond issue, this time for $13.9 million. The new long-range plan announced by the governor called for building the "Supermax" prison as soon as possible using most of the funds from the 1972 bond issue. The balance of this money was to be used to renovate suitable state-owned buildings for use as medium and minimum security facilities so inmates inappropriately held in Maximum Security could soon be moved to more suitable space. The funds being sought in 1976 were to construct a new medium security facility with a capacity of 222 and an intake service center, or state jail, with a capacity of 150. An additional bond issue was planned for 1978 to secure funds for a 72-bed addition to "Supermax," or the High Security Center as it was more formally termed, and for four partial release centers.[98]

To many it seemed that the department had made a tactical error by choosing to build "Supermax" with existing funds and seeking another bond issue for less secure facilities. Given the economic climate and the growing punitiveness of the electorate, it appeared unlikely that any bond issue would be approved, but one for a "Supermax" probably stood a better chance than did one for a diagnostic and classification center. It was scarcely a surprise, then, when the voters rejected the bond issue by a substantial margin. However, the department was not without an alternative plan. Over the summer a number of state owned buildings near the prison complex had been evaluated for penal use. It was decided to renovate these while pushing ahead with "Supermax." Then as the renovated facilities came on line, the population in Maximum Security could be drawn down by funneling appropriately classified inmates into the new units.[99]

Securing funds to staff the new facilities, however, proved difficult in a recessionary economy. Moreover, the recession triggered a sharp increase in the number of prisoners which, having remained stable for two decades, rose by 40 percent from 1973 through 1977 (see figure 3.3). The increase in numbers meant increasing expenditures. Overtime, already comprising 15 percent of total expenditures at the ACI, continued to soar. In 1973-74, it will be remembered, the legislature had approved nearly 100 additional positions for officers. That fact, plus the Brotherhood's successful challenge to Governor Noel's attempt to cut state spending by banning overtime, had prompted a legislative investigation into rumored abuses of sick leave by officers colluding to increase their income. While not uncovering any solid evidence of such abuse, the committee did find substantial evidence of poor management controls and declared there would be no increase in the number of correctional officers until overtime was brought under control.[100]

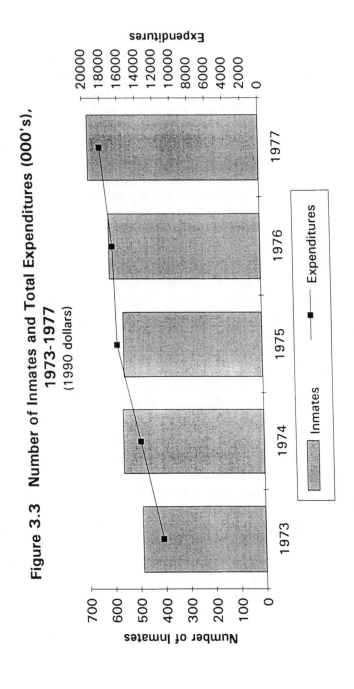

Figure 3.3   Number of Inmates and Total Expenditures (000's), 1973-1977

(1990 dollars)

Ironically, as the finance committee was pursuing its investigation, the state's negotiators were, under directions from the governor, entering into a contract that ensured the overtime issue would continue to be a major problem. The state's primary goal in the negotiations, as discussed above, was to regain some control over the assignment of officers. Thus, in exchange for the removal from the bidding system of posts in certain sensitive areas and the establishment of a procedure by which the correctional managers might challenge the assignment of officers whom they thought unfit for a post, the administration agreed to pay an hour's overtime each week to all officers for a 12 minute pre-shift briefing. In the first year of the contract, pay for the pre-shift briefing added an estimated 10 percent to expenditures for overtime, and led certain legislators to question for whose benefit the prison existed.[101]

Thus, most of the increased expenditure from 1973 through 1977 was for security with only a small proportion going to programs and services for inmates, and that small proportion was from federal grants about to expire. Most of the rehabilitative services for inmates were provided by a 17-member treatment team of social workers, counselors and nurses. Originally funded by LEAA for three years in 1972-73, it had been extended by discretionary grants but the LEAA was adamant in its refusal not to fund it beyond July 1977.[102] The adult basic education program had been cut substantially when its federal funding ended in 1976, and the college level programs funded through the Teacher Corps program were to end in 1977.[103] Despite studies that revealed that 70-80 percent of the inmates had drug problems, and the availability of LEAA funds for drug treatment, throughout 1976 and most of 1977, the department was unable to fulfill its commitment to start a program. At first, this was due to their inability to locate space for a separate residential facility; then, once space was located, to the legislature's unwillingness to fund the additional officers' positions necessary for security.[104]

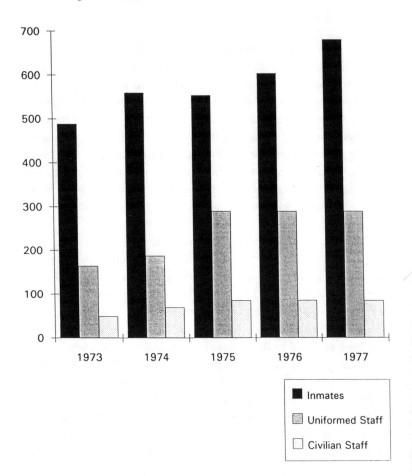

Figure 3.4 Number of Inmates and Staff, 1973-1977

The NPRA Fills the Vacuum

At the time of his appointment, Southworth was told by Governor Noel that his top priority was to regain control of the prison and to restore order there. In pursuit of this dual objective, Director Southworth focused his efforts at developing and implementing managerial procedures and controls and dealing with the department's organizational environment. It was left to his assistant, Bill Laurie, to wrest power from the inmates and reinvest it in the officers.

Four months elapsed between Southworth's appointment as director and Laurie's appointment as his assistant. From his years as a probation officer, Laurie knew most of the inmate leaders and had considerable "street smarts." He had limited administrative experience, however, and had never worked in a prison. It took an additional six months of on-the-job training, therefore, before he began to make changes.[105] In the interim the NPRA expanded its programs and broadened its base of support in the community.

The NPRA continued its legal attack on the department. In April 1976 they filed suit in federal court challenging the mingling of men being detained awaiting trial and those already sentenced and the conditions in which those awaiting trial were forced to live.[106] Several months later they sought a restraining order on the construction of "Supermax," arguing that the 1972 bond issue had made no mention of a high security center and that the facility would not resolve the problem of separating awaiting trial from sentenced men. When this proved unsuccessful, they filed an objection with the state's Department of Natural Resources on the grounds that the site selected for "Supermax" was a wetlands and that Corrections had not received approval to build on it. Although this effort was also unsuccessful, it did delay construction for nearly six months while engineers prepared the required environment impact statements and gained the necessary clearance.[107]

Project Beginning expanded its operations to include misdemeanants sentenced to jail due to their inability to pay a fine, offering them job training through subsidized community service placements. A business loan was secured from the state's Department of Community Affairs in a program underwritten by a grant from the Office of Economic Opportunity. Soon, in its trailer outside the prison and at booths in various shopping malls, the NPRA was selling "Property of the ACI" T-shirts and houses for birds made homeless by the clearing of land for "Supermax."[108] In at least one instance, the NPRA entered into a joint venture with the Department of Corrections. The department received a sizeable grant from the Department of Health, Education and Welfare to teach horticultural skills to medium security inmates who would cultivate an eight acre farm, but lacked the necessary tools. The NPRA arranged for the Providence Corporation to advance the money to the department in exchange for a share of the vegetables which were to be distributed through churches to needy families in Providence.[109]

As the NPRA's operations expanded so did their need for administrative space. Early in April, they obtained a 64-foot trailer on loan from the state's Division on Job Development and Training. Having received permission from Warden Mullen to bring the trailer into the prison, they arranged for volunteers from Local 57 of the International Operating Engineers to lift the trailer over the wall using a crane on loan from a local construction company.[110]

So effective were the NPRA's efforts, and in such sharp contrast to the department's inability to initiate or maintain programs, that even some of the organization's most severe critics joined ranks with them. Raymond Morrissette had founded a victim's rights organization and for years had opposed almost every effort at prison reform claiming that "criminal justice is more often justice for the criminal than for the victim."[111] Late in 1976, it became known to the NPRA leadership that Morrissette was bitterly frustrated at the failure of the state to establish an agency to assist crime victims, and they invited him to meet with them at the prison. Early the next year, the NPRA and Victim Alert, Morrissette's organization, jointly submitted a proposal to LEAA to establish a victim restitution center.[112]

Moreover, violence and disorder were much lower than in the previous two years. In the six months after Southworth's appointment, there were no inmates killed, no suicides and none died of drug overdoses. There were no escapes from Medium or Maximum

Security, there were no major disturbances, and only one call to the state for assistance. What violence there was—several brawls and stabbings—seemed to be isolated incidents. Indeed, the president of the NPRA was quoted in the press to the effect that the NPRA and other organizations were working hard to keep violence in check.[113]

It was widely believed that the NPRA was actively keeping the peace in the prison as part of its effort to defeat the 1976 bond issue for new prison facilities. As if to give credence to this belief, in November, just three weeks after the bond issue was defeated, a number of the "heavies" orchestrated a major disturbance. The brother of one of them had been arrested and charged with the murder of a member of a rival organized crime faction; he was being held in protective custody in Medium Security. Several of the "heavies" approached the captain in charge of the night shift in Maximum Security, demanding to speak by telephone with the inmate and that he be transferred to Maximum where they could protect him. They threatened "all out war" if their demands were not met.[114]

Laurie, called at home, ordered the captain to refuse both requests and alerted the state police who dispatched a SWAT team to the prison. Upon arriving at the prison, Laurie found one cell block in the control of some 200 inmates. The officers were huddled in the captain's office while former warden Mullen, who had arrived moments earlier, was negotiating with the leaders. Laurie did not interrupt the negotiation, but when Mullen agreed to permit the phone call and promised to transfer the inmate the next morning if the inmates returned peacefully to their cells, Laurie vetoed him. The inmates then went on a rampage until the SWAT team was ordered into the wing.

Following this disturbance, Maximum Security remained locked up for a week while the damage was repaired and the prison thoroughly searched. To NPRA's supporters who criticized his action and argued that there would have been no riot had he granted the requests, Laurie responded that such demands are "mutinous activity" and would no longer be tolerated.[115]

A Failed Attempt to Regain Control

During the six months he had spent familiarizing himself with the prison's personnel and operations, those closest to him in the administrative hierarchy advised Laurie to continue the policy of accommodation with the inmate power structure. By temperament, however, Laurie was ill-disposed to such an accommodation, and the November incident merely confirmed what he had come to suspect: that what Mullen and Brule viewed as accommodation was in fact intimidation.

Prior to dealing with the inmates, however, he had first to deal with the officers who were seldom disciplined for being late for work, out of uniform or even insubordinate. Laurie personally took charge of all disciplinary matters, cracking down on such behavior and suspending a considerable number of officers in the process. Union leaders, at first, fought his efforts. After a number of skirmishes, however, the union leaders came to see that his views on the prison were quite similar to theirs and began meeting with him regularly to urge him to take a strong stand with the NPRA and to make a commitment to support them in running the prison through strict enforcement of rules and regulations.[116]

In the months following the November 1976 disturbance, Laurie moved decisively to curtail the activities of the NPRA. As the organization had been sanctioned by the court, he could not abolish it, but for all intents and purposes, he refused to recognize it, declining to meet with its leaders on any issue, however legitimate. Using the budgetary problems as an excuse, he put an end to the nighttime meetings with external groups at which most organization business was conducted, reduced the number of family days and other fund-raising events and stopped purchasing the materials and supplies for the newspaper. Food deliveries to the "take-out stand" began to be searched intensively, turning up alcohol in fruit juice cans and marihuana in coffee containers.[117] And in a move which generated much publicity, he had the organization's telephones removed after one of the "heavies" threatened a state police officer who had charged the prisoner and his brother, also an inmate, with conducting the largest bookmaking ring in state over the NPRA telephones.[118]

Meanwhile, Southworth's efforts, encouraged and supported by a new governor, began to bear some fruit in terms of both long-range planning and program development. The genial and courtly J. Joseph Garrahy had, for the most part, kept a low profile during his tenure as lieutenant governor. Like any informed citizen, he was aware of the problems at the prison but had little inkling of the degree of disarray in the correctional administration. Shortly after taking office, however, he was presented a report that described it in detail.

The report was that of a commission appointed by Governor Noel, in response to a public outcry, to investigate a racially charged incident that had occurred the previous July.[119] In its report, the commission decried the pervasiveness of racial tension in the prison and called for the recruitment of more non-white staff and greater training in intercultural communication. However, it placed even greater emphasis on other factors that, in its view, intensified the racial hostilities brought into the prison from the community: inadequate facilities, the lack of productive activity, blurred lines of authority and the absence of procedures to insure accountability. Echoing Ohmart and Nelson, the commission declared the commingling of prisoners awaiting trial with sentenced men in Maximum Security to be a violation of "every modern principle of correctional administration." Baldly tracing the connection between this practice, the high rate of violence, and the disruption of the classification process caused by the consequent need to convert Medium Security to protective custody, the commission pointedly argued for the construction of an intake center. It also called upon the governor to authorize a detailed management study of the Division of Adult Services, to enlist the help of other state agencies in finding productive work for inmates and urged the department to formalize its policies and procedures.[120]

Declaring that there is "no more important priority in Rhode Island than building an intake and diagnostic center," Governor Garrahy secured legislative approval for a special referendum on a scaled-down version of the bond issue defeated the previous November.[121] This bond issue was approved by the voters late in June, one day after ground-breaking for the High Security Center.

The governor brought together Director Southworth and his counterpart in the state's mental health department to coordinate the latter department's planned program of de-institutionalization and the former's need for buildings suitable for use as minimum security facilities. By the end of April, two such buildings, with a combined capacity of 170, were slated for renovation over the next year.[122]

The state Division of Motor Vehicles was persuaded to renew its contract with correctional industries rather than privatizing the production of license plates as it had planned. Southworth devised a group incentive pay plan for inmates in the plate shop, and the production of plates increased by nearly 500 percent early in 1977.[123] That summer minimum security inmates were put to work clearing brush and making firewood from fallen trees on reservations operated by the Department of Natural Resources.[124]

The department's efforts stalled in April 1977, however, with the trial in the case of *Palmigiano v. Garrahy* (this case is treated in the next chapter). Not only did the trial itself divert time and energy from pursuit of new initiatives, but the massive media coverage of conditions in the prison provided an opportunity for the NPRA and its allies to launch a counterattack against the corrections administration. Arguing that the expert testimony presented in the trial indicated a need for official assessment, State Senator Stephen Fortunato convinced the senate to establish a special committee to investigate conditions at the prison. Like Senator Fortunato, the two other senators appointed to the committee were rather outspoken critics of the administration and supporters of the NPRA, and the committee voted to begin their investigation by meeting in Maximum Security with the leaders of the NPRA.[125]

Convinced that the extensive media coverage given the prison over the past few years was a factor contributing to the inability of the administration to restore order and security, Southworth had recently developed a restrictive media policy. Thus, on the night of the planned meeting between the Fortunato Committee and the NPRA, when members of the commission arrived at the prison accompanied by a large number of media representatives, the reporters were denied access and the meeting proceeded in closed session.[126] Members of the commission and the media were outraged. To Southworth's contention that he had the authority to regulate access to the prison, the commission argued that despite the fact that it was held in a maximum security prison, it was still public business covered by the state's open meeting law, and hence the media had a right to attend. Governor Garrahy, while supporting Southworth's action in the matter, directed him to meet with the committee to establish mutually agreeable guidelines for the future. When announced two weeks later, however, the guidelines agreeable to both the department and the committee proved completely unacceptable to the media, permitting only two reporters, selected by the committee, to attend meetings in the prison. *The Journal-Bulletin* characterized it as an "arrogant and arbitrary exercise of authority."[127]

The committee began its proceedings with testimony from those in the prison administration who supported the NPRA. Associate Director Brule and others attested to the fact that the organizations did more for the inmates than did the state and proclaimed that the only force maintaining the peace amid the explosive conditions in the prison was the NPRA.[128] When it came his turn, Assistant Director Laurie, who viewed the committee as part of the problem and was cheered by some 30 correctional officers who had accompanied him to the hearing, dramatically refused to testify.[129] The *Journal-Bulletin* characterized Laurie's action as "an affront to the duly constituted authority of the state's legislative body and by extension to the electorate it represents," and the senate majority leader demanded that he be fired if he did not testify. Governor Garrahy apologized for Laurie's action and ordered him to testify.[130] However, by the time Laurie appeared again before the committee, the course of events had made the work of the committee anti-climatic, if not redundant.

While the significance of the Fortunato Committee's substantive work was eclipsed by the pace of events, its political significance was great. The actions of Southworth and Laurie in regard to the hearings cost them the support of the media and the legislature at a time when that support was vital. Without it, they stood little chance of regaining control of the institution let alone of implementing the court's comprehensive remedial decree.

NOTES

1. President's Commission on Law Enforcement and the Administration of Justice, *Task Force Report: Corrections* (Washington: USGPO, 1967), p. 59.

2. Personal interview with Anthony Travisono, June 24, 1993. It is instructive to contrast this process with that in Illinois at about the same time. As described by Jacobs that department was created only after a year of study by a task force of prison administrators, treatment specialists and prominent academics. The result, however, at least as measured by disorder and human pain and suffering, was much the same. See James B. Jacobs, *Stateville: The Penitentiary in Mass Society* (Chicago: University of Chicago Press, 1977), pp. 74-80.

3. *Bulletin*, June 29, 1972, p. 1.

4. Included within the new agency were the Juvenile Diagnostic Center, the Training Schools, Juvenile Probation and Parole, Adult Probation and Parole, the Adult Correctional Institutions and the Committing Squad—the function of which is to transport inmates to and from court and which formerly had been administratively housed in the judiciary.

5. *Report of the Citizens' Action Council on the Adult Correctional Institution to Frank Licht, Governor of the State Of Rhode Island*, Edward F. Hindle, chairman (R.I. State House Library, June 1972), especially pp. 7-9.

6. Travisono interview, June 24, 1993.

7. Constantine Karalis, *Adult Correctional Facilities, State of Rhode Island* (Providence: R.I. School of Design, September 1972).

8. Rhode Island Public Expenditure Council, *A Review of Recent Planning for New Prison Facilities in Rhode Island* (Providence: Rhode Island Public Expenditure Council, October 25, 1972), p. 6.

9. For a comprehensive, thoughtful and honest analysis of this decade, see Todd Gitlin, *The Sixties: Years of Hope, Days of Rage*, 1st ed., rev. (New York: Bantam Books, 1993).

10. United States Department of Labor, Bureau of Labor Statistics, "Employment and Earnings" (September 1993) Table A-3; Stephen Margolin and Juliet Schor, *The End of the Golden Age* (Oxford: Clarendon Press, 1990).

11. Robert Martinson, "What Works—Questions and Answers About Prison Reform," *Public Interest* 35 (Spring 1974): 22-54. Also see Douglas Lipton, Robert Martinson and Judith Wilks, *The Effectiveness of Correctional Treatment: A Survey of Treatment Evaluation Studies* (New York: Praeger, 1975) and Robert Martinson, "New Findings, New Views: A Note of Caution Regarding Sentencing Reform," *Hofstra Law Review* 7 (Winter 1979): 243-58.

In the latter piece, Martinson reviews newer research that puts treatment efforts in a more favorable light. This work was largely ignored, however.

12. Ronald Bayer, "Crime, Punishment and the Decline of Liberal Optimism," *Crime and Delinquency* 27 (April 1981): 169-190; Francis T. Cullen and Paul Gendreau, "The Effectiveness of Correctional Rehabilitation: Reconsidering the 'Nothing Works' Debate," *The American Prison: Issues in Research and Policy*, ed. Lynne Goodstein and Doris Layton MacKenzie (New York: Plenum Press, 1989), pp. 23-44; James O. Finckenauer, "Crime as a National Political Issue: 1964-76—From Law and Order to Domestic Tranquility," *Crime and Delinquency* 24 (January 1978): 13-27; Andrew von Hirsch, *Doing Justice: The Choice of Punishments* (New York: Hill and Wang, 1976); James Q. Wilson, *Thinking About Crime* (New York Vintage Books, 1975).

13. Timothy J. Flanagan and Susan L. Caulfield, "Public Opinion and Prison Policy: A Review," *The Prison Journal* 64 (Fall-Winter, 1984): 31-41.

14. *Bulletin*, March 26, 1973, p. 13; March 28, 1973, p. 22; *Journal*, March 30, 1973, p. 2. The following account is based on the findings of an investigative committee. *Report of the Committee to Investigate the Adult Correctional Institution Prison Escape on September 20, 1972* (R. I. State House Library, October 26, 1972).

15. *Ibid.*; *Journal*, November 6, 1972, p. 27. One of the inmates was found dead in Massachusetts several days after the escape. He had been executed gangland style. A second killed a Canadian police officer in June 1973 and was sentenced to be hanged. The two others were arrested together in Atlanta in November 1974; one was charged with rape. In February 1973 a guard and 12 inmates were indicted for assisting in the escape. Charges were dropped, however, when the key witness, an inmate informant, hanged himself in a Connecticut prison to which he had been transferred.

16. Personal interview with Anthony Travisono, June 30, 1993.

17. *Bulletin*, November 27, 1972, p. 1; December 7, 1972, p. 37; *Journal*, November 28, 1972, p. 1; December 20, 1972, p. 57.

18. *Bulletin*, June 13, 1973, p. 59.

19. *Bulletin*, March 26, 1973, p. 13; March 28, 1973, p. 22; *Journal*, March 30, 1973, p. 2.

20. Unless otherwise indicated, this account of the riot and the events leading to it is based upon the investigation and report ordered by Governor Noel, *Report of the Committee to Investigate the Uprising at the Maximum Security Facility of the Adult Correctional Institutions on April 2, 1973* (R. I. State House Library, May 10, 1973). The committee consisted of the

department's legal counsel, Edward F. Burke, and four high- level administrators. In addition to examining state police records, the committee took sworn testimony from 32 staff members and 8 inmates.

21. Personal interview with Jonathan Houston, September 9, 1993. Mr. Houston currently heads a private non-profit group, Justice Assistance. His first job in criminal justice was when hired by this organization, Project Beginning, in March 1973 to write grant proposals.

22. Strife along racial and ideological lines seems to have been endemic to prisoners' rights organizations at this time. See the account by John Irwin, one of the founders of the California Prisoners' Union. John Irwin, *Prisons In Turmoil* (Boston: Little Brown and Company, 1980) pp. 92-122. Also see, Eric Cummins, *The Rise and Fall of California's Radical Prison Movement* (Stanford, CA: Stanford University Press, 1994), pp. 215-251. Although nothing came of it, representatives of the California Prisoners' Union visited Rhode Island and Massachusetts in 1973 to discuss affiliation.

23. *Bulletin*, April 3, 1973, p. 1, quoting John Galligan, President of RIBCO.

24. *Ibid.*, p. 25.

25. *Sunday Journal,* June 24, 1973, p. G1.

26. Travisono interview, June 24, 1993.

27. *Bulletin*, May 7, 1973, p. 1.

28. *Bulletin*, May 16, 1973, p. 47; Travisono interview, June 24, 1993.

29. *Journal*, May 17, 1973, p. 34; May 18, 1973, p. 1; May 21, 1973, p. 29; *Sunday Journal,* May 27, 1973, p. A1.

30. Personal interviews with Warden Ronald Brule, September 16, 1992, and Captain Arnold Anderson, October 7, 1992.

31. *Bulletin*, May 31, 1973, p. 1.

32. *Journal*, June 12, 1973, p. 1.

33. *Journal*, June 13, 1973, p. 19; *Bulletin*, June 14, 1973, p. 1.

34. *Journal*, June 22, 1973, p. 1. The officer, Donald Price, was sitting at the guard's desk at about 12:45 AM. He was engaged in conversation by one inmate while the other came up behind the unsuspecting officer, reached around him and stabbed him deeply in the chest several times with a prison-made knife. The assailants had had virtually no contact with the officer, but one of them was reportedly enraged because his request for plastic surgery had been denied.

35. The statute, which made death mandatory for any person who was convicted of homicide committed while under a sentence of confinement, was eventually declared unconstitutional by the R.I. Supreme Court following the

U.S. Supreme Court decisions in *Woodson* and *Roberts*, but this was not until after two inmates had been sentenced under its provisions. See *State v. Cline*, 121 R. I. 299 (1979); *Woodson et al. v. North Carolina*, 428 U.S. 280 (1976); *Roberts v. Louisiana*, 431 U.S. 633 (1977).

36. *Souza v. Travisono*, 308 F. Supp. 959 (D.R.I. 1973) at 961. Such programs were common around the country at this time. In 1974, the LEAA grant for the program was run through the public defender's office, and the program ended in 1975. Telephone interview with Richard A. Boren, October 18, 1993. Mr. Boren was the supervising attorney of the ILAP.

37. *Ben David v. Travisono*, C. A. 73-5280, (D.R. I., August 8-10, 1973).

38. *Morris v. Travisono*, 373 F. Supp. 177 (D.R.I., 1974).

39. *Journal*, November 16, 1973, p. 27.

40. *Bulletin*, January 3, 1974, p. 1. These observations were made by a reporter who accompanied the new officers into the ACI during their first days on the job.

41. *Bulletin*, December 6, 1973, p. 1; *Journal*, January 2, 1974, p. 9.

42. *Sunday Journal*, February 6, 1974, p. A1; *Journal*, February 11, 1974, p.1.

43. *State v. Cline* (1979).

44. Travisono interview, June 30, 1993; Walter J. Fontaine and C. Marc Bousquet, "Evaluation of Adult Basic Education Programs at the Rhode Island Adult Correctional Institutions, August 1973-March 1976" (R. I. Dept of Corrections, June 19, 1976).

45. Travisono, June 30, 1993.

46. *Bulletin*, January 22, 1974, p. 13.

47. Planning and Design Institute, *Rhode Island Pre-Design Study* (Champaign, IL: Planning and Design Institute, 1974), pp. 8-9.

48. *Journal*, December 14, 1973, p. 1.

49. Travisono interview, June 24, 1993.

50. Howard Ohmart and E. K. Nelson, Jr., *Reducing Administrative Disorganization in Rhode Island Corrections* (University of Rhode Island Library, October 10, 1975), pp. 8-11.

51. *Ibid.*

52. Personal interview with Donald D. Taylor, March 24, 1994. Evidence of Mullen's inattention to administrative detail became clear soon after his appointment. As nearly 100 new officers were added to the guard force in late 1973 and early 1974, he left responsibility for the creation of new posts to his deputies. As a result, 32 more posts than could be filled were created, and

122 *Lawful Order*

without his knowledge, manned through officers working overtime. The skyrocketing cost of overtime eventually forced the diversion of funds from program areas and created extreme tension between the Governor and the union in a time of fiscal crisis for the state. See *Journal*, March 25, 1975 p. B1; March 26, 1975, p. B1; April 4, 1975: p. A1.

53. Ohmart and Nelson, pp. 13-14.

54. *Bulletin,* April 3, 1975: p. A1.

55. An evaluation of the program through March 1, 1976 revealed that 63 inmates had received their high school equivalencies and another 56 had significantly improved their math and reading skills. Moreover, two inmates had received Bachelor's degrees through a distance learning project operated jointly with a small private college. See Fontaine and Bousquet, p. 25.

56. Taylor interview; *Bulletin*, March 22, 1975, p. A21; *Journal,* July 6, 1975, p. A16; August 27, 1977, p. A30.

57. *Journal*, June 3, 1975, p. A1; August 31, 1977, p. A18; *Bulletin*, May 12, 1976, p. A2; June 28, 1976, p. B5; March 1, 1977, p. B4.

58. *Bulletin*, October 21, 1974, p. A1; November 4, 1974, p. B5; November 6, 1974, p. A1; February 3, 1975, p. A2; February 20, 1975, p. B1; February 27, 1975, p. A1; February 28, 1975, p. A1. *Journal*, November 3, 1974, p. A1; January 28, 1975, p. A1; February 11, 1975, p. A1. *Journal-Bulletin*, November 16, 1974, p. 6; March 1,1975, p. 5. *Sunday Journal*, November 10, 1974, p. C10.

In absolute terms, these numbers appear low, but a better perspective on violence at the ACI is perhaps gained by converting them to rates. So, for example, the rate of homicide at the ACI for this period was about 363 per 100,000 while the rate of assaults reported was about 2727. By comparison, the respective rates for the country as a whole in 1974 were 9.8 and 216. See U.S. Department of Justice, Federal Bureau of Investigation, *Crime in the United States, 1975* (Washington, DC: USGPO, 1976), Table 2, p. 49.

59. *Bulletin,* October 21, 1975, p. A11; October 22, 1975, p. A3; October 30, 1975, p.A1; October 31, 1975, p. A1; November 1, 1975, p. A1; January 20, 1976, p. B1; January 22, 1976, p. B3; January 26, 1976, p. B3.

60. Ohmart and Nelson, p. 13. *Bulletin*, November 29, 1975, p. A1. By comparison, it is reported in this news article that among the 850 inmates at the maximum security prison in Connecticut only seven were in protective custody.

61. *Bulletin*, December 16, 1974, p. B4; January 28, 1975, p. B3; January 29, 1975, p. B1; *Journal,* December 19, 1974, p. B1; December 22, 1974, p. B6; December 25, 1974, p. B1; January 30, 1975, p. B1

62. James B. Jacobs and Lynne Zimmer, "Collective Bargaining and Labor Unrest," in *New Perspectives on Prisons and Imprisonment*, ed. James B. Jacobs (Ithaca, NY: Cornell University Press), pp. 142-59; John M. Wynne, *Prison Employee Unionism: The Impact on Correctional Administration and Programs* (Washington, DC: USGPO, 1978), esp. chs. 4 and 6.

63. Ohmart and Nelson, pp. 9 and 25.

64. *Agreement Between State of Rhode Island and the Rhode Island Brotherhood of Correctional Officers, July 1975-June 1977*, pp. 21-22.

65. Wynne, pp. 128-36 and 170-76.

66. *Bulletin*, July 17, 1974, p. A1.

67. *Bulletin*, October 31, 1975, p. A1.

68. *Journal*, December 10, 1975, p. A5.

69. This situation is quite possibly unique to Rhode Island. A study conducted about this time, for example, found that where supervisory personnel such as captains and lieutenants were represented by collective bargaining units, they are usually in a separate unit from lower-ranking officers. No mention was even made of personnel as high as deputy wardens being represented in collective bargaining. See Wynne, pp. 109-116.

70. *Journal*, October 25, 1974, p. A1.

71. *Journal*, March 19, 1975, p. A1

72. *Journal-Bulletin*, December 13, 1975, p. A1. A restraining order forbids a person or class of persons from engaging in a certain behavior but involves no finding that they have actually engaged in the behavior in question and carries no penalty for violation. An injunction is based upon a finding that the parties have engaged in the behavior and orders them to desist. Violation of an injunction may result in a finding of contempt and be punished by a fine or incarceration.

73. *Journal*, February 16, 1975, p. F11.

74. *Journal*, April 9, 1975, p. A1.

75. *Journal*, August 14, 1975, p. A1.

76. Irwin, pp. 94-95; Cummins, pp. 215-51. Irwin lists several other states that had similar organizations at the time: California, Minnesota, Massachusetts, North Carolina and Ohio.

77. *Bulletin*, February 7, 1975, p. B1; *Journal*, January 26, 1975, p. B1; April 30, 1975, p. B1.

78. *NPRA News*, February 1976, April 1977. Personal interview with Thomas DeFusco, November 23, 1992; Personal interview with Anthony Souza, March 12, 1993. DeFusco and Souza were both active members of the NPRA.

79. DeFusco interview; Souza interview; *Journal-Bulletin,* January 5, 1974, p. 7; *Bulletin,* April 3, 1975, p. A1.

80. Defusco interview; Souza interview. Personal interview with Jonathan Houston, September 8, 1993. Mr. Houston had been the deputy director of Project Beginning.

81. *Bulletin,* March 10, 1975, p. A2; April 3, 1975, p. B1; April 16, 1975, p. A1; September 18, 1975, p. B6. The conflict revolved around the chaplains' definition of their role as encompassing the advocacy of social justice versus the state's authority, given payment to the diocese for their services, to restrict them to ministering to the spiritual needs of inmates. In the end, the bishop appointed a new team, but the conflict continued and boiled to the surface every so often over the next decade.

82. DeFusco interview.

83. DeFusco interview; Souza interview. Interestingly, both used exactly the same words suggesting perhaps an actual statement to this effect by Warden Mullen.

There is an amazing consensus among all those interviewed about the activities of the NPRA, and the following description reflects that consensus. The interviewees differ, however, in their views of Warden Mullen's motives. Inmates DeFusco and Souza believe simply that Mullen, like most officers and inmates, was terrified of the "heavies." Staff such as Brule and Taylor think he was exchanging privileges in an attempt to gather information on organized crime for his former superior in the state police. I think these views are quite probably biased by the respective positions and attachments of those holding them.

Warden Brule, incidentally, while admitting that the NPRA leaders were granted illegitimate privileges and virtual immunity from punishment, claims that it was Mullen's policy and not his, that his role was merely that of a loyal subordinate. Brule interview. Warden Mullen died some years ago.

84. All of those interviewed about this period mentioned the goat.

85. *Journal,* October 24, 1975, p. B1.

86. *Bulletin,* September 28, 1973, p. 24.

87. *Bulletin,* April 10, 1975, p. A1; April 11, 1975, p. A1; April 16, 1975, p. A19; July 31, 1975, p. B4.

88. *Bulletin,* July 3, 1975, p. A5.

89. *Journal,* September 10, 1975, p. B1.

90. For example, the editors of the *Providence Journal-Bulletin* had raised serious questions about the proposed facility but in early November had come to the conclusion that "supermax is sorely needed at the ACI." *Bulletin,*

September 12, 1975, p. B2; *Journal*, November 6, 1975, p. A24. Also see *Bulletin*, September 16, 1975, p. B1; *Journal*, September 11, 1975, p. A21; September 15, 1975, p. B1; September 18, 1975, p. A14; October 2, 1975, p. B4; *Sunday Journal*, September 21, 1975, p. F1.

91. Ohmart and Nelson, pp. 27-28.

92. *Bulletin*, February 20, 1976, p. A8.

93. *Journal*, February 20, 1976, p. A18. Governor Noel failed in his bid for the Senate.

94. Personal interview with Bradford Southworth, November 19, 1992. *Journal*, February 23, 1976, p. B1. In point of fact, Southworth was not Governor Noel's first or even second choice for director. A nationwide search had been underway since the previous summer, but interested candidates backed away after becoming familiar with the situation. Governor Noel was prepared to nominate a retired police administrator from another state for the directorship but that candidate was taken seriously ill on the eve of his nomination. It was only then that the governor turned to Southworth.

95. Ohmart and Nelson, p. 10.

96. Southworth interview; *Journal*, February 19, 1976, p. A19.

97. Southworth interview; *Journal,* April 14, 1976, p. A8; April 16, 1976, p. A9; *Bulletin*, May 20, 1976, p. B5.

98. Keyes Associates, *Adult Corrections Complex Long Range Plan: Schematic Phase* (Providence, RI: Keyes Associates, 1976), pp. 4-12.

99. *Sunday Journal*, November 21, 1976, p. C1.

100. *Journal*, February 12, 1976, p. B1; March 25, 1976, p. B4.

101. Personal interview with Lt. Kenneth Rivard, August 4, 1992; *Bulletin*, March 25, 1976, p. A1; *Bulletin*, March 26, 1977, p. A1. Lt. Rivard was on the union's negotiating team and is currently its full-time grievance officer. While legislators were aghast, Rivard maintains that such provisions are far from unique and in his study of correctional unionism Wynne notes the existence of similar provisions in other states. See Wynne, p. 163.

102. Southworth interview; *Journal*, August 1, 1976, p. B10.

103. *Ibid.*

104. Southworth interview; *Bulletin*, June 1, 1976, p. p. A6; June 7, 1977, p. B3; *Journal*, August 31, 1977, p. A18.

105. Personal interview with William Laurie, October 28, 1992.

106. *Bulletin*, April 13, 1976, p. A10.

107. *Journal*, July 8, 1976, p. A15; January 26, 1977, p. B10; March 8, 1977, p. B1; April 14, 1977, p. A1.

108. DeFusco interview; Souza interview; *Bulletin*, August 17, 1976, p. A2; December 9, 1976, p. A1; *Sunday Journal*, December 5, 1976, p. C12.

109. DeFusco interview; Souza interview; *Bulletin*, August 11, 1976, p. A3; *Journal*, June 14, 1976, p. B8; August 31, 1976, p. A10.

110. DeFusco interview; Rivard interview; *Journal*, April 11, 1976, p. B20.

111. *Journal*, November 1, 1976, p. A10.

112. DeFusco interview; *Journal*, March 2, 1977, p. A5. The program, however, was never funded.

113. *Bulletin*, September 17, 1976, p. A3.

114. Laurie interview; *Journal,* November 29, 1976, p. A1; *Bulletin,* December 1, 1976, p. D3.

115. *Bulletin,* December 1, 1976, p. D3.

116. Laurie interview; Rivard interview.

117. Laurie interview.

118. Laurie interview; *Bulletin,* March 26, 1977, p. A1; April 13, 1977, p. B4; April 22, 1977, p. B1; *Journal*, March 23, 1977, p. A1.

119. *Report of the Inquiry Commission on the Adult Correctional Institutions* (R.I. Department of Corrections,December 28, 1976).

120. *Ibid.,* quote from p.14.

121. *Bulletin*, March 8, 1977, p. A1.

122. Southworth interview; *Journal*, April 21, 1977, p. B1.

123. Southworth interview; *Bulletin*, January 25, 1977, p. B3.

124. Southworth interview; *Bulletin*, August 4, 1977, p. A1.

125. *Journal*, June 23, 1977, p. A3.

126. Southworth interview; *Journal*, June 23, 1977, p. A3; *Sunday Journal*, July 10, 1977, p. C1.

127. *Journal,* July 7, 1977, p. A1.

128. *Bulletin,* July 20, 1977, p. C6.

129. *Journal,* August 31, 1977, p. A1; Laurie interview. Laurie claims he was ordered not to testify but refuses to say by whom.

130. *Bulletin*, September 1, 1977, p. A19.

CHAPTER 4

Intervention

Even as public sentiments regarding crime and offenders were hardening in the '70s, federal courts were becoming more deeply involved in protecting the rights of inmates. The earliest cases had involved specific correctional practices and conditions; by the late 1960s, however, courts were faced with a new wave of suits in which the plaintiff inmates alleged that the cumulative impact of a multiplicity of conditions constituted cruel and unusual punishment. The first such case, *Holt v. Sarver*, concerned conditions at the two major prisons in Arkansas. In deciding that case, Judge J. Smith Henley held that in determining whether conditions violated the Eighth Amendment, the various conditions "must be considered together" as they "exist in combination; each affects the other; and taken together they have a cumulative impact on the inmates."[1] Thus even though no single condition is so deficient as to be unconstitutional in itself, the cumulative impact of the totality of conditions may be so severe as to constitute cruel and unusual punishment. In Arkansas, for example, the poor medical care and unsanitary living conditions were exacerbated by the fact that the prisons were for the most part operated by inmate "trusties" with little supervision.

   Holt was quickly followed by a number of other cases, the most significant of which concerned conditions in Alabama's prisons. In *Pugh v. Locke* Judge Frank Johnson found these prisons to be "horrendously overcrowded." Inmates were forced to live in "dilapidated and filthy" facilities, not provided with the means to maintain personal hygiene, fed unwholesome food, denied adequate medical care, forced to spend their days in idleness and subjected to rampant

violence.[2] Where Judge Henley had relied solely upon the defendants
to remedy conditions, Judge Johnson issued a comprehensive remedial
order affecting virtually every aspect of prison administration and
appointed a Human Rights Committee to monitor compliance.[3]

As had been true in Arkansas and has since been true in virtually
all states in which such suits have been successful, the issuance of
Judge Johnson's order touched off a long post-decretal stage marked by
sharp conflict and continual legal maneuvering. In part, this was due
to the sheer multiplicity and complexity of the issues involved. More
important, however, was the unwillingness of state officials to
implement the mandated reforms. Little progress was made in
implementing Judge Johnson's order for nearly two years at which time
he stripped the Alabama Board of Corrections of its authority and
placed the system in receivership.[4]

Judge Johnson's order in *Pugh* was a model for that issued in 1977
by Judge Pettine in Rhode Island. Unlike their counterparts in Arkansas
and Alabama, however, Rhode Island's officialdom, for the most part,
welcomed the order and pledged their cooperation. Nonetheless, it was
a year before there was any substantial progress toward
implementation. As we have seen in the previous chapter, the litigation
occurred in the context of a struggle between a powerful inmate
organization and a neophyte administration for control of the
institutions. That struggle had to end before progress could be made.
Within a year of the decree, there was a new administration and the
inmate organization, whose founding had been sanctioned by the court
and whose leaders had brought the suit, was no longer in existence.

PALMIGIANO V. GARRAHY

In July 1974, Nicholas A. Palmigiano, president of the NPRA, filed a
complaint with the federal court in Providence alleging that the state
was in violation of the Eighth and Fourteenth Amendments and Rhode
Island law by denying inmates adequate medical care and by failing to
classify them appropriately. Palmigiano was no stranger to either the
prison or the courtroom. He had an extensive record as a juvenile and
adult, and at the time of the filing was six years into a life sentence for

the murder of a guard during a payroll robbery. He was, moreover, a jailhouse lawyer of some renown. In 1970 he had successfully challenged the ACI's policies with respect to the censorship of mail. Several years later, when president of the NPRA, he alleged that he had been denied procedural due process by not being allowed to have his attorney accompany him to a disciplinary hearing concerning an incident for which he might face criminal prosecution. That case had made its way to the United States Supreme Court which ruled against him.[5]

The current suit, which initially sought $25 million in damages, was filed *pro se* and accompanied by a petition to proceed *in forma pauperis*. Attorney John Farley of the Inmate Legal Assistance Program[6] had provided advice to Palmigiano in preparing the petition, and early in 1975 he contacted a local attorney to represent him. In just one year of practice at R.I. Legal Services following his graduation from Yale Law School, Bob Mann had established a reputation as an outstanding litigator and a fierce civil libertarian. Although he loved the work he was doing at Legal Services, he chafed at the increasing restraints placed on the cases the organization could accept, and in mid-1974 he had left and established a solo practice. That fall he had been asked to represent the protective custody inmates who opposed the plan developed by the NPRA that would have transferred them from Medium Security to space in "Old Max." His performance in that case had caught Farley's attention as well as that of several other experienced but now somewhat burnt-out prisoners' rights advocates. In concert they prevailed upon Mann to take the case.[7]

Mann successfully sought to consolidate Palmigiano's suit with another filed in February 1975 by Thomas Ross, Palmigiano's successor as president of the NPRA and also an experienced litigator. The principal assertions in the consolidated complaint were that the state subjected plaintiffs to constitutionally impermissible conditions of confinement including gross filth, unsanitary and unsafe living quarters, inadequate medical care and that they were forced to live in near-total idleness amid rampant violence which put them in fear of their lives. Further the petition alleged that the conditions to which pre-trial detainees and those in protective custody were subjected were even worse than those suffered by sentenced prisoners in the general population.[8]

Rather quickly, Mann realized that the issues involved in the case exceeded his resources, and he contacted a number of prisoners' rights organizations requesting assistance. Mann's request was received favorably by Alvin Bronstein, director of the American Civil Liberties Union's National Prison Project (NPP). Bronstein had founded the NPP in 1972 to provide public education about prison conditions, backup assistance to local attorneys and to litigate selected cases. By 1975, the Project employed eight full-time staff attorneys and was generally recognized as the premier prisoners' rights project in the country. In August of that year, they had successfully tried *Pugh v. Locke* before Judge Johnson in Alabama. Reviewing *Palmigiano*, Bronstein saw that it involved many of the same issues. Moreover, his chief assistant, Matthew Myers, had clerked for Judge Pettine and was thus very familiar with the judge's judicial philosophy and his concern for prisoners' rights. To Bronstein, it seemed to be an excellent opportunity to deliver a message he felt important that the nation hear: that wretched prison conditions were to be found throughout the country, in the "enlightened" northeast as well as in the "reactionary" old south.[9]

The Trial

The NPP entered the case as lead counsel early in 1976, amending the original complaint, adding several defendants and requesting that it be certified as a class action on behalf of all prisoners at the ACI. That request was granted in July 1976, and the case went to trial in April 1977. One observer has commented that if litigation were a baseball game the plaintiffs in *Palmigiano* would have won in a shutout.[10] The state was simply no match for the plaintiffs' team with its specialized legal knowledge and heavy-hitting corrections experts from around the country. The case had been assigned for trial to one of the attorney general's most able and experienced litigators, William Brody, but he made his first appearance just eight months before the trial began in April 1977.[11] Prior to that time, the state had been represented by a succession of young assistant attorney generals, most of whom had left the office with the change of administrations in January. Moreover, this was only one of several major cases that Brody was handling, leaving him little time to prepare his witnesses. His key witnesses, Brad Southworth and Bill Laurie, not being corrections professionals, had no sense of the significance of the litigation. Being engaged in conflict on several other fronts, moreover, had left them little time to prepare and they were informed of the trial date only three days before it began.[12]

On the first day of the trial, Paul Keve, a former commissioner of corrections in both Delaware and Minnesota, testified that in his 36 years of experience he had never seen an institution "so uniformly poor in sanitation, housekeeping, general care and maintenance."[13] Theodore Gordon, a specialist in institutional hygiene, described the ACI as "the dirtiest and worst maintained prison he had ever seen" and concluded that it "is unfit for human habitation."[14]

In an unexpected move, Judge Pettine declared a recess in the middle of Gordon's testimony and went immediately to the prison so that he might see for himself "'the junk and garbage and encrustations of filth' that this witness has talked about."[15] In the segregation unit in the basement of Medium—the "green monster"—the judge and his entourage were greeted with obscenities from inmates standing in a passageway strewn with garbage, trash and human feces. In Maximum's kitchen, they observed open food containers stored on top of garbage cans which in turn surrounded a solid waste disposal area infested with flies and pigeons, a few of which were dead. There were mice droppings in the food; a thick layer of grease and grime coated everything from stove hoods to knives, and there was nowhere for those working in the food service area to wash their hands. Conditions elsewhere were much the same, and everywhere he went the judge saw inmates who were not engaged in any productive activity.[16]

Carl Clements, a University of Alabama psychologist who had previously testified in *Pugh,* testified on the third day that the idleness in Rhode Island's prisons was worse than anything he had seen in Alabama. Clements concluded that the lack of programs and services and the absence of meaningful activity meant that "'deterioration [of inmates] is virtually inevitable.'"[17] The next day, the venerable reformer, William Nagel, observed that the idleness of inmates in protective custody was even worse than in the general population and was "more complete than he had ever observed in an American prison."[18]

Another major factor contributing to the near-inevitability of deleterious effects of confinement on inmates, Clements noted in his testimony, was a classification system that had for all practical purposes ceased to function. All inmates—regardless of age, prior record or sentence—were initially classified to maximum security. As had been pointed out earlier by Ohmart and Nelson and by the Governor's Advisory Commission, potential predators thus lived in close proximity to their prospective prey with the result that sexual assault and other forms of violence were rampant. Clements told the court of a case he had found in the classification records. An inmate had suffered a breakdown after being gang-raped several times. At a subsequent parole hearing, he was denied parole because the board thought he needed drug treatment and psychiatric counselling. Neither drug treatment nor psychotherapy were available at the ACI.[19]

Citing a study that the department had itself commissioned in 1975 the court observed that at that time some 15 to 40 inmates remained addicted to heroin while at the ACI and that another 70-80% of the population were users. By contrast, Dr. Anthony Raynes, a specialist in the treatment of addiction, reported only 2 current addicts in the population at the maximum security prison in Massachusetts and only 10 to 20 percent using drugs. Yet Rhode Island, at the time of the trial, had not established a drug treatment unit and treated addiction in a way that Dr. Raynes likened to treating other diseases with leeches.[20]

Dr. Lambert King, medical director at the Cook County Jail in Chicago, found that "the level of medical care falls far below anything I have ever seen in a prison."[21] After giving extensive evidence of the deficient care, Dr. King was asked by Judge Pettine if he had observed anything positive. Thinking for a moment, Dr. King replied that the medical director, who had been hired recently, was aware that changes were necessary. Queried further by the judge, he offered that an x-ray machine recommended three years ago had finally been purchased and that the physician's notes were typed and quite legible.[22]

The state's case was seemingly offered with an eye toward public opinion just two months before a special referendum on a bond issue to construct an intake service center. For the most part, state witnesses conceded that conditions were as described by plaintiffs but blamed the situation on inadequate funds and based their defense on its good intentions and plans for the future. Director Southworth, for example, was forced to admit that an outside expert engaged by the state to counter testimony about living conditions in Maximum Security was not produced at trial because having viewed the conditions "this individual was not able to say much good about these matters."[23] He then laid before the court his plan to open a drug treatment program by the coming August 31, to renovate two abandoned buildings at the state's psychiatric hospital for use as minimum security by June of the following year and to open both the high security center and the as-yet-unfunded intake services center by June 30, 1979. At that point, Southworth testified, Maximum Security—which he held would be too costly to bring up to standards—would be closed.[24]

Opinion and Order

Judge Pettine was not swayed by the state's sanguine prognosis nor by the fact that subsequent to the trial the voters approved the bond issue for the intake services center. On August 10, 1977, he entered an opinion in which he found that Rhode Island's prisons were "unfit for human habitation and shocking to the conscience of a reasonably civilized person." Studies going back as far as 1973 gave ample evidence that these conditions had been in existence for some time, that they had repeatedly been called to the attention of responsible officials yet remained unremedied. That such conditions could have persisted for so long could, in the judge's mind, only mean that officials have consciously disregarded them, thus displaying callous indifference to the grave and substantial risks posed to the health, well-being and safety of the inmates entrusted to their care.[25]

Regarding the defendant's plans, he commented that they seemed "vague and hastily drawn and . . . more accurately described as a compendium of hopes and wishes than as a realistic guide to future conduct."[26] Merely constructing new facilities would not, in Judge

Pettine's view, solve the problem as the new facilities would soon resemble those they replaced if they were operated in the same fashion.[27] In any event, the record in the case is "replete with plans that have never materialized" so that the current plan provides "no reason to depart from the conclusion . . . that the present management of the ACI is basically incapable of creating a safe, orderly, and hygienic prison."[28]

Citing the caution about interfering with the operation of prison systems issued to the federal district courts by the U. S. Supreme Court in the then-recent decision, *Procunier v. Martinez*,[29] Judge Pettine went on to cite federal precedents to support the position that each of his factual findings, in and of itself, was sufficient to support intervention, and proclaimed that:

> Officials who engage in massive, systemic deprivations of prisoners' constitutional rights are entitled to, and can expect, no deference from the federal courts, for the constitution reserves no power to the state to violate constitutional rights of any citizens. . . . Nor can lack of funds, or invocations of the virtues of the legislative process, excuse constitutional violations or judicial default.[30]

On the basis of the factual record before it and its authority under the law, Judge Pettine held that the court had a duty to require Rhode Island officials to remedy the massive constitutional violations plaguing the ACI. To that end, he crafted a comprehensive and detailed remedial decree replete with deadlines and relevant standards.[31] Within three months from the entry of the order, all pre-trial detainees were to be removed from Maximum Security and housed in separate facilities which met the minimal standards set for sentenced prisoners. Additionally, detainees were to be provided access to recreational, educational and treatment programs and, on a voluntary basis, constructive work opportunities. Similar provisions applied to those in protective custody although defendants were given nine months to achieve this.

The maximum security facility itself was to be closed within a year from the date of the order. In the meantime, the population in Maximum was to be reduced via reclassification, and the facility brought into "economically feasible and practicable compliance with minimal standards."[32] If the new high security center was not yet open at the time Maximum was to be closed, those inmates classified to high security could continue to be housed in Maximum provided it was made fit for human habitation and there was compliance with other provisions of the order.

All other facilities were to be brought into compliance with the minimal standards set forth by the United States Public Health Service, the American Public Health Association and the State of Rhode Island's Department of Health. Specific areas of concern included, but were not limited to: heat, light and ventilation; cleaning and maintenance; insect and rodent control; food storage and preparation; toilets and showers and bedding. No inmate was to be confined in a cell of less than 60 square feet.

The department was to reclassify all inmates and develop a written classification or treatment plan for each one within six months from the entry of the order. Three months later, all prisoners were to be assigned to facilities appropriate to their security classification. To implement the classification plans, the defendants were to establish a number of programs with sufficient resources so that all prisoners would have the opportunity to participate regularly. These programs included adult basic education, pre-vocational and vocational training, college extension programs, meaningful work and recreation programs, pre-release and work release programs.

Within three months the department was to establish a program for the treatment of drug abuse that met the minimum standards of the organizations noted above. They were to bring health care into compliance with the standards of these same organizations within six months. And they were to hire an adequate number of mental health professionals to diagnose, treat and care for those prisoners with mental health problems.

The court would appoint a Human Rights Committee within 30 days to monitor the department's compliance with the order. As his opinion makes clear, Judge Pettine saw ineffectual management, indeed an abdication of managerial responsibility, as the root cause of the unconstitutional conditions, and he candidly expressed his doubt about the current administration's ability to bring the system up to acceptable standards. These suspicions had been reinforced in hearings concurrent with *Palmigiano* in which he found that the department had failed to implement virtually any of the provisions of a 1973 consent decree concerning conditions at the Boys' Training School.[33] Thus, he believed close monitoring of compliance was essential, and he thought Judge Johnson's concept of a Human Rights Committee ideally suited for this purpose "because it would bring a whole cross-section of the conscience of the community right into the prison."[34]

Reaction

Remedial decrees mandating massive changes in prison conditions are typically greeted with hostility and resistance. Governor George Wallace of Alabama, in the midst of a campaign for the presidency at the time of Judge Johnson's order in *Pugh*, immediately called a press conference to condemn the order and announce his intention to appeal. Asked whether he thought the order might affect his chances for the presidency, he replied "a vote for George C. Wallace might give a political barbed wire enema to some federal judges."[35] Several years later, Texas officials refused to concede that any aspect of their operations were unconstitutional and for fifteen months outrightly defied Judge Justice's order in *Ruiz* while engaging in an open campaign to denigrate the judge personally.[36]

Some Rhode Island officials reacted to Judge Pettine's order in the same way. Former Governor Noel, for example, proclaimed the order to be "totally unrealistic" and complained that "this guy [Judge Pettine] will tax the people right out of the state."[37] For the most part, however, the response to the order was positive. The editors of the *Providence Journal-Bulletin*, the headlines of which had trumpeted the disorder and turmoil in the prison system for years, unequivocally supported both the order and the judge.[38] In a state the size of Rhode Island, such strong support from the editors of the state's major newspaper, one with statewide circulation, undercut any political opposition that may have developed.

The lack of opposition was also due in large measure to the stance taken by Governor Garrahy, who viewed the situation much differently than his predecessor. Garrahy had only taken office in January and thus could not credibly be held responsible for the situation in the prison. On the day the order was entered, he had little to say beyond the fact that he had directed his staff to study the decision in detail and commenting that "Judge Pettine and I have a common goal—the upgrading of conditions at the ACI."[39]

Two weeks after the decision, the governor let it be known that he was in basic agreement with the decision and was not disposed to appeal it providing the court would extend some of the deadlines and dispense with the Human Rights Committee. To show his good faith Governor Garrahy announced that he was forming a team composed of some top administrators from other state agencies to work full-time to expedite the implementation of the order by assisting the Corrections Department in developing plans, finding personnel and resources and cutting red tape. Further, he had contacted officials in the White House to secure their assistance in locating a corrections expert to assist in the implementation.[40]

Bronstein and Myers had argued in a posttrial memorandum that a Human Rights Committee might not provide the department with the correctional and administrative expertise it so desperately needed and that would be the *sine qua non* of implementation. They had earlier recommended that Judge Pettine appoint a special master under Rule 53 of the Federal Rules of Civil Procedure, an agent of the court who would in essence serve as the judge's surrogate during the implementation process.[41] While the judge had not at first accepted their recommendation, with the governor's open acknowledgement that the state would need expert assistance, he now saw the appointment of a special master as a unique and exciting opportunity for the executive and judiciary to join in a common enterprise. Thus, he modified his order, replacing the Human Rights Committee with a special master to be appointed by the court from lists submitted by both sides. The person appointed was to be a correctional expert who would advise and assist the state as well as monitor compliance.[42] The master was to have unlimited access to all facilities and to all records and files with no advance notice required; was authorized to conduct confidential interviews, without advance notice, with any staff member and to require written reports regarding compliance from any staff member. Moreover, the master was empowered to recommend to the court the hiring, transfer or termination of personnel if such was deemed necessary to implement the order.[43]

On October 27, 1977, Allen Breed was appointed special master. Breed was then a visiting fellow at the National Institute of Justice, having retired the previous year after a decade as head of the California Youth Authority. Athletically trim, constantly in motion and seemingly bursting with energy, Breed arrived in Rhode Island praising the cooperation between the federal court and the state house. The unique situation, he hoped, would make it possible to take "what is widely reputed to be one of the worst systems in the country" and to create the first department accredited under the standards recently promulgated by the American Correctional Association. However, in what was to prove a profound understatement, he cautioned that it might take a year or so to accomplish the court's mandate.[44]

CULMINATION OF THE POWER STRUGGLE

On the day of Breed's appointment, the ACI's Maximum Security entered the third month of a lockup, and it was to be another four months until the lockup ended. During this period, not much was accomplished implementing the order in *Palmigiano*, and the court was to find itself drawn reluctantly into the internal affairs of the department.

The Lockup

As will be recalled from the previous chapter, following a disturbance in December 1976, Southworth and Laurie had allied themselves with the officers' union and begun a crackdown on the NPRA. In the aftermath of the *Palmigiano* trial with the statewide publicity of the horrendous conditions in the prison, the inmate organization whose leadership had brought the suit received widespread public support, and its legislative allies launched a counterattack, in the form of a senate investigation, against the correctional administrators. Thus, by the early summer of 1977, an intense struggle for control was being waged in and around the prison.

Southworth had sought to transfer the NPRA's leaders to federal prisons but these efforts had been unsuccessful, and the administrators felt powerless to abolish the NPRA outright because its existence had been sanctioned by the court in 1972.[45] In June 1977, however, a U.S. Supreme Court decision gave them firmer legal ground on which to take a strong stand. In that decision, *Jones v. North Carolina Prisoners' Union*,[46] the Court held that regulations which prohibited the solicitation of inmates to join a prisoners' union and which banned meetings of the union in prisons did not violate inmates' rights because they were rationally related to the reasonable objectives of prison administration, i.e., the maintenance of security and internal order.

The order in *Palmigiano* two months later provided Rhode Island's officials with a rationale for stronger administrative control, and two weeks later yet another racial disturbance provided the occasion. The incident began earlier that afternoon when a young, black inmate had been denied a visit with his brother and a friend who had travelled from out of state to see him. The reason for the denial had been that it was not his day for visits—as it turned out, this was an administrative error—and he requested a special visit. It was customary for inmates to be granted exceptions under such circumstances, but just two weeks previously Laurie had ordered the practice stopped when a special visitor for one of the white inmate leaders had been found with a pint of Scotch taped to his leg. As this was being explained to the black inmate, there was a call over the loudspeaker for the very same white inmate leader to report to the visiting room. The black inmate knew this had to be a special visit as it was not the white inmate's visiting day either. He flew into a rage, throwing furniture and striking the captain several times before he could be restrained and moved to segregation.(Later investigation showed the black inmate was correct about the visiting days; moreover, the record shows that the white inmate in question received four special visits that afternoon.)[47]

Word of the incident spread during the afternoon, and it was rumored that the inmate had been beaten. Late that afternoon, a group of some 65-70 inmates, mostly black, confronted a captain and several officers demanding to see the inmate in order to determine for themselves if he had been beaten. When this request was summarily denied, they surrounded the officers and assaulted them. Officers coming to the aid of their co-workers extricated them only by forming themselves into a riot control formation and dragging the injured officers out of the wing through some 200 inmates who were milling about and threatening them. All officers then retreated from the wing which remained under the control of inmates for the next two hours.

Learning of the situation, Laurie immediately summoned the state police, a contingent of whom soon appeared in riot gear. The police waited along with some 50 visibly angry and hostile officers in the entry to Maximum Security while Southworth and Laurie deliberated about how to respond. In the meantime, Deputy Warden Brule and Captain Costa had reentered the wing and were attempting to persuade the inmates to reenter their cells peacefully.

Brule and Costa had some success, and those who had assaulted the officers agreed to go to segregation providing there was no general lockup. The two officials agreed to this, and there were several announcements made over the loudspeaker to the effect that if all returned to their cells peacefully, normal routine would resume the next day. As sunset neared, however, some 30 to 40 inmates remained out of their cells with access to the yard. Fearing an escape, Southworth and Laurie ordered the state police into the prison. The inmates offered no resistance, and within five minutes all had returned to their cells.

Reviewing the situation later that evening, Southworth and Laurie were told by union leaders that if they did not institute a lockup, the officers would walk off the job in the morning. In considering this, they also became aware of the opportunity that a lockup presented them. Thus, despite the pledges made by Brule and Costa, the institution remained under lock the next day while the administrators and union leaders met to develop plans to place control back in the hands of the officers.[48]

With the prisoners under lock and key, the NPRA trailer was to be removed and the organization's offices in the industrial building were to be demolished. A cell-by-cell search was to be instituted with the officers instructed to remove all items not specified on a list published by the American Correctional Association. Curtains, refrigerators, hot plates, phones, stereos and such were to be things of the past. Administrative staff and union leaders were to work together to evaluate all posts, update post orders and develop written policies and procedures. And, finally, professional cleaning and exterminating firms were to be brought in to begin implementing the court's orders regarding environmental health and sanitation.

As the administration's objectives became clear, NPRA leaders organized resistance. What began as a lockup soon became a standoff. Inmates refused to leave their cells for showers and exercise, making it difficult for officers to conduct cell searches. At first, the inmates were merely placed on report for refusing an order, and the suspected organizers were placed in segregation. But resistance continued. With segregation filled to capacity, officers began forcibly removing inmates from their cells in order to search them. Inmates were held in restraints while they watched valued belongings tossed out of their cells onto tiers. They began placing soap shaving on the metal tiers to make the officers slip, pelting them with food and excrement and showering them with urine. Frustrated and angry officers with no further resources with which to compel compliance fell back on naked force and exacted retribution in the process: "You whack one of our guys, we're going to take you out. If a guy needed one punch to put him down, he got five."[49]

The inmates who had been placed in segregation following the disturbance began a hunger strike to protest brutal beatings to which they claimed they were routinely subjected. Despite observations of lawyers who had visited the strikers that some of them had lost as much as 30 pounds, Southworth and Laurie claimed both the alleged brutality and the hunger strike were fabrications and refused to meet with the inmates. Moreover, they would not permit the strikers to be interviewed by the press.[50] These actions rekindled resistance to ending the lockup in Maximum Security, and prompted an investigation by the now terribly frustrated and impatient special master.

Public Reaction and Court Involvement

The lockup itself had ignited a public controversy, fanning the flames of an ongoing investigation of the prison administration by a State Senate Committee. At a press conference the day after the incident, the Chairman of the Committee, Senator Stephen Fortunato, accused Southworth and Laurie of "gross stupidity and outright falsification" and requested that Governor Garrahy fire them for "incompetence."[51] It was in this context, it will be remembered, that Laurie refused to testify before Senator Fortunato's committee and publicly blamed the incident on "the federal court, the press and screaming liberals in the state Senate."[52]

Governor Garrahy, while admonishing Laurie, resisted the pressure to fire his administrators. To counter the Fortunato Committee, he appointed his own investigatory committee headed by the highly respected president of a local college, the Very Rev. Thomas R. Peterson. The two committees submitted their respective reports in mid-October within 10 days of each other. The Fortunato Committee relied heavily on the testimony of Deputy Brule and Captain Costa that the lockup was unnecessary and undermined their capacity to administer the prison. It could not reach a consensus on whether Southworth and Laurie should be fired, however, and merely called upon Governor Garrahy to "scrutinize the leadership closely."[53] The report of the Peterson Committee, in contrast, gave great weight to the observations of the state police who were on the scene. It concluded that Laurie's actions in calling the police were justified: that given the general atmosphere in the prison at the time, the lockup was "a sound and judicious exercise of administrative authority."[54] However, the Peterson Committee emphasized the need for the administration to develop a unified philosophy and strongly recommended that privileges be more uniformly distributed among inmates and that there be an investigation of racial discrimination.[55]

While the Fortunato and Peterson Committees were preparing their respective reports, Southworth and Laurie received support from an unexpected source, the federal court. NPRA leaders sought a temporary restraining order to end the lockup. After hearing testimony from both sides, including that of Brule and Costa, and reviewing the administration's plans to end the lockup, Judge Pettine denied their request. Noting that the state's response to his sweeping order of August 10 has been a "refreshing approach, this court has not experienced before," the judge opined that he could find nothing in the allegations to indicate that the inmates were being deprived of necessities. Moreover, the judge's oral opinion suggested a lack of sympathy with the inmates whom he believed were not cooperating with his request to cease resisting the state's plan to phase out the lockup.[56]

As the lockup dragged on into November, however, Judge Pettine decided to receive additional evidence. Director Southworth testified that the continuance of the lockup was necessary to restore order and control and that it was continuing because of the disruptive behavior of inmates. Deputy Warden Brule painted another picture, however. He told the court the lockup was not restoring order and security, that as many inmates were being "booked" for alcohol or drug violations and contraband during the lockup as before. Both Brule and Costa testified that much of the disruptive behavior of inmates was due to harassment by correctional officers. In Brule's opinion, the lockup could be ended within two weeks. He had prepared such a plan and submitted it to his superiors, but they had not responded to it.[57]

Dr. Augustus Kinzel, a forensic psychiatrist on the faculty of Columbia University Medical School, testified that a large number of inmates were having psychotic reactions, experiencing day-night reversal, feeling that their bodies were falling apart, had developed an extreme sensitivity to noise, and were experiencing a withdrawal of interest in social interaction. The department's recently hired psychiatrist, Dr. Frank Perretta, largely corroborated Dr. Kinzel's testimony.[58]

Still, Judge Pettine, anxious to retain the cooperative relationship that had been established with Governor Garrahy, was reluctant to order an end to the lockup. A number of incidents that had occurred during the hearing were now seriously straining that relationship. At one point there had been rumors that the judge intended to relieve Southworth and Laurie.[59] These had been quickly denied but had scarcely died down when the judge angered the governor by requesting that the court be permitted to review a pending agreement with the officers' union before it was signed. Stating that such negotiations are "strictly the responsibility of state government and outside the purview of the federal court" Governor Garrahy firmly denied this request.[60]

Shortly after, however, Brule and Costa were placed on paid leave, pending a departmental hearing, for allowing inmates out of their cells to circulate a petition calling for the court to replace Southworth and Laurie. The suspended subordinates petitioned the court to reinstate them, arguing their suspension was actually in retaliation for their testimony. When Judge Pettine ordered their reinstatement pending a full hearing by the court in early December, the governor leveled a broadside, accusing the judge of a "lack of objectivity" and seemingly drawing a boundary between the court and the state: "When he starts to interfere with the internal management of state government, it bothers me. . . . He can monitor, he can examine, but it's my responsibility to run it."[61]

Fearing that an order to end the lockup would further antagonize the governor, Judge Pettine directed Special Master Breed to assist Southworth and Laurie in developing a realistic plan to end it. Even if it were not ended immediately, a plan with a definite timetable would, the judge believed, render the case moot. Breed informed the judge that he had been encouraging Southworth to ease the lockup and been given assurances that they would begin serving meals in the dining hall during the very next day and increase programming the following week.[62] Despite assurances and public announcements, these plans were not implemented at the promised time. According to Breed, none of the necessary planning, coordination and training was even done. It was not until December 28 that the changes initially planned for the first week of December were made, and still Breed found the plan to be so poorly constructed and implemented that he felt sure the resulting confusion would cause another incident that would provide justification to lock the institution up again.[63] Several incidents did in fact occur and those involved in them remained locked up.

Thus, early in January as Judge Pettine was about to prepare an opinion on the lockup, it was unclear whether the lockup was still in effect. The correctional administrators claimed it had been lifted, that they were aggressively developing programs and that only those who caused additional disruptions were locked in their cells. The NPRA, however, claimed that the vast majority of inmates remained in their cells 21 or more hours per day and that few were involved in programs. Before preparing his opinion, Judge Pettine directed the special master to investigate and report to the court.

In a fifteen-page memorandum, Breed concluded that it is "clear that present conditions do not represent a significant change from lockup status."[64] In support of this conclusion he offered the following examples: (1) the majority of inmates remain in their cells for 20 to 22 hours per day, (2) that only some 50 to 60 inmates out of a population of 400 work on any given day and then only for a few hours, (3) that only another 10 to 15 attend classes on a given day and then for less than two hours, and (4) that the two meals taken out of their cells must be consumed within twenty minutes.

Breed informed the court that in his opinion, "conditions have deteriorated dramatically during the last five months" and that the continuation of the lockup "constitutes an absolute barrier to the implementation" of the order in *Palmigiano*.[65] Among other things he noted that there were fewer work opportunities in January than there had been in August, that not a single new activity had been developed in five months, that many inmates were without blankets even though temperatures in the cell blocks frequently fell below freezing at night and that there had been no serious effort made to improve cleanliness and sanitation. Moreover, as a result of mass "bookings" of entire cell blocks the *Morris* Rules were, in effect, suspended.

Breed acknowledged that the length of the lockup was due, in part, to the refusal of inmates to cooperate with plans to end it and allowed that many might be being pressured to resist. But, he argued, given the plight of those who might cooperate only at considerable risk to themselves, it was irresponsible for the administrators to refuse to negotiate in any way with inmate leaders who expressed a desire to develop a constructive plan.

Taking into account the questionable necessity for the lockup to begin with, its nature and length, the deleterious impact on inmates, and the absence of any current emergency, Judge Pettine concluded that it "runs afoul of every definition of cruel and unusual punishment."[66]

He ordered defendants to submit, within five days of the order, a plan for ending the lockup and to be prepared to implement it within fourteen days of its approval by the court. At the urging of Breed, who was by now convinced that the department was incapable of planning, the order specified precisely what was to be done leaving to the department only the question of how this was to be accomplished.[67]

Implementation and Ouster

By the time the order ending the lockup was entered, Breed was convinced that Southworth and Laurie had to be replaced. That conviction had formed in light of their apparent inability to plan an end to the lockup early in December but grew in proportion to the department's inertia with respect to implementing the court's order in *Palmigiano.*

Governor Garrahy, two weeks after the remedial decree, had established an Implementation Team to assist the department in developing plans and securing resources. This team, composed of three high-ranking and highly regarded senior officials, in turn formed a number of task forces—health, mental health, education, vocational training, etc.— to determine what needed to be done, to set priorities, and develop plans. Nonetheless, for four months there was little progress made in implementing the remedial decree, fueling Breed's doubts about the capacities of Southworth and Laurie. The lack of progress is most clear with respect to classification.[68] As there could be no realistic planning for facilities or programs without a profile of the inmate population in terms of security risk and treatment needs, Judge Pettine strongly believed that the reclassification of all inmates was the cornerstone of his remedial order and had ordered the department to complete such within six months. Early on, the department had decided that it would be necessary to retain an external consultant to assist in the process, and the Implementation Team had secured the necessary approvals. Nonetheless, the hiring process alone took three months. In the meantime, no staff were reassigned to gather the information that would be necessary for reclassification nor were any additional staff hired. The classification board merely continued business as usual, meeting several times a week to process furlough and work release applications.

When the consultant was hired on November 5, he requested the reassignment of several staff to prepare social histories on 100 inmates over the next two weeks so that he might begin to reclassify them. When he returned two weeks later, not only had the social histories not been completed, no staff had even been assigned to the task. It was to be another month before staff were assigned to do the social histories, and the professional staff needed to administer and interpret psychological tests were not hired until mid-January, just three weeks before the deadline for the completion of reclassification.

Informed of the situation on December 7, Breed directed the department's classification consultant to work throughout the day with the classification staff to establish a plan to meet the court's order and to inform him of the needed resources. The plan presented to him the next day indicated the need for a large number of additional staff, and Breed then "laid out with the head of the classification section what would be necessary for him to do to get temporary staff and asked that he get back with me in forty-eight hours if he had run into any bureaucratic roadblocks."[69]

Breed had at first tried to define his role as that of a detached observer but as the above example suggests, found himself continually being thrust into a leadership role.[70] Meetings seemed to go nowhere until he made his views known, at which point these seemed to become the group consensus. Bewildered staff came to him individually, venting frustration at the lack of direction and support from their superiors and seeking his advice and assistance in determining what they had to do in order to meet the court's mandate with respect to their area of responsibility.[71] Breed was thus confronted with a dilemma. Should he shore up the current administration, doing all that he could to see that the order was implemented and run the risk of leaving the department with inadequate leadership? Or should he remain detached and see nothing accomplished in the expectation that the resultant crisis would force the governor to recruit a new and hopefully more capable director?[72] As suggested by the example above, he adopted a middle course. On a number of occasions, he galvanized the department into action, defining the problem and assisting in securing technical experts and needed resources but left the detailed planning and implementation to Southworth and his staff, carefully documenting their failures.

Almost as soon as he had formed an opinion of Southworth's ability, Breed had shared it with Governor Garrahy. The governor indicated that he might be willing to replace the director if a suitable replacement could be found but seemed reluctant.[73] At this point, the governor was becoming deeply concerned about the intrusions of the court into executive prerogatives. Moreover, with the legislature about to convene in January, he was coming under pressure about the estimated costs of compliance. To avoid the appearance of being weak, he had begun, as we have seen, to take a stronger stand with the court. In addition to his continued public support for Southworth, he now threatened to appeal the order of reference appointing Breed on the grounds that the charge to the special master exceeded the scope of the remedial decree by directing him to establish a grievance procedure at the ACI and authorizing him to conduct his own hearings.[74]

Despite the growing tension, Breed began a campaign to persuade the governor to take action on Southworth and Laurie. In addition to documenting their failures, he encouraged disgruntled staff and implementation team members to make their views known to the governor or his staff. He arranged for Raymond Procunier, former director in California and known in corrections circles as "the Pro," to evaluate Southworth and Laurie and communicate his views personally to the governor, and he made sure that the governor was aware of the opinions of other consultants brought in to assist the department.[75] Finally, after completing his investigation of the lockup, he publicly stated in an interview that the ACI "is one of the worst institutions in the country . . . falling apart piece by piece . . . and Southworth and Laurie do not have the necessary skills to be able to put it together."[76]

By the time of Breed's statement to the press, Governor Garrahy had been persuaded to interview several people whom Breed had recruited. Although perhaps not planned as such—Breed gave the interview reluctantly and understood it was to be used only as background material[77]—the salvo in the newspaper angered the governor and spurred him into action. The day after the interview appeared Governor Garrahy indicated to Breed, even while expressing his extreme displeasure with the interview, that he was very impressed with the first candidate and wanted to check his references further. Within the week, Southworth's resignation had been secured and John Moran, who had himself been recently ousted as director of corrections in Arizona, named to replace him.

Although successful, the effort to orchestrate a change in leadership had exacted a price. To appease the governor and avoid an appeal, Judge Pettine did modify his order appointing Breed, removing that section charging the special master to establish a grievance procedure within the Department of Corrections. That action may have influenced the governor to agree to search for a replacement for Southworth, but the lack of a grievance procedure was to be a problem in the years ahead.[78] Moreover, the governor's cooperation was to be rather short lived. Garrahy felt personally betrayed by his adviser's unauthorized remarks to the press.[79] With an experienced corrections professional in his camp, the governor was no longer dependent on this court-appointed outside expert, and the once-close relationship between the state's chief executive and the federal court became increasingly distant and tense.

A NEW REGIME

Moran was the first seasoned prison administrator appointed to head Rhode Island's correctional system since the appointment of Warden Gough in 1956. At forty-seven, he had nearly twenty years of management experience in both juvenile and adult corrections in four states. When he was appointed director of corrections for Arizona in 1973, conditions in that state's major prison were not unlike those in Rhode Island in 1978; it was by all accounts a dirty and unsafe facility manned by an untrained and demoralized staff. Even his sharpest critics, and there were apparently more than a few, were forced to admit that Moran had made remarkable improvements during his five-year tenure. In the process, however, the blunt and outspoken administrator from New England had alienated a number of allies of veteran Arizona politician, Wes Bolin. When Bolin became governor in 1977, one of his first moves was to replace Moran.[80]

Within days of his ouster in November, Moran was contacted by Allen Breed who saw a natural fit between Moran's background and Rhode Island's needs. Through his many New England contacts, however, Moran was well aware of the state of affairs in Rhode Island and was not interested in the position. But Breed tried again in January, and by this time two months of inactivity had caused the normally frenetic Moran to be more receptive. Arriving with a snowstorm on January 18, Moran met the next day with Governor Garrahy. Rapport between the two Irish-Americans—the tall, affable governor and the diminutive, intense administrator—was immediate, and the governor never interviewed the three other candidates Breed had recruited.[81] The Senate was equally impressed and a month later his appointment was confirmed without a dissenting vote. In the words of one key legislator, Moran seemed to be just what the state needed: "a guy able to stick to his guns without caving in to outside pressure whether that comes from the prisoners or a master or the media."[82]

In time, Moran would delight in telling people he worked for "the six P's"—Public, Politicians, Personnel, Prisoners, Press, and Pettine—and that the hardest part of his job was to keep these various interests and factions together and moving in the same direction.[83] Early in 1978, however, all six "P's" had the same priorities—an end to the lockup, a cleanup of the prison and movement toward compliance with the remedial decree. But looking at the enormity of the task ahead, Allen Breed was doubtful "that John Moran or Moses himself could do a great deal . . . considering the almost total lack of any ability on the part of senior staff."[84]

Reshuffling the Old Guard and Going It Alone

Soon after Moran's appointment, the results of the management study commissioned the year before by Southworth became public. Though far more detailed than any of the earlier studies, it echoed these evaluations and supported the court's conclusion in finding that "the major problem is the lack of any formal management processes within the department."[85] Six weeks after his appointment Moran reorganized the department in accord with their recommendations. The division of support services—classification, education, and health care along with training and research and planning—was eliminated and its functions placed in the other divisions. This change gave the assistant directors for youth services, on the one hand, and adult services, on the other, virtually complete control over all aspects of their respective operations. To handle the increased responsibilities, two new positions were created within adult services—deputy assistant directors for rehabilitation and for institutions.

Although he liked Bill Laurie personally, Moran replaced him because the lockup had become a "personal power struggle between him and the prisoner leadership" and "he didn't know how to get out of it."[86] Laurie was reassigned to youth services and his assistant, the affable 30 year veteran Bob Houle, appointed assistant director for adult services. Former acting Director Taylor who had been in charge of support services was named deputy assistant director for rehabilitation under Houle, but the other deputy's position—that for institutional operations—was left vacant until a suitable replacement could be found. Moran, in any event, intended to immerse himself in institutioɪ. :l operations until control was regained. To facilitate this, in March 1978 Moran provided himself with an administrative assistant. Matt Gill, a teacher at the ACI for several years whose administrative talent immediately attracted Moran's attention, thus became the one new face among the top management.

In Breed's estimation, the placement of support services in the other divisions put "too great an emphasis on custody." Breed, however, now saw his role to be "one of reinforcing and strengthening the director rather than to try to move in any way independently."[87] Nonetheless, he hoped that the elevation of Houle might change what he saw as Moran's unnecessarily negative views on the inmate leadership. Where Breed and Houle believed in a negotiated order, involving inmates in decision making, Moran emphasized strong centralized control and thought inmate participation anathema. These differences in philosophy became clear as master and director attempted to deal with inmate grievances. Inmate petitions had been piling up as

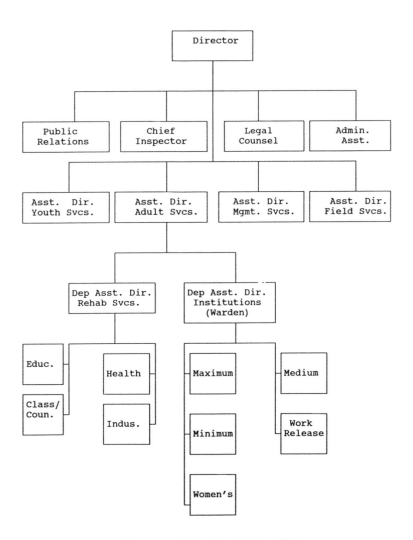

Figure 4.1 Table of Organization, 1978

a result of the lockup. By March 1978 Breed thought it imperative that a grievance process be established quickly to resolve them. In Breed's view, a grievance process without inmate participation and an ultimate appeal to an external, neutral agent would lack any credibility and thus be ineffective. To Moran, a grievance process should be completely internal, involving appeals through successive levels of administration, and not involve inmates in any way. This clash of viewpoints caused a two-month stalemate until finally Breed, assisted by Bob Houle but without inmate participation, decided to settle those petitions related to the remedial decree.[88]

Moran's aversion to outsiders extended even to experts providing technical assistance. Where Breed, as we have seen, had been drawing upon his extensive network to bring in experts to assist the department, early on Moran let it be known that he had no need of any more studies or help, that he wanted to see what his staff could do by themselves. Although Breed continued to offer, Moran steadfastly, and sometimes adamantly, refused any outside help.[89]

By early April 1978, Breed's role had become that of a monitor. Most of his time was expended in establishing standards, writing and reviewing reports, conducting and attending hearings. Although he met with Moran informally on occasion, it was to listen to his problems not to assist in solving them; indeed he found that his suggestions, whether about implementing the order or administering the prisons, were resisted. Gradually, he was coming to the conclusion that the "force or leverage that the court can use through the master is more effective where the tool of coercion is used or at least is readily available rather than through an approach which utilizes persuasion and advocacy."[90]

The Demise of the NPRA and the End of the Lockup

On February 3, 1978 Judge Pettine had given the department five days to submit a plan to end the lockup which had been in effect since the end of August. However, an unexpected blizzard buried the state under four feet of snow on February 8, bringing everything except emergency services and snow removal to a halt for nearly a week, and the court extended the deadline to February 23. On the job less than a week, Moran was hard pressed to meet even that deadline, however. The plan he submitted proved to be a mere rehashing of Southworth's earlier efforts and totally unacceptable to Breed. A continuance was granted until March 17 while a departmental task force headed by Matt Gill put together a more detailed plan. The scheduled hearing, though begun on that date, was never completed as the lockup became a boycott and then degenerated into open warfare.[91]

At his confirmation hearing on February 22, Moran publicly proclaimed his opposition to the NPRA and any other inmate organization that tries to assume "the strength and authority to tell inmates what to do."[92] Internally, he let it be known that it was his policy not to speak to any inmate who claimed to be representing others. Two weeks later his policy was put to the test when the NPRA organized a boycott of the expanded programming then being put in place. The boycott began in support of an inmate's request to be transferred to a hospital. The inmate in question had been on a hunger strike since February 1 to demand increased visiting privileges and had requested transfer to the prison's hospital. Laurie denied the requests, and after having being assured that the inmate was being examined daily and was not in any immediate danger, Moran backed Laurie's decision, letting it be known that "we're not giving in to temper tantrums."[93]

As the boycott continued, other underlying concerns surfaced. The NPRA presented Moran with its own programming proposal which he rejected out of hand. They also requested that inmates rather than private contractors do the court-ordered cleanup, a request Moran also rejected summarily for security reasons. In response to the boycott, Moran publicized the fact that it was jeopardizing a college-level program funded by LEAA and CETA and that there were sufficient jobs and activities to allow inmates out of their cells six hours per day if they would only come out.[94]

The boycott received no support from the public. The editors of the *Journal-Bulletin* labeled the leaders "confused malcontents" and likened the NPRA to a "creature, bent on self-destruction, consuming itself starting with its own tail."[95] At a scheduled hearing in federal court on programming, Judge Pettine questioned the motivation of those plaintiffs present and advised them that the role of the court was to "define a constitutionally acceptable pattern of living" and that may be "a far cry from what may be desired."[96]

As the lack of public support became clear, the boycott gradually wound down. In the course of its two weeks, however, it had become clear to Moran that the personal animosity between Bill Laurie and the inmate leadership was a major element in the power struggle. Thus, while he firmly agreed with Laurie's policy orientation and supported his decisions, he replaced him at the end of the month with Bob Houle. On April 3, 1978, the very day Laurie's removal was announced, the inmate ended his 59-day hunger strike, and it appeared that the lockup, now into its eighth month, could at last be ended.[97]

Plans were made to put a modified lockup into place, inmates being allowed three hours per day out of their cells. The plan, however, encountered resistance from the officers who refused to work, claiming they had not been sufficiently briefed and were not prepared to carry it out. Moran was out of town and Houle, on his own initiative, agreed to delay implementation for a week.[98]

To Breed, it seemed that the real reason for the officers' refusal was that over the past year "they have harassed the inmates and the inmates in turn have threatened that they will get them when they get out of their cells. Consequently, the officers will do anything within their power to see that the lockup continues."[99] From inmate reports, it appears that the harassment by officers intensified during the next week and culminated in brutality when an inmate who spit on a nurse was severely beaten by the lieutenant transferring him to segregation. Moran placed the lieutenant on immediate leave and ordered a disciplinary hearing following which the officer was demoted and transferred to another facility.[100]

Despite this decisive action, the situation spun out of control. Inmates who were now being given outside recreation and fed in the dining hall in small groups began refusing to return to their cells to protest the harassment. Those in their cells began throwing their furniture and belongings out. And just prior to a court-required sanitation inspection, inmates eating lunch threw their trays and food all over the dining hall. The next morning, a larger group followed suit with their breakfast and a total lockup was again implemented.[101]

Thus, early in April 1978 began what is known as the "garbage war." Locked in their cells 24 hours a day, over the next two weeks inmates threw their garbage and waste out onto the tiers. Moran ordered inmates to clean the mess but refused to meet with inmate leaders who wanted to negotiate some terms for their cooperation. Nor would he order the officers to do the cleaning. By the end of April, there were "two to three feet of debris piled in the flats [floors] in the cell block areas." It reminded Moran of what you might see after "a heavy winter snow storm . . . garbage and filth up to your knees with pathways winding through it."[102] While he had hoped to force the inmates into cleaning it themselves, conditions became so unhealthy that he had to retain a private contractor. Small sections of cell blocks were emptied of their occupants who were given showers and recreation in the yard while the area was cleaned and then returned to their cells. Perhaps because their rage had been spent, or because their desperate protest had come to seem futile or perhaps just because it felt good to be clean again and to feel the warm May air, on returning to their cells the inmates kept them clean, and within a week the long lockup ended.

The "garbage war" lost the NPRA whatever external support it had left. Judge Pettine was "greatly disturbed" and warned that its continuation in light of the good-faith efforts of the administration "will be counterproductive."[103] The press branded it an "outrage" and called upon the governor and the legislature to give their full support to Moran in his battles with both the inmates and the officers.[104] And the turn of events even silenced those who had vociferously defended the organization when the lockup began. Thus, it went almost without notice when Moran met with some external members of the NPRA in the basement of a church in Providence and frankly told them that he had abolished the organization and had no intention of resurrecting it.[105]

Order Restored

The end of the lockup brought an end to collective resistance. Nonetheless, tension remained high, and from the beginning of June through the end of August, several brief lockups were implemented in Maximum Security in response to isolated incidents of violence among inmates. Rumors of a plot to kill an officer, however, surfaced in August 1978, but no specific information could be developed. Then, just after the noon count on September 19, a rookie officer, on the job only three weeks, was bludgeoned and near-fatally stabbed by three inmates who had draped themselves in sheets.[106]

Moran immediately ordered another lockup and met late that afternoon with Governor Garrahy to inform him of the situation. With the governor's consent, he called Norman Carlson, director of the Federal Bureau of Prisons and an old friend, to see if he would accept some transfers. Carlson agreed to take 15 men. That night and the next day, Moran and several of his top staff reviewed the files of those inmates on a list of "leaders and hatchet men" that Moran had been preparing since his arrival in February. Thus, just two days after the stabbing, most of the inmates who had formed the core leadership of the NPRA and other organizations were taken from their cells by correctional officers and driven by state police to the federal prison in Danbury, Connecticut.[107]

Five years previously, as has been discussed in Chapter 3, Judge Pettine had ruled that prisoners could not be involuntarily transferred out of state without being given a hearing except in the case of an emergency. Prior to the transfer, Governor Garrahy had declared the prison to be in a state of emergency, and, as required by Rhode Island law, Director Moran had notified the Secretary of State that he was suspending disciplinary and classification regulations. Judge Pettine seemed willing to accept that definition of the situation. In an unusual move, he issued a written statement that strongly endorsed the action although not without qualification:

> . . . [T]hey had a moral and legal obligation to act quickly and decisively—even though later assessment may show the difficulties to be unfounded and the transfers unjustified. . . . I applaud [the governor's] willingness to take whatever steps he feels necessary to bring about safety and order at the ACI. I share his determination to achieve that result.[108]

By the end of October, all the transferees had been brought back to Rhode Island for hearings before the classification board. The transfer was upheld in each case. In the interim, however, the inmates had filed suit challenging its legality. As none of them had been involved in the stabbing, they argued that the transfer was in retaliation for their organizational activities and involvement in litigation.[109] That claim was not given a hearing for eighteen months, however, by which time several of the plaintiffs had been paroled and one was dead, having been executed gangland style shortly after his parole.

The two-week trial was held at the prison for security reasons. It was, for the most part, a test of credibility between Moran and the inmates. Admitting that the plaintiffs were not involved in the stabbing, Moran nonetheless maintained that "individually and collectively they contributed in a substantial way to the total breakdown in discipline that made the assault . . . more likely." It was for this reason that they were transferred, he testified, not because they were outspoken leaders or because they had successfully sued the state.[110] The inmates' own prison records—of assaults on both staff and inmates, extortion and theft from inmate funds they controlled, inciting riots, etc.—meticulously brought out on cross-examination by the state lent considerable weight to Moran's contention. Judge Pettine certainly believed him. After delaying a decision for another year, in 1981 he ruled in favor of the state, labeling the inmates' First Amendment claim "a transparent veneer that does not hide the dangerous game they were playing."[111]

At the time of the transfer, Moran had justified it by claiming that "it marks a new beginning that will allow us to build order at the prison day by day."[112] In 1980, at the time of the hearing, it had become abundantly clear that the transfer had accomplished this objective. Within a month of the transfer, the lockup had ended and new programs were brought on line with no disruption. Those who had sought protective custody now sought to rejoin the general population, and the number in protective custody rapidly fell from about 140 to about 25. The medium security facility, which for years had been used as protective custody and thus frustrating any meaningful classification, could once again be used as intended.

Riots and violence at the ACI were no longer daily news items. In the five years prior to the August 1977 court order, the press reported seven murders, three escapes from Maximum Security and 31 violent disturbances. From January 1, 1979 through December 31, 1985, by contrast, there were no escapes from Maximum Security, only one murder and six minor disturbances. This decline in violence and disorder, moreover, occurred despite an 83 percent growth in the number of inmates from 1980 through 1985 and substantial disruption and confusion caused by construction and renovation to meet the requirements of the court's order in *Palmigiano*.

It was not, of course, the transfer of the 15 inmate leaders alone that brought about the restoration of order. But, as Moran said at the time, it gave him breathing space to rebuild order. Over the next several months, as we shall see, he strengthened middle management, developed new policies and procedures and retrained the officers. Moreover, the utility of interstate transfer as a management tool was not lost on the staff, and transfers among the New England states became routine. Administrators began to meet several times a year to arrange transfers, in effect trading inmates the way sports team owners might trade players.[113]

In 1981 Rhode Island's long-awaited "Supermax" was opened. This high-tech prison is quite unlike the others, the most recent of which had been built fifty years before. Rather than cell blocks, the basic units in the High Security Center (HSC) are modules containing either 12 or 24 inmates. Each module is sealed off from the others by virtually impenetrable doors operated electronically from a central control station and monitored by closed-circuit television. Most inmates remain in the modules, either in the dayroom or in their cells, for 23 hours per day, the only hour out being for recreation in either a small courtyard or a depressingly spartan gym. When those transferred in 1978 were returned to Rhode Island, they were kept in this facility where they were under constant close surveillance and had little contact with inmates other than the eleven who shared their "pod."

With the new controls in place, "nobody wanted to step up to head some group or lead a charge."[114] Power struggles between cliques of inmates occasionally erupted into violence, but the cliques were ephemeral and the conflicts short lived. Competition between staff and inmates for control of the institution was a thing of the past.

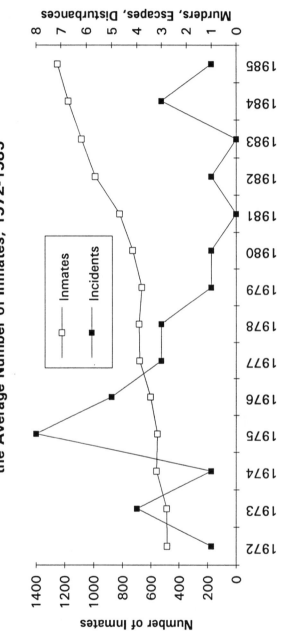

Figure 4.2 Annual Number of Murders, Escapes, Disturbances and the Average Number of Inmates, 1972-1985

Blending Youth and Experience

In ending the lockup and restoring order, Moran won strong support in both the state house and legislature. When, in 1979, he was offered the job of commissioner of corrections in Massachusetts, Democratic state chairman and Senate Majority Leader Rocco Quatrocchi let it be known that "this guy took the ACI off the front pages. If we have to do a few things to keep him, I'd be most sympathetic."[115] What they gave him was a substantial pay raise and a contract through the end of 1984, in essence granting him an unprecedented seven-year contract and implicitly the ability to administer the department with minimal political interference.[116]

This support was to prove essential in strengthening the middle levels of his administration. In his first annual report to the court in the fall of 1978, Special Master Breed observed a "leadership void in the positions below Moran."[117] In part, Breed was referring to the lack of talent in middle management, but he was also referring to the fact that key positions were vacant. When Moran had removed Laurie from the assistant director's post and replaced him with Bob Houle, he had left the position of warden vacant. Continual tension and frequent clashes between the authoritarian director and the consensus-seeking assistant led the 30-year veteran Houle to take his retirement just six months after his appointment, however, leaving Moran with the two major positions under him vacant.

Fred Chiarini, the union official and former director of Medium Security, began to campaign for the assistant director's position. He was backed by several prominent Democrats, and Moran feared that he might have to accept a political appointment. To fend off this pressure, he commenced a hurried national search for a qualified replacement. Several were interested but none would take the job at the salary offered. Moran then decided to gamble by teaming youthful enthusiasm and energy with nuts and bolts experience. In December 1978, he offered the job of assistant director to his administrative assistant, Matt Gill. Only thirty at the time, Gill had a master's degree in education and had been the director of education for four years before being named Moran's assistant in March. While he had no line experience, he had impressed Moran with his intelligence, administrative ability and, particularly, his aggressiveness. Moran was convinced he could handle the job if teamed with someone who had the requisite operational knowledge.[118]

To supply the experience Gill lacked, Moran turned to John Brown, a recently retired corrections veteran looking to supplement his pension. Brown was appointed warden at the time Gill was appointed assistant director. The fifty-five-year-old Brown had retired in 1976 after thirty years with the Federal Bureau of Prisons. Starting as a correctional officer, he had worked his way through the ranks to become a captain and then chief of security. Since his retirement he had been working as a security consultant to state prison systems, Rhode Island among them.[119]

At the time of these appointments, Moran had been running the prison virtually by himself for nearly a year. His intent now was to vest responsibility for internal operations in Gill and Brown and devote his attention to external matters such as securing needed resources, planning, overseeing the new facilities coming on line and implementing the court order. Gill was to be in overall charge of all the institutions but was to focus his attention on the expansion of programming and dealing with labor-management relations where he was instructed by Moran to take a hard line. Brown, in addition to advising Gill on operational matters, was to focus his attention on "putting the basics in order."[120]

Over the next several years, Brown immersed himself in the myriad operational details of running the prison on a day-to-day basis, from food preparation and serving through sanitation and maintenance to custody and security. He developed policy and procedure manuals to replace the long-outdated and ignored procedures that had been in place since 1957; he established a chain of command grievance procedure; a manual of rules and regulations for inmates was once again published; and an extended pre-service training program for officers was designed and implemented. In all of this, Brown worked closely with the officers and, at times, with union officials, imbuing them to some degree with his operational expertise.[121]

One example of Brown's influence and success is the tactical team he developed in 1979. The team, composed of 30 selected officers, was to be used to handle other problem situations and to quell disturbances. Brown provided them with extensive training in a wide variety of tactics from merely making a show of force through use of riot batons, attack dogs, tear gas and shot guns. The team was first used on March 24, 1980 when a number of inmates in segregation refused to return to their cells and climbed onto the window bars. After the melee, the inmates, one of whom suffered a broken leg, charged brutality but an investigation by the FBI found that the team had used only necessary force and cleared it of all charges.[122] Thereafter, calls for assistance from local and state police, once common, became rare.

Although less visible and dramatic, other changes made by Brown were more pervasive and probably more important in the long run. An in-service training program was developed with components for all staff. For the first time since 1956, when Warden Gough had retrained officers, staff were released from their jobs to attend classes in subjects ranging from hostage negotiations to food preparation. Middle managers and superior officers, lieutenants and captains, were given leave to attend programs at the training center run by the National Institute of Corrections in Colorado and at training academies in other states.[123]

Brown's tenure was short lived, however. Early in 1981, he resigned, allegedly for personal reasons. Moran contends that Brown's appointment was to have been short term; others, however, cite sharp and increasingly frequent conflict between Brown and Gill as the reason. In part these differences concerned Gill's hard line in dealing with the officers. In even larger measure, however, they involved differences in priorities. The inmate population, stable for over a decade, had begun to increase exponentially in 1979. New facilities were opening and accommodating the increase, but operational costs were escalating at the same time as the cost of court-ordered improvements had already placed the department under intense budgetary pressure. To balance his budget, Gill increasingly ignored Brown's operational advice and took actions that in Brown's eyes, not to mention those of the officers under him, unduly compromised security and the safety of the staff. They clashed over whether this post or that post was absolutely necessary, how many perimeter patrols were needed, and whether a special 1 to 9 PM program shift could be cut and its members reassigned to other posts to reduce overtime.[124]

Brown was replaced with Donald Ellerthorpe who had 22 years experience as a military police officer specializing in corrections. Just prior to his retirement from the army in 1980, he had served as director of custody at the military's largest prison, the U.S. Army Disciplinary Barracks at Fort Leavenworth, Kansas, and had come from that position to Rhode Island to open the High Security Center. Similar to Brown in his operational expertise, Ellerthorpe was, however, more inclined than his predecessor had been to identify with the administration and to sympathize with their budgetary and political considerations.[125] Thus, with Brown's departure, the officers lost an advocate in the administration and the administration lost an important link with the line. As a result conflicts over budget versus security more clearly split labor and management, intensifying ongoing struggles over matters such as the use of excessive force and seniority.

Conflict and Accommodation

Gill had begun his career as a teacher and the officers frequently referred to him as "the Principal."[126] He seemed to relish the appellation, and if he felt insecure at all, it only served to make him all the more aggressive. On the day of his appointment, he let it be known he was "not going to be Mr. Nice Guy," and the first day on the job he showed that he meant what he said. For reasons unknown, the winter uniforms had not been issued although it was mid-December. The officers decided to wear flannel shirts and blue jeans. Getting wind of what was to happen, Gill locked in the night shift and met the day shift at the entrance to Maximum Security where he sternly told them "no uniforms, no work, no pay." When the officers continued to mill around in the parking lot, he ordered them off state property and summoned the state police to enforce the order. That afternoon, the 3:00 PM shift appeared in uniform.[127]

The press saw Gill's forceful approach as a dramatic announcement that the administration was "no longer going to be pushed around."[128]

That announcement was reinforced just two months later. On the morning of February 28, 1979 an inmate who had been denied parole the day before slashed the throat of an officer who was letting him out of his cell for breakfast. The inmate was placed in segregation but the next day had to be taken to the hospital where he was treated for a fractured skull, a deep cut in his left ear and multiple bruises. The inmate claimed to have been beaten; the officers claimed his injuries occurred because he was unruly and had to be subdued. There were no other witnesses.[129]

Questionable incidents involving the use of force had continued to occur with disconcerting frequency even after the relative quietude brought about by the transfer of prisoners to the federal system in September 1978. With superior officers in the same union as those they supervised, and with only a small investigative staff, Moran had found it difficult to get credible information to justify further disciplinary actions. This incident was so serious and seemingly so blatant, however, that he, Gill and Brown thought it was essential to get a handle on it before the situation degenerated into another all-out war. The best way to do this, they thought, was to have a full-blown investigation of the incident by an impartial body. Thus, without taking any internal action, they referred the case to the attorney general who placed it before a grand jury.[130]

In a widely publicized report that May, the grand jury concluded that the inmate had been beaten but that there was not enough evidence to bring an indictment against any correctional officers. However, it went on to chastise the officers as a body for their lack of discipline and poor job performance. In Gill's view, the grand jury report "went miles in establishing the tone we wanted."[131] On the one hand, it reinforced Brown's efforts in training; on the other it justified the hard line Gill took with respect to discipline. But, public criticism by an external agency whose support had been enlisted by the administration also incensed most officers and further strained the already tense relations between the administration and the union.

For years, as we have seen, labor and management had been in conflict over the seniority principle governing virtually all assignments of union members. The strength of the union's commitment to that principle was evident in its support of sexual integration of the guard force in the early '80s.[132] That issue presented the brotherhood with a serious dilemma. The vast majority of the rank-and-file agreed with management that to put female officers on the line in men's prisons would seriously jeopardize security. But for the brotherhood to admit sex as a valid factor in determining assignments would undercut their claim that seniority should be the sole criterion. Even a compromise that would permit women to bid into non-contact positions was unacceptable as these were almost invariably the positions desired by the most senior male officers. It would, moreover, provide the administration with a rationale for the displacement of more experienced officers into more sensitive positions.

Nonetheless, commitment to unionism and the principle of seniority prevailed over male biases. Beginning in 1979, the brotherhood brought several grievances against the department on behalf of female officers been denied posts in a men's facility. These grievances were successful, and by 1981 the department no longer had any sex-specific posts and the bids of male and female officers were handled in a uniform manner.

The opening of the High Security Center, the first new prison since the officers had unionized, also generated conflict over seniority as it was unclear how the complicated bidding system was to apply in staffing it. During the summer of 1980, the department hired 113 new officers and created three new captains and six new lieutenants to provide adequate staffing for the facility scheduled to open in November, and Ellerthorpe arrived in August to train with those who had bid into it. Already two years behind schedule at that point, the opening was again delayed when the union complained that the bidding process that had been used violated the contract. Rather than contest the claim, which would have delayed the opening even longer, the department redid the bidding, and Ellerthorpe spent an additional two months training a new cadre.[133]

The delay in opening the HSC cost the state about $500,000 at a time when it was already experiencing fiscal distress due to an expanding population, court-mandated improvements and an economic recession. Moreover, the year before an arbitrator had ordered the department to pay officers approximately this same amount to compensate for over 50,000 hours of coffee breaks they had been denied during the turmoil of 1975-77. The department had delayed making this payment for several months, and after the delay in opening high security began giving signals that it was going to appeal this decision (which it did, ultimately losing four years later and having to pay over $ 1 million).[134] On February 19, in a thinly disguised job action to demand the back pay, the day shift called in sick. Moran and Gill had been expecting such an action, and without any attempt at negotiation, they immediately went to court to seek a restraining order. That afternoon, Superior Court Judge Domenic Cresto, former legal counsel to Governor Garrahy, found the officers in violation of their contract. He ordered them back to work and issued an injunction prohibiting any further strikes.[135]

The injunction had a chilling effect on the union, and for two years there were no further job actions. Throughout 1982 and into 1983, however, both sides waged an intense campaign through the media. Every incident of disorder became an occasion for the brotherhood to protest staff cutbacks and warn of an impending riot and for the administration to assail them for their "self-serving theatrics."[136] Meanwhile backstage, the state's negotiators were taking a hard line in contract negotiations seeking changes in the contract that would dilute seniority rights, giving the administration more discretion in staffing levels and assignments with the intent of reducing overtime. The impasse dragged on for 18 months; then, Moran and Gill moved aggressively to seize control, again calling upon the power of the court.

Allegations of excessive force by officers in Medium Security had been increasing for some time. That unit had over the years become a haven for officers who shared the authoritarian views of Chiarini and his successors and were resistant to the authority of the central administration. The strong subculture made complaints of brutality difficult to sustain. Incidents took place at times and places where there were no witnesses other than the officers and the inmate. The version of events given by the officers invariably justified the force used, and lieutenants and captains, who should be the first line of defense against brutality, were more often than not implicated in the allegations.

In July 1983, some 20 inmates went on a rampage to protest the repressive conditions. The disturbance was quickly brought under control; no one was injured and the amount of damage was estimated at less than $1000.[137] Moran and Gill, however, seized upon the incident as a pretext for removing the deputy warden in charge and replacing him with Ronald Brule. Brule, it will be remembered, had been in charge of Maximum Security during the turmoil of the '70s. At the time, he was blamed by most officers for "giving the joint away," and he, in turn, had been publicly critical of the officers and the union. The enmity had not died in the years since then. Thus, it was scarcely a surprise, and may even have been intended by the administration, when the officers in Medium staged a job action one month later to protest several policies Brule had put into place. But the swiftness and severity of the administrative response caught most off balance. Within hours, Moran had again secured a court order forcing the officers back to work, and those who had refused to work were given two-day suspensions without pay.[138]

Just two months later, following another incident, the administration went back to court charging the union with civil contempt for violating the 1981 injunction. On the morning of November 9, the day shift was over a half hour late in reporting for work, causing the night shift to be held over for that time. According to union officials, the officers were late because a union meeting, called to inform members of what was going on in the contract negotiations which were now in their 18th month, had run on longer than anticipated due to the pent-up frustrations of the membership. Moran and Gill, however, viewed it as a job action and saw in it a chance to strike a decisive blow at the union.[139] At a hearing in December, the union was found in contempt of court and ordered to pay a fine of $1750. Further, the judge recommended that the state's attorney general consider charging union officials with criminal contempt.[140] Although these charges were never brought against the officials, the threat was effective—there has not been another job action by the officers since then.

The Brotherhood retained significant power at the bargaining table, however. Seniority rights were preserved in the contract and remain substantially unchanged even today. In 1984, after the contract was negotiated, Moran resigned himself to having to live with fewer management prerogatives than he believed he should have. He filled the employee relations position which had been vacant for years with a labor relations specialist from outside the department.[141] This action moderated the conflict by removing most disputes from the chain of command and providing the union with a presumably neutral party whom they had reason to believe would be more sympathetic to their position.

One indicator of the new accommodation was the longevity of Brule who remained warden of Medium Security until his retirement in 1996 and the relative peace that prevailed during his tenure. Brule, who had felt like a sacrificial lamb on taking the job in 1983, came to see himself like a "big bowling ball hitting the pins and scattering them all over the place—guys quit, guys bid out—and the deck was clean."[142] In the years to come, Medium Security was to be the object of intense scrutiny by the federal court but for overcrowding not brutality. And, indeed, on several occasions the unit drew the praise of the court which allowed the cap on its population to be raised in light of the high quality of its management and operation.

NOTES

1. 309 F. Supp. 362 (1970) at 372-3.
2. 406 F. Supp. 318 (1976) at 322-26.
3. While upholding the essence of the order, the U.S. Court of Appeals reversed several of its provisions and instructed that the Human Rights Committee be replaced with a monitor for each institution. *Newman v. State of Alabama*, 559 F. 2d 283 (1977).
4. For a detailed study of the origins of this case, the litigation and the problems of implementation, see Lawrence W. Yackle, *Reform and Regret: The Story of Federal Judicial Involvement in the Alabama Prison System* (New York: Oxford University Press, 1989).
5. *Palmigiano v. Travisono*, 317 F. Supp. (1970); *Palmigiano v. Baxter*, 487 F. 2d 1280 (1973); *Baxter v. Palmigiano*, 425 U. S. 308 (1976).
6. With the dismantling of the Office of Economic Opportunity by the Nixon Administration, responsibility to provide governmentally subsidized legal services for the poor was lodged in a public corporation, the Legal Services Corporation. The legislation creating this corporation prohibited its member

organizations from representing clients in a number of controversial areas, prisons rights among them. Thus, R.I. Legal Services could no longer represent inmates suing the state, and the Inmate Legal Assistance Program, now run by the state's public defender, had become rather dormant and, in any event, could not represent inmates seeking damages from the state.

7. Personal interview with Robert B. Mann, November 16, 1992.

8. Robert Harrall, *Section 1983 Prison Cases: A Study of 'Palmigiano v. Garrahy'* (Ph.D. Dissertation, University of Connecticut, 1988), pp. 161-62.

9. Personal interview with Alvin Bronstein, October 3, 1992.

10. Harrall, p. 168.

11. Daniel Pinello, "Case History of *Palmigiano v. Garrahy*," in *Remedial Law: When Courts Become Administrators*, ed. Robert C. Wood (Amherst, MA: The University of Massachusetts Press, 1990), p. 98.

12. Personal interviews with Bradford Southworth, November 19, 1992, and with William Laurie, October 28, 1992.

13. *Bulletin*, April 13, 1977, p. A1.

14. *Bulletin*, April 14, 1977, p. A1.

15. *Ibid.*

16. *Palmigiano v. Garrahy*, 443 F. Supp 956 (1977) at 962-63; Personal interview with Judge Raymond J. Pettine, October 21, 1992.

17. *Bulletin*, April 15, 1977, p. A1.

18. *Palmigiano v. Garrahy* at 970.

19. *Ibid.* at 965, 975-76.

20. *Ibid.* at 972.

21. *Ibid.* at 973.

22. *Bulletin*, April 19, 1977, p. A1.

23. *Palmigiano v. Garrahy* at 964.

24. *Journal*, April 21, 1977, p. B1.

25. *Palmigiano v. Garrahy* at 973, 979.

26. *Ibid.* at 978.

27. *Ibid.* at 984.

28. *Ibid.*

29. *Ibid.* at 978 citing *Procunier v. Martinez*, 416 U.S. 396 at 404-405.

30. *Ibid.* at 979.

31. *Ibid.* at 986-90.

32. *Ibid.* at 987.

33. Pettine interview. The day before he entered his opinion and order in *Palmigiano*, Judge Pettine entered an order in this case. That order gave the department six months to come into compliance with the decree. They did not

meet this deadline, and subsequently a master was appointed. *Bulletin*, August 10, 1977, p. A20. The 1973 consent decree followed an extensive remedial decree issued the previous year. See *Inmates of the Boys Training School v. Affleck*, 346 F. Supp 1354 (1972).

34. John Jenkins, "Prison Reform, the Judicial Process," *Criminal Law Reporter* (August 2, 1978): 5; Pettine interview.

35. Yackle, p. 105.

36. Steve J. Martin and Sheldon Ekland-Olson, *Texas Prisons: the Walls Came Tumbling Down* (Austin: Texas Monthly Press, 1987), p. 176.

37. *Journal*, August 11, 1977, p. A25.

38. *Journal*, August 11, 1977, p. A26.

39. *Bulletin*, July 8, 1977, p. A7; *Journal*, August 11, 1977, p. A1.

40. *Bulletin*, August 23, 1977, p. A10.

41. Jenkins, p. 5; Bronstein and Myers had made a similar recommendation to Judge Johnson in *Pugh*. See Yackle, p. 103.

42. *Journal*, September 13, 1977, p. A3. Just three weeks later that portion of Judge Johnson's order in *Pugh* appointing a Human Rights Committee was overturned on appeal. See Yackle, pp. 135-137.

43. *Palmigiano v. Garrahy* at 989-90.

44. *Bulletin*, October 27, 1977, p. A14.

45. Southworth interview; Laurie interview.

46. *Jones v. North Carolina Prisoners' Union*, 433 U.S. 119 (1977).

47. This description of events is summarized from the account of the commission appointed to investigate the incident. *Report of the Governor's Commission to Investigate the Incident Which Occurred at the Adult Correctional Institutions on August 26, 1977*, Rev. Thomas R. Peterson, O. P., chairman (R.I. State House Library, October 14, 1977).

48. Laurie interview; Southworth interview. Personal interview with Lt. Kenneth Rivard, August 26, 1992.

49. Personal interview with Warden Walter T. Whitman, September 23, 1992.

50. *Bulletin*, January 11, 1978, p. A3; *Journal*, January 17, 1978, p. A1; January 18, 1978, p. B3; January 19, 1978, p. A1.

51. *Bulletin*, August 30, 1977, p. B9.

52. *Bulletin*, August 30, 1977, p. A18; *Journal*, August 31, 1977, p. A1.

53. *Bulletin*, October 12, 1977: p. A3; *Journal*, October 13, 1977: pp. A1, A11.

54. *Peterson Commission*, p. 50.

55. *Ibid.*, p. 51.

56. *Bulletin,* September 27, 1977, p. A20.

57. *Jefferson v. Southworth,* 447 F. Supp 179 (1978) at 182-83.

58. *Jefferson v. Southworth* at 184-85.

59. *Bulletin,* November 15, 1977, p. C10.

60. *Journal,* November 17, 1977, p. A1. Judge Pettine's request had been made following Director Southworth's testimony that the present contract hampered the ability of the department to make major changes in operations.

61. *Bulletin,* November 23, 1977, p. A1. Brule and Costa were later reinstated but given different assignments.

62. Allen Breed, *Special Master's Diary* (Providence, RI: U.S. District Court), entry for December 7, 1977, pp. 5-6.

63. Breed, *Diary,* December 8, 1977, p. 4; December 28, 1977, pp. 10-11; *Jefferson v. Southworth,* C. A. 77-554, "Master's Memorandum to the Court" (D.R.I., January 18, 1978) at 11-12.

64. *Jefferson v. Southworth,* "Master's Memo," p. 2.

65. *Ibid.,* pp. 1-2.

66. *Jefferson v. Southworth* at 188.

67. *Ibid.* at 191-92.

68. This description of the state's inaction is a summary of the facts set forth by Judge Pettine in an unpublished opinion supporting his finding the state in civil contempt for its failure to meet the classification deadlines. *Palmigiano v. Garrahy,* C. A. Nos.74-172 and 75-032, at 5-22 (D.R.I., March 28, 1978). Hereafter referred to as *Palmigiano Classification Order.*

69. Breed, *Diary,* December 8, 1977.

70. From a detailed analysis of a number of cases, including *Palmigiano,* Susan Sturm has developed a typology of judicial approaches to managing the implementation process: the deferrer, the director, the broker and the catalyst. See "Resolving the Remedial Dilemma: Strategies of Judicial Intervention in Prisons," *University of Pennsylvania Law Review* 138 (1990): 805-912. Sturm concludes that the catalyst approach is most likely to be effective but also recognizes that each approach has its strengths and weaknesses and may be more or less appropriate in different circumstances. Breed, at this point, alternated between being a catalyst and a director, but as circumstances changed in *Palmigiano,* as we shall see, so did the approach adopted by the court.

71. Breed, *Diary,* November 30, 1977; December 15, 1977.

72. *Ibid.,* December 29, 1977.

73. *Ibid.,* December 7, December 8, December 19, 1977.

74. *Bulletin*, November 23, 1977, p. A1; *Journal-Bulletin*, November 26, 1977, p. A1.

75. Breed, *Diary*, December 6, December 12, December 15, December 19, 1977.

76. *Sunday Journal*, January 22, 1978, pp. A1, A7.

77. Breed, *Diary*, January 18, 1978.

78. Breed, *Diary*, December 23, December 27, 1977, January 31, 1978. The lack of a grievance procedure was not an issue at trial. Between the trial and the issuance of the order, however, Judge Pettine had directed to Magistrate Jacob Hagopian to chair a committee of staff and inmates to attempt to dispose of the large number of petitions filed with the court by inmates. This committee had been so successful that the judge wished to institutionalize a similar procedure and had so charged the special master.

79. *Ibid.*, January 23, 1978.

80. Personal interview with John J. Moran, June 10, 1992; *Journal*, February 5, 1978, pp. A1, A8.

81. Moran interview, June 10, 1992; Breed, *Diary*, January 23, 1978.

82. *Journal*, February 5, 1978, p. C7, quoting Sen. John C. Revens, then deputy majority whip.

83. Personal interview, John J. Moran, June 17, 1992.

84. Breed, *Diary*, February 7, 1978.

85. Touche, Ross and Company, *Rhode Island Department of Corrections Management Study* (RI Department of Corrections, December 31, 1977). Not surprisingly, this study echoed earlier reports and the findings of the court. Roles and responsibilities were found to be so ill defined that middle mangers did not know what was expected of them and were afraid to make decisions. There were few written policies and procedures, and in their absence the performance of line staff was ineffective and their supervision inadequate. No inmate records contained treatment plans, 95percent were missing reports of medical exams and 65percent were missing social histories. The classification board was not considering such information in making its decisions, and their decisions were meaningless anyway as there were no operative vocational education, industries or recreational programs, and the education program was fragmented, underequipped and underutilized.

86. Moran interview, June 10, 1992.

87. Breed, *Diary*, February 16 and March 21, 1978.

88. *Ibid.*, March 6 through April 27, 1978.

89. *Ibid.*

90. *Ibid.*, April 27, 1978.

91. Breed, *Diary*, March 3 through April 17, 1978.

92. *Journal*, Feb. 22, 1978, p. A4.

93. *Ibid.*, March 8, 1978, p. A3.

94. *Ibid.*, March 15, 1978, p. B9.

95. *Ibid.*, March 20, 1978, p. A14.

96. *Ibid.*, March 21, 1978, p. A3.

97. *Bulletin*, April 3, 1978, p. B2.

98. *Journal*, April 9, 1978, p. A7.

99. Breed, *Diary*, April 16, 1978.

100. A year later, in a suit filed by the inmate a jury found in his favor but awarded only $1.00 in compensatory damages and no punitive damages. *Bulletin*, April 4, 1979, B7.

101. *Bulletin*, April 14, 1978,p. A3; April 17,1978, p. A3; *Journal*, April 13, 1978, p. A3; April 16, 1978, p. A1.

102. Moran interview, June 10, 1992.

103. *Journal*, April 18, 1978, p. A1.

104. *Journal*, May 4, 1978, p. A26.

105. Moran interview, July 7, 1992.

106. *Journal*, September 19, 1978, p. A1; September 20, 1978, p. A1.

107. Moran interview, June 10, 1992; *Bulletin*, September 21, 1978, p. A1.

108. *Bulletin*, September 22, 1978, p. A1.

109. They also argued that they should have been given a written statement setting forth specific reasons for the transfer and at least a brief opportunity to rebut them. That argument, however, ran afoul of the Supreme Court's ruling in *Meachum v. Fano* (427 U.S. 215, 96 S. Ct. 2532) in which the Court held that the involuntary transfer of prisoners from one institution to another does not require due process guarantees absent a state-created right to remain in the prison to which initially assigned. In March 1979, Judge Pettine ruled that Rhode Island law does not create such a liberty interest and dismissed that portion of the inmate's suit (*Bulletin*, March 2, 1979, p. A1).

110. *Journal*, June 4, 1980, p. C12; *Bulletin*, June 24, 1980, p. B16.

111. *Bulletin*, July 28, 1981, p. A7.

112. *Journal*, September 21, 1978, p. A10.

113. Personal interview with Matthew Gill, July 22, 1992. From 1978 through 1985, Mr. Gill served as Moran's administrative assistant and then as assistant director for Adult Services.

114. *Ibid.*

115. *Journal*, August 14, 1979, p. 3.

116. Moran interview, June 10, 1992.

117. *Journal*, September 17, 1978, p. C3.

118. Moran interview, June 10, 1992.

119. *Journal*, December 7, 1978: p. A1.

120. Moran interview, June 10, 1992.

121. *Ibid.*

122. *Bulletin*, August 14, 1980, p. A3.

123. Memo to John Moran and Matthew Gill, from John Brown, Warden, ACI. (RI Department of Corrections, January 29, 1980).

124. Personal interviews with Donald Ellerthorpe, October 7, 1992, and with Warden Ronald Brule, October 10, 1992; Moran interview, July 7, 1992; Gill interview; Rivard interview.

125. Ellerthorpe interview.

126. Gill interview.

127. *Ibid.*; *Journal*, December 17, 1978, p. A9.

128. *Journal*, December 17, 1978, p. A9.

129. *Bulletin*, March 2, 1979, pp. A1 and A4.

130. Gill interview; Moran interview, July 7, 1992.

131. Gill interview; *Bulletin*, May 25, 1979, pp. A1 and A10.

132. Sexual integration of the guard force became an issue after amendments, in 1972, to the 1964 Civil Rights Act prohibited discrimination against women by public employers at the state, county and local levels. The issue first arose in Rhode Island when a female lieutenant working in the women's prison was denied her bid for a vacant post in the men's medium security prison despite being the most senior person bidding for it. A full treatment of the issue in Rhode Island and of the problems surrounding sexual integration can be found in Lynn E. Zimmer, *Women Guarding Men* (Chicago: University of Chicago Press, 1986).

133. Ellerthorpe interview; *Journal*, December 11, 1980, p. B7.

134. *Bulletin*, November 21, 1985, p. A2.

135 Gill interview; Moran interview, July 7, 1992; *Bulletin*, February 20, 1981, p. A14.

136. *Bulletin*, February 8, 1982, p. A1; *Journal*, February 14, 1982, p. B14.

137. *Journal*, July 27, 1983, p. A1.

138. Brule interview; Moran interview, July 7, 1992; *Journal-Bulletin*, October 8, 1983, p. B20.

139. Moran interview, July 7, 1992; Rivard interview, August 26, 1992; *Journal*, November 10, 1992, p. A3; November 22, 1992, p. A8.

140. *Journal-Bulletin*, December 17, 1983, p. A5.
141. Moran interview, June 10, 1992.
142. Brule interview.

CHAPTER 5

Implementation

The implementation of judicial decrees mandating widespread structural reforms typically takes years and sometimes more than a decade. Even in cases such as *Palmigiano,* where the decree is met with pledges of cooperation rather than resistance, this protracted process is likely to be marked by periodic conflict as changing external circumstances combine with internal pressures to create moments of high drama. As was seen in the previous chapter, pressure may arise from sheer incapacity or inertia on the part of the defendants. Or the plaintiffs, having been vindicated in court, may develop unrealistic expectations about what can be accomplished or the speed at which it can be done. Concerned with maintaining its integrity by implementing an adequate remedy, on the one hand, but also not wanting to risk its legitimacy by unduly intruding upon government policy and practice, on the other, the court may be caught in the middle and forced to make a number of mid-course changes in its order.

Such pressures and tensions are largely endemic to the process, but their operation in particular cases is shaped to a great degree by the larger social and political context in which they are embedded. As *Palmigiano* entered the post-decree phase, this larger context was in the process of radical change: the economy was unstable, the numbers of prisoners began to grow at an exponential rate, and more stringent doctrinal limits were being established by higher courts.

The recession of 1974-75 had been followed by several years of modest expansion, but in 1978 inflation exceeded 10 percent largely as a result of increases in fuel prices due, in turn, to the production and pricing policies of the oil-exporting countries. As the dollar fell to record lows and massive trade deficits developed, the GNP slumped; in 1979 economic growth was only about one-third of what had been expected. Feelings of impotence and rage swept the nation, intensified by our inability to free 52 hostages held by the Iranian government, and President Jimmy Carter openly worried about a "crisis of confidence" that he saw as a "fundamental threat to American Democracy."[1]

Carter's efforts to control inflation via tight money and voluntary wage and price controls fell most heavily on wage earners, alienating many traditional Democratic voters. Moreover, they plunged the economy into a short but severe recession just prior to the 1980 election. Carter thus became the first incumbent President to be defeated in a re-election attempt since 1932, losing to Ronald Reagan in a landslide.

Extolling traditional values and telling America to "stand tall," Reagan promised to bring an end to America's economic woes by a new strategy, one in line with the conservative swing in the national mood. Rather than raise taxes, as planned in Carter's budget, he proposed a tax cut to revive the economy and steep cuts in domestic spending to keep the budget in balance. Critics thought Reagan's supply-side policy was based on incorrect assumptions and would cause a massive budget deficit that would stifle economic growth. These fears proved correct. Inflation slowed to a five percent annual rate, but in July 1981 the economy entered a 22-month recession during which unemployment reached its highest level in 40 years and the budget deficit grew to heretofore-unparalleled heights.

Confronted with a severe recession and mounting dissatisfaction with his economic policy as the mid-term Congressional elections approached, Reagan once again exploited the growing cultural conservatism. Despite the fact that the crime rate levelled off and even dropped in the late '70s and early '80s, fear of crime remained pervasive. For a decade conservative politicians had been successfully channeling the public angst arising from a host of issues from Viet Nam to economic stagnation into support for law and order.[2] During the 1980 campaign, Reagan had called for a renewed emphasis on combatting street crime and providing assistance to its victims. Now he proposed the establishment of multi-jurisdictional task forces to make war on drugs. The war was initiated the following year with a staff numbering over 1600 and a budget of nearly $130 million.[3]

Prison populations had been growing since the mid-70s largely as a result of the adoption of mandatory and determinate sentencing statutes by a large number of states.[4] At year's end in 1975, there were 240,593 sentenced prisoners in state and federal institutions; by the end of 1980, this number had increased to 315,974 or by 31.3 percent. Due largely to the national hysteria over drug abuse, this already rapid rate of growth accelerated over the next five years. On December 31, 1985, the number of sentenced prisoners was 480,568, an increase of 52.1 percent over 1980. Thus, in the decade between 1975 and 1985, a time when there was little or no increase in serious crime, the number of prisoners per capita had nearly doubled, going from 111 per 100,000 population to 200.[5]

As prison overcrowding became a serious problem, polls showed that the majority of Americans thought we needed more prisons and half were willing to pay higher taxes to build them. At the same time, however, there was widespread resentment at federal judges who ordered improvements in prison conditions.[6] Reflecting popular sentiment, the Burger Court, as we reviewed in Chapter 1, began in the mid-1970s to restrict prisoners' rights and to limit the involvement of federal courts in prison litigation. To prisoners' rights advocates such as Alvin Bronstein, not only the substance of these decisions but the language in which they were couched foreshadowed a return to the "hands off" doctrine.[7] Interspersed throughout *Meachum v. Fano*, for example, was language recognizing the existence of "a wide spectrum of discretionary actions that traditionally have been the business of prison administrators" and that "the-day-to-day functioning of state prisons" involves "issues and discretionary decisions that are not the business of Federal judges."[8] Language chiding lower court judges for becoming too involved in the "minutiae of prison operations," along with quips that the Constitution embodies no "one man, one cell" principle, also distinguished Justice Rehnquist's opinion in *Bell v. Wolfish*.[9]

Overcrowding had not been an issue in the *Palmigiano* litigation; it was to become a major factor in the implementation of the decree, however. In the decade prior to the trial, as we saw in the previous chapter, Rhode Island's prisoner population had varied from 500 to about the system's capacity of 600, but in the five years following the decree the number of inmates increased by nearly 50 percent, going from 680 to 990. The need to accommodate this rapid growth while implementing the decree during a prolonged recession placed a severe strain on the state's resources. And, while the plaintiffs had the remedial decree and the power of the court behind them, the changes in the law weakened their ability to press for compliance. The result was an extended period of bargaining and negotiation, failed promises and threats, amendments and modifications that one of the participants has likened to a "minuet of delay."[10]

CLASSIFICATION AND FACILITIES

Judge Pettine's remedial order mandated the closing of Maximum Security within a year and required that all other facilities be brought into compliance with minimum standards of the United States Public Health Service, the American Public Health Association, and the Rhode Island Department of Health within nine months. Simultaneously all prisoners were to be reclassified and gradually moved into facilities suitable to their security classification. It was assumed that the reclassification would reduce the population of Maximum Security to those destined to be housed in the High Security Center (HSC) then under construction. If necessary, these inmates could be retained temporarily in the old prison provided the area in which they were housed "can be made fit for human habitation" and that the state complied with the other provisions of the order.[11]

Classification

Reclassification was essential in order to develop a profile of the population in terms of both risk and needs. Judge Pettine accordingly regarded it as the cornerstone of the remedy, and he ordered it to be completed within six months, by February 10, 1978. As discussed in Chapter 4, as late as December, the department had made no progress beyond hiring a consultant. Upon learning of the situation, Special

Master Breed worked with the consultant, Dr. James Cowden, to develop a plan of action. It was six weeks before sufficient staff could be secured to begin the process, however, and as of February 10 only 37 inmates of some 525 had been reclassified. Judge Pettine cited the department for civil contempt. Rather than impose a penalty, however, he took note of the department's recent efforts under Moran and extended the deadline until May, threatening a fine of $1000 per day only if the new deadline was not met.[12] In a whirlwind of activity, the department was able to complete enough of the reclassification within the month to purge itself of contempt and avoid the fine.

In Judge Pettine's view, carrots are more effective than sticks. Threatening a fine provides an incentive for defendants to comply with requirements set by the court, but imposing a fine on the state is equivalent to taxing its citizens, something he will do only with greatest reluctance.[13] Thus, this first confrontation between the state and the court initiated a pattern that was to weave itself through the case establishing a basic rhythm. Time and again, the state failed to meet deadlines. The deadlines were usually extended with contempt findings and fines sometimes threatened and then withdrawn given a good faith effort by the defendants. In only a few instances were fines actually imposed, and only once did this involve a substantial sum.

The intent of the order went beyond a one-shot reclassification of the current population, however. To comply, the department had to develop a meaningful system by which inmates could be rationally classified on an ongoing basis. Over the next year, Cowden worked with the staff to organize a management information system so as to make the relevant data on each inmate accessible and ensure that each inmate was seen for reclassification at least every six months. He trained staff in the preparation of treatment plans. More objective measures of risk and needs assessment, then in use in Wisconsin, were normed for Rhode Island inmates and staff trained in their use.[14]

Cowden's system was never fully implemented, however. By law, Moran had to approve every classification decision, and he took this responsibility seriously. He was skeptical of objective classification systems and even more so of the information on which they might be based as the institution seldom received pre-sentence reports from the courts and lacked sufficient staff to verify what was reported by inmates. Thus, while information was gathered, testing done and objective scoring forms completed, decisions continued to rely heavily on insight and experience with the inmate.[15]

The percentage of inmates classified as requiring maximum security failed to decline as predicted. Although two independent assessments by classification experts agreed that no more than 20 percent of the population required maximum security, by mid-1980 nearly 40 percent of the population were so classified and a crisis loomed. If Maximum Security, which the court had allowed to remain open, were to be closed when the long-delayed HSC opened, there would be over 150 homeless maximum security inmates. Bronstein urged the court to deny the department's request that it be allowed to retain use of a portion of Maximum Security, arguing that the crisis was, in large part, brought about by the "defendants systematically making irrational decisions which result in the gross overclassification of inmates."[16] In the end, however, the plaintiffs were persuaded by the logic of Special Master J. Michael Keating who had found the defendants in full compliance with this provision of the 1977 order. As he interpreted it, the order did not mandate a specific classification scheme nor that specific percentages be classified to any particular level of custody; it required only that the department develop and implement a process that would permit the making of reasonable decisions and that these decisions be reviewed at least once per year. The choice to classify 40 percent of the population to maximum security may be "excessive or unwise" but was not prohibited.[17]

A New Master

Special Master Keating had been recruited by Breed in July 1978 to serve as his deputy. Six months later Keating succeeded Breed as special master when the latter left to become director of the National Institute of Corrections. A lawyer who had worked for a number of years developing systems of alternative dispute resolution in corrections, Keating brought a much different style to the mastership than had Breed. An outstanding correctional administrator, Breed had the experiential base to provide credible advice on operational matters and, as we have seen, occasionally orchestrated major administrative changes. Keating, in contrast, while willing to assist where he could, defined his role more in terms of monitoring, evaluating and mediating. As he saw it "my real obligation [was] to the terms of the order, to gain compliance as quickly and as fully as possible, and where the terms proved to be unreasonable, to negotiate changes so that what was done was reasonable."[18] Moreover, shortly after his appointment, Keating moved to Rhode Island rather than commute, as had Breed, from Washington, D.C. Being a full-time resident made him more sensitive to community responses and thus may have moderated his approach. It also gave him the opportunity to become part of Judge Pettine's official family, to develop a close personal as well as a professional relationship with him. Differences of opinion between judge and master were rare and resolved quickly, in private, so that there was never a hint of division between them in public. Within a relatively short time, all parties were aware that the master's position on disputed issues was almost certainly the position to be adopted by the judge, providing the parties with both an incentive to negotiate and a benchmark for a settlement.[19] Concerned with gaining compliance to the terms of a decree won by plaintiffs, theoretically Keating was more on their side than the defendants . In reality, however, his participation probably benefitted the defendants more than plaintiffs, making up to some extent for what all agree was inadequate legal representation of the state whose counsel changed frequently and who were typically young, inexperienced, not well versed in correctional law and possessed little knowledge of the case and its history.[20]

Renovations

Keating's first job as deputy special master was to work with expert consultants to translate the various standards noted in the order into a list of specific renovations to be made in the medium and minimum security units. As these standards were not written with correctional institutions in mind, this was a complex and difficult task that consumed nearly six months. In the meantime, funding the renovations nearly precipitated a confrontation between the federal court and the state legislature.

The legislature meets in January each year and remains in session until their work is completed, usually in May or June. It was not in session when the remedial order was issued by Judge Pettine nor were legislative leaders consulted by Governor Garrahy on the decision about whether to appeal. Feeling left out of the decision making but responsible for paying the bill, a number of legislative leaders came to the January 1978 session determined to demonstrate the power of that branch vis-a-vis both the state's executive and the federal court. Rather than grant Governor Garrahy's request for a supplemental appropriation to complete the renovations, the legislature decided to put the issue before the voters in the November 1978 election. The referendum was six months beyond the initial deadline set for the renovations, and defeat seemed certain in the volatile economic climate. Judge Pettine nonetheless extended the deadline, but when the predicted defeat became a reality, he immediately ordered the improvements to be made.[21]

Governor Garrahy, concerned about his leadership within his own party and still smoldering over what he perceived as betrayal by Allen Breed on the Southworth issue, directed the attorney general to appeal this order. The judge and special master wanted to avoid the delays in implementation that an appeal would entail. Even more, they were concerned about what the appeals court might rule in a situation in which the lack of funding was an expression of the sovereign will of the people, not mere legislative intransigence. And further, they feared that losing on appeal might provoke the state to outright defiance opening wide the fissures now appearing in their relationship.

Hoping to avoid a confrontation, Keating used his extensive contacts in Washington in an attempt to find federal funds for the renovations. When officials of the Law Enforcement Assistance Administration (LEAA) indicated funds might be available given an equal state match, Keating worked with the department's planners and grant writers in preparing the necessary application all the while keeping up a drumbeat of appeals to the agency. As the legislature convened its January 1979 session, the department submitted an application to LEAA which "squeezed every possible sympathy of the federal court's imposition of standards on it."[22] Director Moran and

Governor Garrahy, meanwhile, were lobbying legislative leaders, presenting them with a scenario in which continued refusal to appropriate funds would result in the forfeiture of substantial federal funding, leaving the state with the prospect of facing fines for civil contempt and then having to foot the bill by itself. A moment of high drama occurred early in May 1979 when on the very eve of oral arguments before the First Circuit Court of Appeals, LEAA awarded the grant and the legislature approved the matching funds.[23]

The successful resolution of this issue, and the major role played by the master in achieving it, restored a substantial measure of good will between the state and court. As we shall see, however, other issues introduced additional tensions. Moreover, repeated delays in actually making the renovations tried the patience of both judge and master. Although funding for the renovations to the medium and minimum security units became available in July 1979 and a deadline for completion set for April 1980, the work was not finished until August 1981. The delay was caused not by the Department of Corrections but other state agencies upon which it was dependent and which were bureaucratically insulated from the pressures it faced. Neither the rhetoric of the court, nor findings of contempt, nor the threat of fines, could speed the plodding pace of these agencies as they lumbered through the maze of statuatory and administrative requirements governing public construction.

A case in point was the construction of a Butler Building.[24] One of the most glaring inadequacies of Medium Security was its lack of program space. The solution developed by the department was to construct a prefabricated building to house work and vocational programs for 90 inmates. Another matching scheme with LEAA was arranged and funds became available in July 1978. With the manufacturer's assurance that the structure could be erected in four weeks and allotting several months to equip it, the court set a date of December 31, 1978 for its completion. But control of the process was in the hands of the purchasing division of the state's budget office, hands which are guided by an elaborate set of rules designed to prevent them being soiled by graft and corruption. The fact that this contract was developed to comply with an order of a federal court did not, it became apparent, mark it for expedited treatment. In repeated hearings, an increasingly frustrated Judge Pettine was introduced to a world of checks and balances and diffused responsibility in which contracts were seldom, if ever, completed on time and in which several 120-day extensions were routine. The Butler Building, designed to be erected in four weeks, took nearly two years to complete and even then was rushed to completion after a finding of contempt and the threat of a substantial fine.[25]

Despite such delays, Keating was able to inform the court late in 1983 that the defendants were in substantial compliance with all of the directives regarding Minimum and Medium save one, that there be 75 square feet of personal living space for each inmate in the dormitories. There were 245 prisoners living in space the court considered sufficient for no more than 186.[26] On the basis of Keating's report, Judge Pettine in January 1984 ordered the department, *inter alia,* to reduce the number of inmates in Medium Security or to begin planning to increase the availability of bedspace, and gave the department 18 months to comply.[27] When the special master inspected Medium Security again in July 1985, however, he found the situation even worse; there were 268 inmates in the same space. The state had, however, developed a plan to construct a new 515-bed facility financed in a creative way, and the court took no further action at the time.[28] As we shall see in the next chapter, unanticipated obstacles delayed the construction of this facility and provoked a serious confrontation between state and court over the issue of overcrowding.

Maximum Security

The order to close Maximum Security within a year had been framed so as to coordinate with the construction of HSC and the Intake Services Center (ISC), both of which were slated to open within a year to 18 months. However, the same types of problems that plagued the construction of the Butler Building were to plague these facilities as well. HSC did not open until January 1981, 28 months after the original scheduled date of completion, and ISC originally scheduled to open in December 1979 was not occupied until July 1982. As these delays were becoming evident late in 1977, Special Master Breed had recommended to the court that the defendants be permitted to continue to use Maximum Security until the new facilities came on line, provided the old structure was made fit for human habitation and those awaiting trial were separated from sentenced inmates.[29]

Maximum Security was rather quickly separated into two parallel facilities by using the two cell blocks north (MNO and PQR in Figure 5.1) of the central rotunda as a jail while retaining the four cell blocks on the south side for sentenced inmates.[30] But it took seven months for the court and department to reach agreement on what was required to make the old prison habitable. Meanwhile, conditions in the facility were actually becoming worse as the lockup continued and inmates engaged in a "garbage war" with staff (see Chapter 4). Plaintiffs moved the court to find the state in civil contempt and requested imposition of sanctions of $5000 per day. By the time of the hearing in late June 1978, however, the lockup had ended, conditions had improved and thirteen specific changes relating to basic health and safety had been identified and agreed upon. These were ordered by the court with all 13 remedies to be accomplished by September 7, 1978.[31] This deadline was more than a year after the court had ordered "immediate" improvements and one month after the original deadline for Maximum to be closed. Yet it was still to be six months beyond that date before the master could report substantial compliance with the interim measures.

No sooner had the department complied with the 13 remedies than all parties were confronted with new and disturbing facts. As discussed above, the reclassification of the population had not resulted in the expected reduction in the percentage of inmates classified as maximum security. Moreover, the inmate population, after more than two decades of stability, had begun to grow in 1975 and this growth accelerated in the years after the remedial degree. The plans to close Old Max had been based on the assumption of a stable population of about 600 inmates with about 100 needing maximum security, but by the end of 1978, there were nearly 700 inmates with over 200 estimated to need

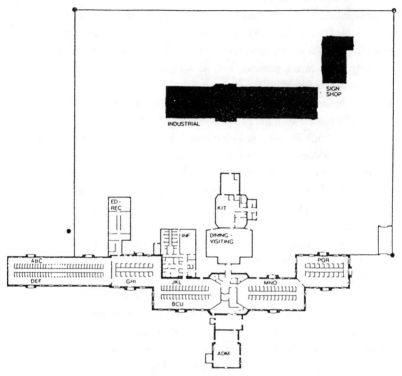

Figure 5.1 Diagram of Maximum Security, 1980
(The shaded buildings were razed after a riot in 1991)

maximum security. HSC, then expected to open late in 1979, had a capacity for only 96. Closing Maximum when HSC opened thus would leave more than 100 maximum security inmates homeless.

In May 1979 Director Moran requested that the department be permitted to retain use of two cell blocks in Maximum. The request posed a genuine dilemma for the court, one that prompted Judge Pettine and Special Master Keating to examine the "place of the courts in the constitutional fabric and the limits on judicial remedies."[32] On the one hand, to permit continued use of a portion of the facility was completely antithetical to the court's determination that it be closed and would in all probability encourage the state to seek permanent use of the entire decrepit structure. On the other hand, with the number of maximum security inmates more than double the capacity of the new facility, for the court to insist upon the prompt closing of Maximum Security would throw the correctional system into chaos. Moreover, the growth of the inmate population was beyond the control of the department and the court saw the proportion of inmates classified as maximum security as a management decision, not something the court could impose upon the department.[33] Thus, they decided that if the state was now willing to spend the money necessary to bring portions of the prison up to acceptable standards, the court had no real choice but to approve the plan. To preserve the integrity of the order, however, the court was bound and determined that the renovations should be real and complete. Thus the special master retained experts to inspect the cell blocks over the summer to determine precisely what would need to be done to bring them up to minimum standards, and then the state was required to submit its plans for the court's review and permission before the renovations were begun.

Almost as soon as the process of identifying what repairs would have to be made in the two cell blocks had been completed, the department submitted an amended plan. Claiming that the growth of the population was now outstripping the plan developed in May, they now sought to more than double the size of HSC, the opening of which labor problems had by now pushed back to late 1980, and to continue using all of Maximum until the expansion was completed and ISC, which had also been delayed, opened.[34]

Pointing out contradictions in projected numbers and facility capacities among various plans submitted at different times, Judge Pettine rejected this latest submission and directed the department to work with the special master to develop "a common, mutually acceptable definition of the population problem . . . based on sound research and analysis."[35] Rather than the cooperate as the court had hoped, however, the department went its own way and prepared a plan that reiterated its view that the most feasible approach was to increase the capacity of HSC from 96 to 256 and retain use of Old Max until the expansion was completed in 1984.[36] Keating characterized the plan as "ill-conceived, badly structured and inadequate . . . "[37] and presented the results of his own extensive research. His analysis suggested that the surge in prison admissions was probably a temporary phenomenon, that no more than 15-20 percent of the ACI's population need be held in maximum security, and that several available buildings might well be converted to house medium security prisoners. Therefore, Keating concluded that the state could resolve the problem by the less costly expedients of reclassification and renovation. Finally, he raised the question of what would happen if the bond issue scheduled for a special referendum on July 22 were defeated.

The early summer campaign was marked by intense public conflict between the director and the special master. Moran labelled Keating as "little more than an 'expert visitor' engaged in writing 'novels' about the prison" and accused him of making recommendations that "risk the public safety"[38] while Keating, unfettered by the judge to defend his evaluation, publicly challenged the effectiveness of Moran's "seat-of-pants management style" and likened him to a "'messiah' feeding 'true believers' a diet of glittering generalities."[39] In the July referendum, the public sided with Keating, rejecting the bond issue by a 3 to 1 margin and leaving the state in the uncomfortable position of being under a court order to close its maximum security prison without a plan to house its prisoners. It was a dilemma, the *Journal-Bulletin*, declared "of the state's own making and one for which Governor Garrahy must take full responsibility."[40]

The state, however, had laid the groundwork for a way out of its dilemma. Concurrent with the plan to expand HSC, the defendants had moved the court to reverse its 1977 decision that conditions in Maximum were unconstitutional, arguing that the improvements made thus far had reduced substantially the sum of the "totality of conditions" upon which the court had based its condemnation. While not specifically requested, such a reversal would, in effect, allow the state to use the facility indefinitely. Judge Pettine had reserved judgement on this seemingly contradictory motion until after the referendum. Now, with the defeat of the bond issue, he directed the special master to hold hearings to evaluate the state's request. In a report submitted in September 1980, Keating found that Maximum is "now a clean, freshly painted, sanitary facility in which staff have a new confidence in their ability to control effectively both the institution and its population."[41] Nonetheless, such improvements only met the "habitable" standard imposed by the court in 1977 for short-term use. Expert testimony, however, did indicate that additional repairs to three cell blocks could make them sufficiently habitable for use through 1984 and that they could possibly be brought up to the minimum standards set for all facilities in the 1977 order. Thus, Keating recommended that the defendants be allowed to continue to use these three cell blocks (GHI, JKL and MNO in Figure 5.1) given the necessary repairs, at least through 1984 and possibly indefinitely. Basic structural problems in the other cell blocks, however, were so severe that he recommended they be closed as soon as the new facilities, now scheduled to open in December 1980 and July 1981, came on line.[42]

Bronstein objected strenuously to Keating's report. Conceding that "there has been much painting and some improvement in housekeeping," he argued "there has been no major change in the fundamental physical conditions."[43] Rather than continue to warehouse people in this "outmoded and obsolete facility" as the special master recommended, he moved the court to appoint a receiver to supervise its closing. Judge Pettine gave serious consideration to Bronstein's motion, but in the end rejected it after consulting with Moran and the inmate plaintiffs.[44] In November 1980 he entered the master's recommendations as an order and warned the defendants that "the Court will entertain no further excuses for failing to meet these deadlines."[45] Thinking compliance was at hand and concerned about the cost to taxpayers, Judge Pettine also reduced the mastership to a part-time enterprise.[46]

The population pressure was relieved slightly when the long-awaited High Security Center opened in January 1981, and that spring the legislature provided the department with a supplemental appropriation to make the repairs needed to keep the three cell blocks open. However, the growth of the population accelerated so that by mid-1981 there were 950 inmates, about 185 of whom were pre-trial detainees being double-celled in Maximum; this was more than the capacity (168) of the yet-to-be-opened Intake Services Center. Staffing HSC and overtime made necessary by the crowded conditions, moreover, also increased the department's operating expenses by a substantial margin just as federal funding was cut and the nation entered a recession. Offsetting this to some degree were savings realized when the small but expensive juvenile corrections division was transferred to a newly created department designed to coordinate all state services for children, youth and families. The creation of that agency increased the overall burden on the state, however, and Governor Garrahy announced plans to delay the opening of ISC until July 1982 to save over $1 million in new operating costs, to divert most of the monies allocated for the renovations of the cell blocks into the operating budget and to cut program staff. Coincident with these decisions the state petitioned the court for an indefinite stay of its order to close any portion of Maximum.

The state's plan meant that a record number of pre-trial detainees would continue to be double-celled in patently unconstitutional conditions for several months while a new facility, ready for use, remained vacant. Nonetheless, because of the short time involved and because double-celling had not previously been raised as an issue in the case, Judge Pettine believed there was not much the court could do about this "promiscuous mingling of accused petty criminals and major felons in harsh, dangerous and unsafe physical conditions."[47] But he denied the state's motion for a stay and categorically ordered that all cell blocks which had not undergone renovations (four of the six) be closed permanently when ISC was occupied on July 1, 1982.

The court and the state came eye to eye when the defendants hinted that it might not obey this order, and there followed two months of quiet tension during which it seemed to Keating that the state was "sitting on its hands waiting for the Court to reverse it."[48] Further adding to the sense of crisis were public warnings of an impending riot from the officers' union which at this time was locked in a struggle with the administration over staffing levels and seniority rights (see Chapter 4) and were seizing upon each and every incident of disorder to gain public support for their claims. In the end, it was the state that blinked. In April Moran decided to divert sufficient funds from other areas in the corrections budget—specifically probation and parole—to pay for the renovations to two of the four unrenovated cell blocks (MNO and PQR in Figure 5.1) which then the department proposed to use until December 31, 1984. With the opening of ISC, 168 inmates housed in the two unrenovated cell blocks were to be moved out of Maximum Security leaving these blocks vacant. However, increases in the population meant the department would need to retain temporary use of two cell blocks ordered closed (ABC and DEF in Figure 5.1) while it renovated the vacated blocks. Impressed by what the department had accomplished with its renovations of two cell blocks (GHI and JKL) the previous year, the plaintiffs did not oppose this plan. Following two days of negotiations during which a list of specific renovations was developed, Judge Pettine entered an order incorporating the agreement and directing that the improvements be completed by April 1, 1983. The remaining two unrenovated blocks (ABC, DEF) were ordered closed by June 30 of that year unless they also underwent sweeping renovations.[49]

With this plan and the opening of ISC in July 1982, yet another crisis had been averted. But as the population continued its seemingly inexorable increase, it soon became clear that there would not be sufficient bedspace if Maximum Security were closed at the end of 1984. Moreover, closing it would waste the several million dollars already spent on repairs and renovations, and it was estimated that for an additional investment of $5 million, the entire structure including those blocks with extensive structural damage could be brought into compliance with the minimum standards set in the 1977 order. What had once been too costly to consider, now had become the cheaper alternative, and the legislature placed a bond issue for $8.5 million—$3.5 million of which was to begin construction of a new medium security prison (see above)—on the November 1982 ballot. The grip of the recession, however, was stronger than the exhortations of the coalition of political leaders, business watchdogs and prison reformers supporting the bond issue, and it was defeated.

Once again the voice of the voters left the state in an uncomfortable situation. The failure of the bond issue meant the state had no funds to renovate the other cell blocks that the still surging population necessitated they keep open but which the court had ordered closed. Compounding the problem, the renovation of the two blocks vacated when the ISC had opened was not complete by the April 1, 1983 deadline. On June 7 Judge Pettine found the state in contempt for its failure to complete these renovations and once again ordered the two blocks being used temporarily closed as soon as the renovations were complete.[50]

Director Moran responded that they would not close the cell blocks on June 30, as had been ordered, despite not being able to renovate them and was publicly backed by Governor Garrahy who, reciting the list of improvements already made, gratuitously declared that Rhode Island's prison system was now the best in the country.[51] Despite his pugnacious public posture, the governor was at the same time lobbying the legislature to get the funds to complete the renovations, and secured an appropriation of $500,000 in the next fiscal year for that purpose. Additionally, he gained legislative approval for a special referendum in November 1983 in which the voters would be asked to approve a scaled-down bond issue of $4.9 million to be used solely to bring Old Max up to the minimum standards necessary for the court to approve its indefinite use.

By this time the two-year recession had ended. Once again leaders of both parties and various interest groups endorsed the bond issue, and it was presented clearly to the public as the least costly alternative; the other being to construct a new facility. With the issue so sharply drawn, the voters for the first time since 1977 approved a bond issue for corrections.

Squabbling between the court and the department continued for a year over matters such as deadlines for plans and blueprints, but in the summer of 1985 the mastership was reactivated to assess the defendants' compliance. Despite the continuing specter of overcrowding, Keating found the institution in substantial compliance with the orders to renovate.

The refurbishment of the old Maximum Security Building is fundamentally complete, and the results are simply astounding.... Once a seething bedlam of noise, dirt, fear and violence [it] is now a remarkably quiet, incredibly clean and relatively placid facility.... The defendants' decision to retain the old structure, developed slowly and incrementally in response to immediate needs, has been fully vindicated. The presently reconstituted structure will serve for generations, and its rehabilitation has probably cost less than a fourth of what a wholly new facility of comparable size might have required.[52]

Following a status conference on September 17, 1985 the court accepted Keating's recommendations and granted defendants' motion that they be allowed to continue the use of the facility for the housing of prisoners indefinitely so long as it is maintained in compliance with the standards set forth in the August 1977 order.[53] Thus did Old Max, ordered demolished in the year of its centennial, gain a new life.

HEALTH SERVICES

Medical and Mental Health Care

The 1977 remedial decree directed the defendants to bring the health care delivery system into compliance with minimum standards set by relevant agencies within six months and to hire an adequate number of mental health professionals to diagnose, treat and care for those prisoners with mental health problems. At the time the department had a medical director who, although a full-time employee, worked at the prison only fifteen hours per week and was on-call for emergencies. Two part-time physicians provided another 24 hours of care per week. There was neither a psychiatrist nor a clinical psychologist and no provision for short-term treatment. The nursing staff was undermanned and operated largely without supervision. There was no pharmacist and little control over medications. Nurses routinely diagnosed illnesses and dispensed medications without prescription and without consulting or informing the physicians. Basic emergency equipment such as a defibrillator was lacking. There were no written protocols or policy manuals, and medical records were nonexistent.[54]

Although it took longer than six months, the department moved into compliance with the health care provisions more rapidly than with any other aspect of the decree. Even before the order had been entered, a medical services coordinator had been hired to upgrade the system, and the medical director was replaced soon after. By June 1979 this work had been completed, and the special master found defendants in compliance with the provisions of the order with respect to both medical care and mental health.[55]

Four years later, however, the increase in the prisoner population was straining the medical and mental health systems that, with the same staff and resources as in 1979, were attempting to meet the needs of nearly twice the number of inmates. In January 1984, Judge Pettine ordered the department to expand medical and mental health services to keep pace with the increase in population, but despite additional staffing and facilities, 18 months later, the special master reported that "the general picture of a system in danger of being swamped has not changed. . . . "[56] Nonetheless, there had been no massive breakdown in care and there were some promising developments. Located on the same grounds as the prisons are the state's Institute of Mental Health and its General Hospital. Moreover, the prison complex is less than 10 miles from several major hospitals in Providence, all of which are affiliated with the Brown University Medical School. The department had always made use of the hospitals for emergencies and long-term treatment. Now, however, it was seeking to negotiate cooperative agreements with them and the medical school that would involve some sharing of staff, internships, and case conferencing to facilitate the coordination and delivery of appropriate services. Thus, Keating concluded with respect to medical and mental health care, the defendants remained in "substantial but tenuous compliance."[57]

Drug Treatment

Various studies prior to 1977 estimated that as many as 70 percent of the inmates were abusing drugs even while incarcerated. Yet the prison had no detoxification unit, staff made no attempt to identify and provide help to substance abusers, and the medical personnel were woefully ignorant of proper methods of treatment. The decree mandated that within one month the department place the treatment of addicts under a physician willing and able to do so and establish a medically sound detoxification program for those physically addicted to drugs or alcohol. Within three months, they were to develop a drug abuse treatment program which complied with the relevant standards.[58]

The department moved quickly to establish a detoxification unit by sealing off a portion of the infirmary in Maximum Security, developing written protocols for detoxification and treatment, and securing a license from the Food and Drug Administration to distribute methadone. Thus, by July 1978 they were in substantial compliance with that portion of the order.[59]

The development of a drug treatment program progressed more slowly, however. Whereas physical addiction is a serious medical condition which prison authorities cannot deliberately ignore, non-medical treatment for those with a history of substance abuse has no such legal standing. Plaintiffs thus chose not to push too hard on this aspect of the order, and it was not a high priority for Director Moran who believes that concerns about confidentiality in a prison setting render such treatment ineffective there.[60]

On March 9, 1978—nearly three months beyond the initial deadline—Director Moran submitted to the court for its approval an organizational and staffing plan for a drug treatment program. In addition to detoxification, the plan established a screening process at intake, counselling in each facility, crisis intervention, a residential drug treatment unit for 20 inmates, and post-release information and referral services. The plan was dependent upon the state funding 31 additional positions, but the legislature appropriated monies for only 24. Judge Pettine, however, ruled that the plan must be fully implemented within 60 days, and if it were not, he would appoint the special master as limited receiver for the purpose of developing and implementing it.[61] Given this threat, the legislature which came into session in January 1979 quickly appropriated the funds for the additional positions, and the plan was implemented, a year after the original deadline.

The drug treatment unit, however, was hampered by the fact that it was a minimum security unit and inmates had to be within 6 months of release to be eligible. At no time were there 20 residents and usually only 10-11. Turnover among the counselling staff was common, and the unit was frequently without a full complement of correctional officers as the growth in staffing requirements in other areas took precedence. Finally, with the demise of LEAA in 1981, Moran dismantled the unit. At the same time, he reduced the counselling staff substantially to meet an order from the governor that all departments reduce their budgets by five percent to cope with a fiscal crisis occasioned by the 1981 recession. In a report filed early in 1982, Keating observed that there is "little left of the defendants' brief efforts to conform with the court's order" to establish a drug treatment program.[62]

Moran's actions had been unilateral, and on April 21 Judge Pettine warned the defendants that they were technically in contempt of court and directed them to either conform to the relevant orders or file a motion to modify them within 10 days.[63] Claiming that the master's report overlooked a number of treatment resources available to inmates the defendants petitioned to be relieved of the responsibility of operating a residential treatment unit. At the time, however, all parties were preoccupied with the issues surrounding Maximum Security, and the motion was allowed to languish for nearly a year. In April 1983, Bronstein, impressed by the success of the previous year's negotiations in developing a list of specific improvements to be made in Maximum, suggested that one of the experts who had testified for the plaintiffs at trial evaluate the current program and make specific suggestions for improvement that could then be negotiated. The expert, Dr. Anthony Raynes, had likened the institution's treatment of substance abusers in 1977 to the use of leeches; now, however, he submitted an upbeat report which found the program to be a good one that needed only an additional full-time counsellor and some minor changes to meet minimum standards.[64] These requirements were met, but by 1985 the pressure of the growing population was straining this service as well. Although finding them in compliance, Keating noted that only some 137 prisoners were receiving counselling while it was estimated that as many as 865 had substance abuse problems. Thus, while drug treatment was a far cry from the absence of programming which existed in 1977, it nonetheless was capable of serving only a small portion of those in need.[65]

PROGRAMS

Finding almost a complete lack of work, vocational, educational or recreational opportunities in 1977, the court had ordered the department to develop a meaningful job for each prisoner and sufficient programs in the other three areas so that each inmate would have the opportunity to participate on a regular basis.[66] In comparison to the closing of Maximum Security, this undramatic portion of the order received little public attention but proved to be every bit as vexing.

Although, as in *Palmigiano,* the lack of meaningful rehabilitation programs may be one of the grounds supporting a finding that the totality-of-conditions in a prison constitute cruel and unusual punishment, courts have repeatedly held that the lack of such programs is not, by itself, a defect of constitutional magnitude.[67] Thus, Bronstein, knowing he had a strong order which guaranteed at least some programming, was reluctant to push in this area for fear that the defendants might, on appeal, argue successfully that remedies of other conditions were sufficiently substantial as to bring the totality of conditions within the orbit of the Constitution even without programs.[68]

Almost as if reflecting the uncertain constitutional grounds of a right to treatment, the order in *Palmigiano* itself was indefinite in this area. Unlike other portions of the order, these directives contained no set deadlines. Moreover, there was no definition of such terms as "meaningful" and "opportunity to participate on a regular basis." After several months of bickering over these terms and more specific matters such as how many students there should be per teacher in an adult basic education class, bickering which itself delayed implementation, complex standards were abandoned in favor of a simple pragmatic guideline: the department was to provide sufficient program opportunities to occupy five hours in the daily life of each inmate.[69]

Finally, programming was affected by the state's financial problems more than any other aspect of the order. The Department of Corrections was receiving annual budget increases of 15-20 percent while increases for other agencies were less than 5 percent. Most of these increases were eaten up by overtime, renovations and the need for additional correctional officers, all due to the burgeoning population and basic issues that in Moran's eyes took precedence over programs. As he put it, "You can't go into the Finance Committee that just gave you a 20 percent increase and ask them for another $5 million to add 100 more treatment positions."[70]

Education and Recreation

Rhode Island had fewer than 20 female prisoners in the mid-1970s. Due to their small number, providing programs for women had been a long-standing problem to which the department in 1975 had found a partial solution by contracting with a local YMCA for recreational programs. The Rhode Island Council on the Arts had also funded a small Arts-in-Corrections program by which local artists provided instruction to inmates in a wide variety of endeavors from poetry to glass blowing. Following the order in *Palmigiano*, these programs were extended to all facilities. Within weeks, the Y was offering a full range of craft programs in each facility, even in Maximum during the lockup, and supervising inmates in making needed physical improvements in the recreational areas. By the summer each unit had a softball team in the town league—though the teams in Maximum and Medium played only home games—and there was an intramural league in both softball and basketball with teams representing each cell block and dormitory. Additionally, interested inmates in each unit could sculpt, learn to make films, paint etc.

Funding for Arts-in-Corrections ran out, and the Y contract was not renewed in 1981-82 in an effort to cut costs. Recreation was merged into one unit along with education and vocational training, and the court feared that the program would deteriorate. That fear, however, proved to be unfounded. In 1983 the special master found that the "quantity and scope of avocational and recreational activities . . . are exceptional and meet the requirements of the . . . order."[71]

The ability of the department to maintain high-quality programming was due in part to the training full-time staff had received while working with the vendors and to the strong initiative of middle managers, who had moved quickly to find alternative sources of funding and redesign programs. As noted in Chapter 4, an adult basic education program had been implemented with LEAA funds in 1974. In addition to providing services to inmates, this program had for years been the only conduit into the institutions for administrators without a background in custody. Gill, for example, had begun his ACI career as a teacher and served as director of education before Moran named him his assistant and then assistant director.

Late in 1977, Gill, then in charge of the Education Division, sought additional state funds from the Department of Education and federal funding under such programs as Title 1 and CETA. By the Fall 1978 the division had a staff of 16 including a school psychologist, an educational counselor, a reading specialist, an English as a Second Language instructor and 11 teachers. Classes were offered during the day in each facility and several nights per week for those who worked during the day. The instruction was about evenly split between basic education and high school equivalency although an LEAA grant underwrote a small college-level program for those with a high school diploma or GED.

In conjunction with their 1980 motion to have Maximum Security declared constitutional, the defendants argued that educational programming was more than adequate, noting that the ACI educational expenditures, per inmate, were now 40 percent greater than the average per pupil expenditure in the state's public schools. The plaintiffs, however, took a different view. One of their experts, touring the facility for five hours, found few inmates either at work or in class and characterized the department's figures as "a sham."[72] The special master, after considering both viewpoints, came down on the side of the state declaring "the focus of the programming requirement is on the defendants' effort to provide opportunities. If the Department of Corrections provides educational opportunities for 100 but only 20 take advantage of it, the defendants cannot be said to have violated the mandate of the order."[73]

The failure of inmates to take advantage of education was only one among many problems, however. The close proximity of the facilities permitted teachers to divide their time between the different units so that theoretically about 70 to 80 hours of instruction could be provided each week in each of the four major facilities. However, that did not take into account other schedules. Daytime teachers worked from 8 to 3, for example, but generally were not allowed into Maximum and Medium Security until after the morning count had been cleared which could be as late as 9. Customarily inmates were not summoned for class until after the teachers were there and recall for lunch was at 11. Thus, four hours of potential instruction was usually reduced to 90 minutes. Moreover because the court required that educational programming be made available to all inmates, the limited resources had to be spread thinly across many small segments of the population which could not be mixed, for example, those awaiting trial or in protective custody and the few women, rather than concentrated on those wishing to take advantage of them.[74]

With the demise of LEAA and cutbacks in state funding, the full-time educational staff was cut in half just as the number of clients shot up. Although funds were secured from the state's Department of Education to pay for part-time instructors and a number of innovative arrangements made—such as an exchange of inmate maintenance services for instructional services with the state's community college—resources came to be spread ever more thinly through the early '80s. Nonetheless, while recognizing these problems, in his 1983 report, Keating found that "for the overwhelming majority of prisoners . . . access to basic educational programs is more than adequate" and recommended the court enter an order indicating a satisfaction of judgement with respect to this provision.[75] Plaintiffs, however, objected, and Judge Pettine, in a rare instance of disagreement with his special master, decided to continue the court's supervision in this area as the possibility of recurrence had not "become attenuated to a shadow" as required by precedent.[76] Two years later, as we shall see, the question was once again before him.

Jobs and Vocational Training

Success in implementing the court's mandate with respect to work and vocational training varied greatly by level of custody. The department moved aggressively to market the labor of minimum security inmates to other government agencies, and by the summer of 1978 crews of inmates cleaning highways and parks were a common sight. Moreover, grants from LEAA and CETA, and later from the state's Division of Vocational Rehabilitation, subsidized nighttime and weekend vocational training for both minimum security inmates and those on work release at established sites in the community. Although jobs for the small number of female prisoners did not increase during 1978, by early 1979 two-thirds of the sentenced women were employed in a garment repair shop working under the supervision of a professional seamstress.[77]

Compliance in the larger and closer custody institutions was more difficult, however. The development of a self-sufficient correctional industries program had not been a high priority of the treatment-oriented administrations, and the frequent disturbances and disruptions had resulted in the loss of much of the equipment and most of the market. When Moran arrived in 1978, the industries division was so eroded that he had to contract with other states to purchase much of the supplies and materials needed to make the improvements required by the court. Moreover, renovations to the facilities provided few opportunities beyond some simple cleaning and painting due to union restrictions and concerns about liability[78]

Although vocational training had received some emphasis in the early '70s, programs were developed in response to the availability of federal funding and died when the grants expired. In 1978, there simply was no vocational training in either Maximum or Medium Security and neither the space nor equipment with which to begin a program. Moran, like his predecessors, thought vocational education inappropriate for inmates in Maximum Security given the long sentences most were serving, and sought to concentrate it in Medium

Security. The star-crossed Butler Building, discussed above, was to
house workspace and classrooms so as to integrate basic and vocational
education with actual work. Originally scheduled for completion in
December 1978, the building, as we have seen, was not ready for use
until February 1980. In the meantime, nearly two-thirds of the 150
inmates were without jobs and relatively few of these chose to take
advantage of the educational programs offered. Despite pressure from
the plaintiffs, however, the court was reluctant to impose sanctions
since responsibility for the delays lay with other state agencies, not
Corrections which seemed itself to be victimized by the process. When
the Butler Building opened at long last, its automotive repair and
upholstery shops offered program opportunities for less than half of the
by-then approximately 200 inmates. Moreover, by that time, federal
funding for vocational education had all but disappeared and the need
to provide beds and security for a rapidly growing population took
precedence when it came to the allocation of state funds.

Job development in Maximum Security was delayed by the
disturbances and lockup which lasted into the summer of 1978. In
January 1979 Keating reported 168 jobs and vocational slots for the 225
sentenced inmates in that facility.[79] However, over the next six months,
in the quietude following the September 1978 transfer and with
plaintiffs threatening to seek sanctions, considerable progress was
made. The plate shop, which two years previously had almost lost its
contract for Rhode Island license plates, was now operating six days
per week to turn out plates for both Rhode Island and Maine, and
additional state contracts for printing and carpentry permitted some
expansion in these shops. Virtually all sentenced inmates had jobs, but
there was substantial idleness as most of the assignments were janitorial
and required only some 2-3 hours per day,[80] and even this delicate
balance of population and jobs was soon destroyed by the growth in the
number of sentenced inmates.

The situation in Maximum was relieved to some degree by the
opening of HSC Center in 1981 and ISC the following year, but the
inexorable increase in prisoners outstripped the capacity of the
department to create jobs. In 1983, Keating reported that one-third of
the sentenced inmates in Maximum and Medium were without even a

part-time job assignment. The idleness combined with overcrowded dormitories in Medium to create a situation he viewed as "downright dangerous."[81] Moreover, the opening of the new facilities had merely spread the idleness. HSC, designed for control, contained only a small print shop, and ISC, double-celled as soon as it opened, was designed for short-term detention and had no job opportunities other than institutional maintenance. In his 1983 report, Keating listed only 12 industrial jobs and some 30 part-time housekeeping assignments for the 100 inmates in HSC and only 45 portering jobs for the 200 detainees in ISC. With respect to the latter, he remarked that "even an ambitious detainee, who has a job and is involved in education, is able to occupy no more than a few of hours of his day with meaningful activity. . . . The typical detainee simply fills his day with television."[82]

From 1983 through 1985, moreover, there was little expansion in work and vocational opportunities. Stitching together programs funded with small grants from a variety of sources, the department was able to offer vocational education to only 100 inmates at any given time, about 10 percent of the population, and these courses were for the most part short term, classroom based programs offering little actual work.[83] While there was some modest gain in the number of inmates employed in the three close custody institutions, Keating thought the increase was "nothing more than statistical legerdemain, dividing jobs long identified . . . as requiring no more than an hour or two a day to perform among more people to reduce system-wide unemployment rates."[84] The number of kitchen and portering jobs at ISC had been increased to about 75 since 1983, but the population had soared by 30 percent to 327, nearly double the design capacity of the 3-year-old facility, leaving even more detainees unemployed than two years before.[85]

Keating did note a ray of hope, however. One of the major obstacles to expanding industries was that all profits reverted to the state's General Fund leaving the department with no funds to invest in new equipment. Moran had successfully lobbied the 1983 legislature to amend the law so as to permit Correctional Industries to retain up to $50,000 per year for that purpose. With a grant from the National Institute of Corrections, the department retained consultants to identify potential markets and products, to recommend ways to boost sales and to develop a master plan for implementing these recommendations. This work had been completed by mid-1985 by which time accumulated profits, some savings from the renovations to Maximum and a supplemental appropriation from the legislature left the department with nearly $2 million with which to expand its industries.[86]

Thus, while Keating thus found the department still remained "hopelessly out of compliance" with the provisions of the order requiring them to provide work and vocational opportunities, they were "now armed with a reasonable blueprint and surprisingly large resources," and seemed "on the verge of making this once apparently utopian requirement a reality."[87] Moreover, as noted above, the refurbishment of Maximum had been completed and the transformation was astounding, and following two defeats of bond issues newly-elected Governor Edward D. DiPrete had recently announced plans to use an emergency mechanism to fund construction of a new medium security prison with adequate space for work and programming. In the summer of 1985, then, it appeared to all parties that the case might soon be brought to a close. That optimism, however, was soon shattered by the explosive growth in the prisoner population brought on by an intensified war on drugs.

NOTES

1. *New York Times*, July 16, 1979, pp. A1, A10.

2. Diana R. Gordon, *The Justice Juggernaut: Fighting Street Crime, Controlling Citizens* (New Brunswick, NJ: Rutgers University Press, 1991), ch. 7.

3. *New York Times*, October 15, 1982, pp. A1, A20.

4. A survey by the Council of State Governments in 1980 revealed that 18 states enacted mandatory sentencing statutes in 1979 while another five had adopted fixed or determinate sentencing thus continuing a movement begun in the mid-70s to limit the discretion of judges and to curb the power of parole boards. Because such statutes imposed tougher sentences or meant that a larger portion of the sentence would be served, the number of inmates continued to increase. *New York Times,* March 30, 1980, p. A27; April 5, 1982, p. A18.

5. Kathleen Maguire and Ann Pastore, eds., *Sourcebook of Criminal Justice Statistics 1993* (Washington: USGPO, 1994), Table 6.29, p. 600.

6. *New York Times*, April 5, 1982, p. A18; May 18, 1982, p. A1.

7. Alvin J. Bronstein, "Prisoners and Their Endangered Rights," *The Prison Journal* 65 (Spring-Summer 1985): 3-17.

8. *Meachum v. Fano*, 96 S.Ct 2532 (1976) at 2540.

9. *Bell v. Wolfish*, 99 S.Ct. 1861 (1979) at 1886.

10. Personal interview with J. Michael Keating, Jr., June 2, 1992. Mr. Keating was Allen Breed's deputy from July 1978 to January 1979 when he succeeded Breed as special master.

11. *Palmigiano v. Garrahy*, 443 F. Supp. 956 (1977) at 486-87.

12. *Palmigiano v. Garrahy*, C. A. No. 74-172, (D. R.I., March 28, 1978).

13. Personal interview with Judge Raymond J. Pettine, October 21, 1992.

14. *Palmigiano v. Garrahy*, C. A. No. 74-172, "Final Report on the Re-classification of Inmates at the ACI and on the Development and Validation of a Re-classification Monitoring Instrument," prepared by James E. Cowden (D. R I., July 1979).

15. Personal interview with John Moran, July 7, 1992.

16. *Palmigiano v. Garrahy*, C. A. No. 74-172, "Plaintiff's Objections to Special Master's Findings of Fact and Recommendations" (D. R.I., October 10, 1980) at 7.

17. *Palmigiano v. Garrahy*, C. A. No. 74-172, "Special Master's Findings of Facts and Recommendations" (D. R.I., September 18, 1980) at 14-18.

18. Personal interview with J. Michael Keating, Jr., June 2, 1992.

19. J. Michael Keating, Jr., "A Personal Account of the Adventures of a Master" (Providence, R. I., October 28, 1981). This account was prepared to provide data for the Federal Judicial Center's evaluation of the use of masters.

20. Personal interview with Alvin J. Bronstein, Washington, DC, October 3, 1992; Personal interviews with J. Michael Keating, Jr., June 22, 1992 and John Moran, June 17, 1992. Weak legal representation of the state is a common feature of structural reform cases due to the specialized nature of the law and the length of time required to implement decrees.

21. *Palmigiano v. Garrahy*, C. A. No. 74-172, (D. R.I., November 9, 1978).

22. Keating, "A Personal Account," p. 23.

23. *Ibid.*, pp. 22-28.

24. *Ibid.*, pp. 30-44. Butler is the name of the company which patented and produced the structure.

25. *Palmigiano v. Garrahy*, C. A. No. 74-172, (D. R.I., December 3, 1979).

26. *Palmigiano v. Garrahy*, C. A. No. 74-172, "A Summing Up: The Special Master's Final Report on Compliance with the August 10, 1977 Order" (D. R.I., October 20, 1983) at 25-33, 61.

27. *Palmigiano v. Garrahy*, C. A. No. 74-172, (D. R.I., January 25, 1984).

28. *Palmigiano v. Garrahy*, C. A. No. 74-172, "Special Master's Findings and Recommendations"(D. R.I., July 22, 1985) at 24-29.

29. Hon. Raymond J. Pettine, "A Practical Experience: Implementing Court Orders in a Class Action Prison Suit" (unpublished, c. 1981), p. 5.

30. Somewhat ironically, this arrangement conformed to the original design of the building in which the northern blocks were the Providence County Jail and those on the south formed the R. I. State Prison.

31. *Palmigiano v. Garrahy*, C. A. No. 74-172, (D. R.I., July 7, 1978).

32. Keating, "A Personal Account," pp. 54-55.

33. *Ibid.*, p.57.

34. *Ibid.*

35. *Palmigiano v. Garrahy*, C. A. No. 74-172, (D. R.I., January 21, 1980) at 12.

36. Letter from John J. Moran to Judge Raymond J. Pettine, May 1, 1980.

37. *Palmigiano v. Garrahy*, C. A. No. 74-172, "Special Master's Report on Defendant's Draw-Down Plan of May 1, 1980" (D. R.I., May 22, 1980) at 28.

38. *Journal-Bulletin*, May 24, 1980, p. A1.

39. *Sunday Journal*, June 15, 1980, p. C1.

40. *Journal-Bulletin*, July 24, 1980, p. A12.

41. *Palmigiano v. Garrahy*, C. A. No. 74-172, "Special Master's Findings of Fact and Recommendations" (D. R.I., September 18, 1980) at 13.

42. *Ibid.*, at 25-30.

43. *Palmigiano v. Garrahy*, C. A. No. 74-172, "Plaintiff's Objections to Special Master's Findings of Fact and Recommendations" (D. R.I., October 10, 1980) at 2-3.

44. Pettine, "A Practical Experience," p. 12.

45. *Palmigiano v. Garrahy*, C. A. No. 74-172, (D. R.I., November 19, 1980) at 15.

46. *Ibid.*

47. *Palmigiano v. Garrahy*, C. A. No. 74-172, (D. R.I., January 4, 1982) at 16-17.

48. *Bulletin*, February 11, 1982, p. A3.

49. *Palmigiano v. Garrahy*, C. A. No. 74-172, (D. R.I., July 21, 1982).

50. *Palmigiano v. Garrahy*, C. A. No. 74-172, (D. R.I., June 7 and July 21, 1983).

51. *Bulletin*, April 13, 1983.

52. "Special Master's Findings," July 22, 1985, at 4-5.

53. *Palmigiano v. Garrahy*, C. A. No. 74-172, (D. R.I., September 30, 1985).

54. *Palmigiano v. Garrahy*, 443 F. Supp. 956 (1977) at 973-976, 988.

55. *Palmigiano v. Garrahy*, C. A. No. 74-172, "Special Master's Report to the Court on Defendant's Compliance with the August 10, 1977 Order" (D. R.I., June 17, 1979) at 34-36.

56. *Palmigiano v. Garrahy*, C. A. No. 74-172, (D. R.I., January 25, 1984); "Special Master's Findings," July 22, 1985, at 21-24.

57. "Special Master's Findings," July 22, 1985, at 24.

58. *Palmigiano v. Garrahy*, 443 F. Supp. 956 (1977) at 989.

59. *Palmigiano v. Garrahy*, C. A. No. 74-172, "Master's Tentative Findings of Fact and Recommendations to the Court" (D. R.I., July 20, 1978) at 4-6.

60. Moran interview, July 17, 1992.

61. *Palmigiano v. Garrahy*, C. A. No. 74-172, (D. R.I., October 23, 1978).

62. *Palmigiano v. Garrahy*, C. A. No. 74-172, "Special Master's Quarterly Report" (D. R.I., February 10, 1982) at 9.

63. *Palmigiano v. Garrahy*, C. A. No. 74-172, (D. R.I., April 21, 1982).

64. *Palmigiano v. Garrahy*, C. A. No. 74-172, "Report on Substance Abuse Treatment at the ACI" (D. R.I., June 6, 1983).

65. "Special Master's Findings," July 22, 1985, at 24-5.

66. *Palmigiano v. Garrahy*, 443 F. Supp. 956 (1977) at 988.

67. *Holt v. Sarver*, 309 F. Supp. 362 (E. D. Ark. 1970), *aff'd* 442 F. 2d 304 (8th Cir. 1971); *Wilson v. Kelley*, 294 F. Supp 1005 (N.D. Ga. 1968). *aff'd per curiam*, 393 U.S. 266 (1969).

68. Bronstein interview.

69. *Palmigiano v. Garrahy*, C. A. No. 74-172, "Final Recommedations to the Court on Compliance with Programming Requirements of the August 10, 1977 Order," (D. R.I., January 31, 1979) at 6.

70. Moran interview, June 17, 1992.

71. "A Summing Up," October 20, 1983, at 39.

72. "Special Master's Findings," September 18, 1980, at 18.

73. *Ibid.*, at 23.

74. Richman interview.

75. "Special Master's Findings," September 18, 1980, at 37, 63-64.

76. *Palmigiano v. Garrahy*, C.A. No. 74-172, (D. R.I., January 25, 1984).

77. *Palmigiano v. Garrahy*, C.A. No. 74-172, "Tentative Findings and Recommendations on Programming at the Women's Institution," (D. R.I., March 30, 1979); "Special Master's Report to the Court on Defendants' Compliance with the August 10, 1977 Order," (D. R.I., June 19, 1979) at 24.

78. Moran interview, July 7, 1992.

79. "Final Recommendations," January 31, 1979, at 4-5.

80. "Special Master's Report to the Court," June 19, 1979, at 22-23.

81. "A Summing Up,"October 20, 1983, at 42-44.

82. *Ibid.*, at 16.

83. "Special Master's Findings," July 22, 1985, at 15-17.

84. *Ibid.*, at 18.

85. *Ibid.*, at 10-13.

86. "A Summing Up," October 20, 1983, at 41-42; "Special Master's Findings," July 22, 1985, at 18-20.

87. "Special Master's Findings," July 22, 1985, at 31.

CHAPTER 6

Threat

Following the 1981-1982 recession, the fits-and-starts that had crippled the American economy throughout the '70s disappeared. In 1984, the economy expanded by 6.8 percent, the greatest growth in a single year since 1951.[1] Thereafter, although at more modest levels, growth was sustained until mid-1990, marking the longest period of peacetime economic expansion in American history. The Reagan administration claimed, and most people agreed, that this long period of steady growth without inflation clearly vindicated their supply-side economic policies.

Despite sharp cuts in domestic spending, however, the increases in revenues brought about by sustained growth were never sufficient to reduce the burgeoning budget deficit incurred by the massive increases in military spending which were fueling the recovery as much, if not more, than were the revisions to the tax codes and deregulation. Moreover, the predicted "trickle-down" effects never occurred, and most Americans entered the 1990s no better off financially than they had been in the early '70s.[2]

Splits in the economy, developing for over a decade, were thrown into sharp relief by the unevenness of the recovery and expansion. Even as high-tech knowledge industries experienced unprecedented growth, plants closed, over 10 million manufacturing jobs disappeared, and a barrage of corporate takeovers spurred by tax incentives and deregulation resulted in the loss of middle management positions for the first time since the Great Depression. Jobs lost were disproportionately replaced by jobs paying lower wages, carrying fewer benefits and, because many of them were temporary, giving employers greater flexibility. And those who retained their jobs were not appreciably

212 _Lawful Order_

better off as for the first time since World War II, sustained increases in productivity did not result in higher wages for workers but were reinvested in labor-saving technologies or paid out to stockholders or high-level managers in the form of dividends, higher salaries and bonuses.[3]

Sociologists such as William J. Wilson began to speak of a growing underclass composed of individuals locked in urban ghettos from which capital had been withdrawn, suffering long-term unemployment or having dropped out of the labor force altogether and caught in a tangle of crime, drug addiction, illegitimacy and welfare dependency.[4] Other analysts such as Christopher Jencks[5] took exception to Wilson's terminology and the causal chain he traced but agreed that life in major American cities was coming to look and feel increasingly like that in third-world cities: posh restaurants and glittering shops filled with people spending money like Indian rajahs and Arab sheiks set amid public places littered with beggars living in cardboard boxes over subway grates.

The government's principal response to the plight of the inner-city poor was to intensify the war on drugs. In a recent book, Diana Gordon[6] argues convincingly that the growing ranks of marginalized people were characterized by leaders and perceived by the public in the same way as the "dangerous classes" of an earlier era, a teeming mass whose existence calls into question the legitimacy of the established political order and whose behavior poses a threat to its stability. The war on drugs capitalized on this threat. In promising to reduce the threat while simultaneously reinforcing traditional values it offered to politicians of both parties a relatively costless political strategy.

Crack, a powerfully addictive and thus immensely profitable form of cocaine, appeared on the illegal drug market late in 1985, disrupting control of the trade and resulting in an epidemic of violence. During the 1986 Congressional elections politicians of both parties vied for the most ferocious anti-drug posture, and just prior to the election President Reagan signed a new comprehensive anti-drug bill which, _inter alia_, increased federal penalties, required drug testing of federal employees and private sector workers in some sensitive occupations, put thousands of new law enforcement agents into the field and allowed the use of the military to combat the flow of drugs into the country.[7] Over the next several years, additional legislation further increased penalties and added the death penalty for homicides committed in the course of drug trafficking, expanded the role of the military and provided law enforcement with new weapons such as asset forfeiture and eviction from public housing. Drug sweeps by specially trained police tactical teams became routine fare on the evening news, AWAC planes flew the Caribbean to detect drug smugglers, U.S. helicopters and planes sprayed insecticides over coca fields in South America and American forces invaded Panama to bring suspected drug kingpin, General Manuel Noreiga, to trial in Miami. From 1986 to 1990 funding for the war on drugs grew from about $1.5 billion to nearly $8 billion[8] despite general agreement that it was a hopeless war that fell far short of its objectives.

If the war on drugs had little impact on drug abuse, it nonetheless had a dramatic impact upon the nation's criminal justice system. In 1984 there were 568,032 arrests for drug abuse violations; by 1990 the number had increased to 782,758.[9] During that same period the number of court commitments to prison for drug offenses more than doubled and, because of stiffer penalties, the estimated average minimum time to be served by newly sentenced drug offenders increased by approximately 40 percent[10] The jail and prison population rose by 54 percent, from 744,111 in 1985 to 1,145,915 in 1990, and as governments rushed to expand capacity, correctional expenditures increased by 94 percent.[11] To cut costs, local and state governments began to experiment with a variety of alternative sanctions from intensive probation to home confinement and short-term incarceration in so-called correctional "boot camps" and, in some cases, contracted with private corporations to either build or operate some correctional facilities.

The war on drugs was fought as vigorously in Rhode Island as elsewhere, causing a surge in the prison population. Indeed, in 1988 and 1989, Rhode Island surpassed all other states in the percentage increase growth in the number of prisoners. This rapid and largely unexpected growth in the prisoner population threatened to overwhelm the ACI and destroy the improvements that had been made over the seven years prior to 1985, transformed the focus of the on-going litigation from prison conditions to jail overcrowding and drew the state and court into another confrontation.

POPULATION GROWTH AND ITS IMPACT

From 1956 through 1975, the population of the ACI remained stable at about 500 inmates. Beginning in 1976, the number of inmates increased slightly each year over the next few years before beginning a steeper climb in 1980, going from about 700 in that year to almost 1200 at the end of 1984 (see Figure 6.1). As recounted in the last chapter, this sharp increase in growth greatly hampered the implementation of the *Palmigiano* order. It was, however, but the prelude to what happened over the next five years during which the population more than doubled, going from 1200 to over 2500. A number of changes contributed to the increased rate of growth. In 1983, for example, the state's parole board, composed of six part-time political appointees, adopted a set of administrative guidelines that greatly increased the percentage of their sentences most inmates would have to serve before being considered for release. Although all became legally eligible after completing one-third of their sentence, most would not be released until completing 50 percent or two-thirds depending upon the nature of the offense of which they were convicted. A management study commissioned by the department found that in fiscal year 1988, only one-third of those appearing before the board were granted parole, down from nearly 60 percent before the guidelines were developed, and a court-appointed expert in 1990 concluded that Rhode Island's rate of parole was far below that of other states.[12]

The attorney general in 1988 established a unit within his office to identify probationers who had been arrested on new charges. Up to this time, probation violators typically had not been identified until their arraignment in Superior Court. The new unit, however, screened the criminal records of all people arrested on felony charges at the time of their initial appearance in District Court and recommended that violators be held without bail pending a probation revocation hearing.

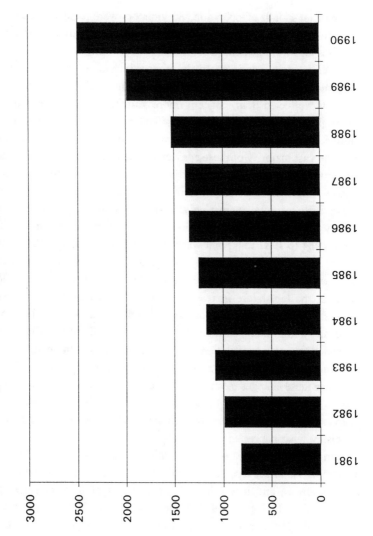

Figure 6.1 Average Annual Population, 1981-1990

In the first month of operation, 86 violators were identified and held without bail, 60 of whom pleaded guilty to the violation or the new charges and were sentenced to prison.[13]

While such administratively imposed changes may have been inspired by the war on drugs, other changes with more dramatic impacts reflected that concern more directly. Local news media spotlighted the disposition of drug offenders by the courts bringing to public attention that many offenses were treated as misdemeanors and that the vast majority of those convicted of felony offenses were placed on probation or given suspended sentences.[14] Officials scrambled to absolve themselves of responsibility, and quickly tightened the net. Drug offenses were increasingly treated as felonies. The number of felony filings for drug offenses rose by 217 percent in just three years from 1984 to 1987 to a point where they constituted almost half of the felony cases in Superior Court, and the percentage of those convicted who were sentenced to incarceration doubled.[15] In its Spring 1988 session, the legislature increased the penalties making even the mere possession of as little as 1 ounce of heroin or cocaine subject to a mandatory minimum sentence of 10 years. Later that year, the voters amended the state constitution to authorize judges to deny bail in cases of drug offenses carrying a sentence of 10 or more years.[16] Taken together these changes meant that even quite minor drug offenses could result in detention prior to trial and an extremely long sentence if convicted. In the midst of the national hysteria over drugs, that is precisely what happened.

In Rhode Island, as in five other states and the District of Columbia, jails are operated by the state rather than by counties or municipalities, and it was here that the impact of these changes fell most heavily. In January 1990, there were close to 800 inmates in the state's jail. Of this number, some 500 were pre-trial detainees, nearly two-thirds of whom were being held without bail. About 230 of the 800 were housed in a building formerly used to house patients at the state's psychiatric hospital, and 550 were housed in the Intake Service Center (ISC) which had opened in 1982 with a design capacity of 168.[17] Jail overcrowding, which had not been an issue in the original case, had become its focal point.

A Delayed and Inadequate Response

Although the full dimensions of the overcrowding problem did not become evident until 1988, the relentless growth in the number of prisoners beginning in 1980, as related in previous chapters, continually eroded the state's efforts to comply with court orders. Early in 1984, Governor Garrahy appointed a panel to examine the issue and to recommend steps that should be taken throughout the criminal justice system to address it. The panel presented its report to the governor on May 1, recommending that, *inter alia,* the state should build a new medium security prison for 160 inmates, that bail guidelines be developed for use by judges in all of the state's courts, that more resources be provided to probation and parole, and that the state expand existing alternatives to incarceration such as restitution and develop new alternatives such as halfway houses, home confinement and weekend incarceration. Additionally, the panel listed some 89 other options that it had not had the time to examine in detail and recommended that the governor appoint a permanent committee composed of the top administrators of each component of the criminal justice system to study other possible options and effect better coordination among the various components of the system.[18]

A $10 million bond issue for the construction of the recommended prison was placed on the November 1984 ballot. However, despite the revitalized economy, the voters, having just approved $5 million for renovations to Maximum Security at a special referendum the previous November, solidly defeated the proposal. Forced back to the drawing board, Moran and his staff working closely with the chief aides to newly-elected Republican Governor Edward DiPrete came up with an alternative method of financing the construction. A Public Buildings Authority (PBA) had been created by the legislature in 1958 and empowered to issue revenue bonds for the construction of public buildings. Unlike general obligation bonds, these bonds require neither voter nor legislative approval and the PBA, moreover, is exempted from state laws requiring competitive bidding. The Authority, in effect, functions much as a private enterprise, raising capital through its bonds, hiring a construction manager to coordinate and monitor construction and then leasing the buildings to state agencies and paying off the bonds with rents paid out of the agency operating budgets. Intended only for emergency situations, the PBA had been seldom used in its 25 years. Governor DiPrete asserted, in announcing his plan, that the voters' rejection of the bond issue in the face of court orders to reduce prison overcrowding created precisely the sort of emergency situation for which the PBA was created.[19]

Despite promises that with the streamlined process the prison could be built in two years, it was not until November 1990 that the first sections of it opened and the entire prison was not operational until 1992. Unexpected problems at the original site raised cost estimates and led the PBA to spend about a year looking for an alternative. In the meantime, the ACI's skyrocketing population forced continual increases in the design capacity, and as the projected costs escalated, the governor's chief aides determined to investigate whether abandoned buildings at another state facility, a residential facility for retarded people no longer needed due to deinstitutionalization, could be suitably renovated at less cost.[20] Then, after it was determined that these buildings could not be renovated to provide sufficient security and the decision was made to build near to the original site, the PBA ran into local opposition to the construction.

A clause in the legislation creating the PBA requires local approval of the construction. The Cranston City Council gave its approval in 1985 in exchange for $300,000 annually to reimburse the city for services to the ACI, a long-standing grievance, and the transfer to the city of the old prison and its grounds once the new facility opened. By mid-1988, however, as construction was about to begin, the state—under court order to reduce overcrowding at the ACI, threatened with serious financial penalties if it did not, and seeing no end in sight to the growth in the population—informed the city that it must retain the old prison in addition to building the new one and adding an 800-bed expansion to ISC. The City Council angrily rescinded the 1985 agreement and threatened to file suit to block the construction should the state seek to proceed without their approval. There followed another year of difficult negotiations before an agreement acceptable to all could be developed and construction begun.[21]

Calling the occasion a "sad, sad day," Director Moran, speaking at the groundbreaking ceremony for the new prison in August 1989, warned the assembled dignitaries, politicians and officials that "we cannot build our way out of this" and called upon them to allocate more resources to preventive programs.[22] One of those in the crowd, Elena Natalizia, found herself pleasantly surprised at Moran's remarks and, perhaps for the first time, in agreement with him. Natalizia had come to work at the ACI in 1984 as part of the Catholic Chaplaincy Team. Where others, perhaps exhausted from a six-year struggle and basking in the glow of an assumed constitutionality, saw only improvement, Natalizia could scarcely contain her frustration with the lack of programs and opportunities for inmates and the absence of alternatives to incarceration. In 1985, she founded R.I. Justice Alliance to educate the public and policy-makers about prison conditions and ways to alleviate overcrowding without building more prisons. Over the next four years she and the director, who viewed the new organization as a reincarnation of the NPRA, had sparred in private meetings, public forums and the press.[23]

To critics such as Natalizia, both within and outside his administration, Moran was an old school prison warden who had little understanding of the differences between jails and prisons, let alone an appreciation of the need to develop a balanced continuum of sanctions. Moreover, resources which might have been devoted to developing alternatives were consumed by what some saw as an obsession with security. Warden Roberta Richman, then director of education, for one, thought Moran's concerns to prevent disorder and escapes led him to approve the creation of too many posts for correctional officers and to fill each one, giving great control but driving up overtime and leaving insufficient resources for programs and the development of alternative sanctions.[24]

Moran and his supporters, however, contended that faced with a rapidly expanding population, there was no choice but to maintain security and fund the essential activities and services such as medical care. Just meeting those immediate institutional requirements, Moran argued, necessitated budget increases of nearly 20 percent per year for several years running at a time when other state agencies were getting annual increases of five percent or less. He could not get more than 20 percent no matter how hard he lobbied. Moreover, as he saw it, neither the public, nor its elected representatives in the legislature, nor the state's judges were of a mind to accept non-incarcerative alternatives voluntarily. The roots of the problem lay in the other branches of state government over which neither the department nor the governor exercised any control, and which, though not entirely unmindful of the problem, were unwilling to assume any substantial responsibility for its management or resolution.[25]

Both Moran and his critics can point to evidence to support their views. The voters, as we have seen, approved an amendment to the state's constitution giving judges the discretion to deny bail to suspects in drug cases where the sentence upon conviction was 10 years or more. The General Assembly enacted legislation increasing penalties for drug offenses to such a degree that this discretion could be exercised in cases involving possession of even relatively small amounts of drugs, and judges chose to exercise that discretion. Even as the dimensions of the overcrowding crisis were abundantly evident, the editors of the *Providence Journal-Bulletin* argued against embracing alternative sanctions cautioning legislators and officials that while "necessity may be the mother of invention , . . . desperation can give birth to wishful thinking."[26] And the legislature heeded their caution. Home confinement, for example, first used in Rhode Island in 1985 when a judge imposed it as a condition of probation, was not given a statutory basis until 1989 at which time the legislature was virtually forced into action by threats from the federal court.[27] At the same time a series of journalistic exposés of murderers placed on work release or paroled to the community without notification to the police as required by law prompted legislative hearings resulting in laws toughening eligibility standards and reducing the discretion of both the department and the parole board by granting the attorney general and local police a greater role in both processes.[28]

Early in the 1970s there had been three federally-funded halfway houses for ex-felons in Rhode Island. When federal funding ended, however, the department did not pressure the legislature to pick up the funding and the houses closed. Viewing Rhode Island essentially as a city-state, Moran chose instead to expand the capacity of the work release unit located on the prison's grounds and to use it in many respects as a halfway house. In the short run this saved funds and avoided potential conflict with local communities. However, it also contributed marginally to the growing population as work release inmates eligible for parole often had to choose whether to return to their hometown or to retain their current job, and the parole board was reluctant to parole those who chose the former.[29] More importantly, however, it left the department vulnerable to community opposition at a critical point. Caught between pressure from overcrowding and pressure from the court to relieve it, the department frantically and unsuccessfully sought in 1989 to establish a halfway house in a corner of the state far from the prison complex. With no record of safely operating such facilities and no time to build the necessary relations with community leaders, the department was in no position to counter opposition aroused by stories about "killers on work release."[30]

Governor DiPrete never appointed the criminal justice coordinating committee recommended by the 1984 Task Force on Overcrowding, and thus the responses of different components of the system remained uncoordinated. Even as judges were exercising discretion to deny bail to drug offenders and cooperating with the attorney general to deny bail to suspected probation violators, the courts were attempting to make pre-trial release more possible for others. In 1987, a Bail Information Unit was established by the courts with the aim of making available to judges more information about defendants' community ties and finances at the time of initial appearance in court. The unit also supervised those released pending their trial and referred them to shelter and needed services in the community.[31] In June 1988 its efforts were complemented by a Jail-Based Notification Unit established within the Department of Corrections to assist bailable detainees to find the money or property to guarantee their release.[32] The efforts of these agencies, although not insubstantial, were not nearly sufficient to stem the tide then flowing into and swamping the jail, however.

So uncoordinated were the responses of different agencies, the existence of the probation violation unit in the attorney-general's office was not even known to the Department of Corrections until it had been in operation for a year.[33] The development of this unit was prompted in part by the failure of the adult probation unit to provide the courts with timely information to identify potential probation violators. Although much of its work is in the courts, Rhode Island's adult probation unit is structurally a part of the Field Services Division within the Department of Corrections. As is a danger with such hybrid organizations, it had come to be a poor stepchild. Between 1985 and 1990, the number of people on probation in Rhode Island had increased at a rate faster than the number of inmates but the proportion of the department's budget going to field services had declined slightly, from 6.8 to 5.8 percent. The number of supervisors did not keep pace with the increase in probationers and the average caseload, already twice the national average in 1985, shot up from 236 to 282 in 1990, when it was the highest in the nation.[34] Furthermore, probation officers received little or no training and had no access to computers. At a time when other states, even those nearby such as Connecticut and Massachusetts, were employing formal risk assessments to determine the level of supervision necessary, no such instruments were available in Rhode Island. Until 1989 when a minimum supervision unit was established to track those cases thought to no longer require active supervision, probation officers made this decision informally and "banked" such cases on their own.[35]

The consultants retained by the department concluded that there is "little understanding that a well-managed probation/parole program with adequate resources can assist in managing the inmate population."[36] In their view many fewer inmates would be sent to prison if judges were presented with detailed presentence reports which included referrals to appropriate agencies in the community for assistance and if they had confidence that those placed on probation would receive adequate supervision. With an untrained staff, antiquated information system and overwhelming caseloads, however, Rhode Island's probation department had long since ceased preparing presentence reports and was incapable of inspiring such confidence.

The Impact on Facilities, Programs and Services

The ACI in 1985 was a much better institution than it had ever been. In August of that year a British Broadcasting Corporation television production on the debate surrounding privatization of prisons featured Old Max as an example of what government could do by way of improving prison conditions.[37] That same month, security consultant J.J. Clark who had visited the institutions just after the original order in *Palmigiano* returned to conduct a post analysis. So struck was he by the transformation that he wrote "At the time of my visit . . . in 1978, I had never witnessed a more totally bankrupt management system in my long correctional experience. . . . The basic operations and conditions found during this visit match or exceed any state system this consultant has visited . . . and could serve as a model for other state and local corrections operations."[38]

There remained nonetheless serious deficiencies. These had drawn the attention of Elena Natalizia, leading her to form Justice Alliance, and were the subject of some concern in Special Master Keating's report to the court in July 1985. While expressing amazement at the physical transformation of Maximum Security and hope that the department was on the verge of developing an industries program that would provide meaningful jobs for all inmates, Keating nonetheless found pervasive idleness and a medical system, that was, in his opinion, in only tenuous compliance with the court's orders.[39]

Over the next four years, despite significant increases in resources, the situation became dire. Although the facilities remained in far better condition than they had been twelve years before, population pressures threatened to undermine the improvement in environmental and sanitary conditions. For example, the central kitchen, in which most meals were prepared before being shipped to kitchens in each unit, had been designed to prepare about 800 meals a day but was now preparing about 6600. A health inspection in March 1989 had listed 41 code violations, half of which had been previously reported but not corrected by the overburdened maintenance staff. The same inspection cited 45 violations in the kitchen in Maximum and noted that the food storage

rooms in that unit were in such poor condition as to "defeat all
reasonable efforts at maintaining sanitary and vermin-free conditions."[40]

The cooperative program with Brown Medical School and its
teaching hospitals, which had been under negotiation in 1985 and in
which Keating placed great hope, never materialized. In 1989, the
management consultant team retained by the department concluded that
"the current level of front line medical service and clinical supervision
is such that the State of Rhode Island would be extremely vulnerable
to lawsuit."[41] At the time of their study, two key administrative
positions—that of medical director and that of health program
administrator—had at that time been vacant for several months due to
the department's inability to recruit qualified candidates at the salary
levels offered. Physician coverage was available only four days per
week, far less than the estimated 120 hours or so needed for some 2000
inmates, and the nursing staff was not of sufficient size to enable
24-hour on-site coverage for each facility. To provide the necessary
coverage, nurses routinely worked 2-3 consecutive shifts and extensive
use was made of temporary help which seriously disrupted continuity
of care. The consultants found it difficult to assess service utilization
as the maintenance of records had deteriorated under the crush of
numbers. It was clear, however, that physical examinations of incoming
prisoners were not being completed in a timely fashion, orders and
progress notes were being entered in incorrect form in patient files,
policies defining appropriate operational standards were routinely
violated due to insufficient staffing, and the medical services unit had
no tracking system for the routine follow-up of inmates with such
chronic diseases as diabetes, heart disease and tuberculosis.[42]

Justice Alliance was at this time receiving numerous complaints
from families of inmates about delays in treatment or, in some cases,
lack of treatment for apparently serious conditions. The deaths of two
inmates in 1989 under circumstances suggesting possible negligence or
incompetence prompted Natalizia to hold several press conferences to
highlight allegedly poor treatment and demand an investigation and
public accounting. Moran and his deputy in charge of rehabilitative
services, Jeffrey Laurie, steadfastly denied the allegations, asserting
such complaints were thoroughly investigated but could not be made

public. Two years later, at a forum to review medical policies and procedures that had ordered by the legislature, the Justice Alliance representative could find no evidence of conscious neglect or incompetence.[43] By then, however, action by the court had reduced overcrowding and the department had secured the resources to remedy many of the deficiencies noted by the consultants in 1989. Nonetheless, there was still cause for concern about the level of care provided.

Although not in the same perilous state, mental health services and substance abuse treatment were also sorely taxed. Four psychologists and a contracted psychiatrist were attempting to offer a comprehensive program involving needs assessment, crisis intervention, some long-term therapy for violent offenders and sex offenders, and a suicide prevention program. But their efforts were outstripped by the rapidly increasing population, and particularly by a dramatic increase in the number of suicidal inmates.[44] Despite the war on drugs, the small drug treatment program established begrudgingly by the department had been allowed to languish for several years. By 1989, consultants estimated that over 80 percent of the inmate population had histories of substance abuse. Prodded by Natalizia who had been actively searching for funding sources, the department that year secured a grant from the National Institute of Corrections to contract with a local drug treatment agency, Marathon House, to provide education and counselling in the prisons and post-release services to parolees. While crediting the program as a good beginning, the consultants saw the level of service as far less than what was needed and expressed concern that even that might be terminated because the space in which the program was located had been converted to housing to accommodate the accelerated population growth in 1988-89.[45]

Keating's hope, expressed in his July 1985 report, that the department would soon be able to provide meaningful jobs for all inmates was based in part on a plan to construct new space for prison industries. Most of this space was to be in the new medium security unit, the rest in a new industries building to be constructed outside the walls of Maximum. By mid-1989 ground had yet to be broken for the new prison and construction of the industries building in Maximum, though underway, was not yet completed. While according to department records, only some 20 percent of the sentenced population was idle, and then mostly because they were ill or in segregation;[46] idleness was, in fact, far more pervasive.

The management consultants observed that the missions of correctional industries to provide on the job training in various trades and to generate sufficient income to be self-sustaining had, in the face of the population increase, been compromised by pressure to provide employment of as many inmates as possible. In an effort to reduce idleness, shops in Maximum, where most of the inmates employed in industries worked, ran two half shifts each day although inmates were paid for a full day's work. Moreover, they found that 39 percent of the population were employed in institutional support activities, far higher than the 22-25 percent that their experience had shown to be necessary, with the result that much of what inmates were doing was make-work requiring at best an hour or two per day.[47]

By 1989 the classification system had virtually fallen apart under the crush of numbers. Background information to make risk assessments continued to be collected and evaluated, but testing, needs assessment and tracking had gone by the way, seriously affecting programming. Moreover, overcrowding made space scarce as areas originally designed for program usage, like that for drug treatment, were converted into housing areas. In Maximum Security, the gym was converted into a dorm and basketball games were played in the chapel. And in ISC where the crowding was most severe, administrative offices were vacated and converted into dorms as were all program areas including the chapel, law library and classrooms. Thus, by 1989, it had become extremely difficult to determine what programming an inmate might need and virtually impossible to even find the physical space in which to offer it. Not surprisingly less than six percent of the population were involved in academic work of any kind, and only some 2.5 percent received any vocational preparation. Moreover, even those enrolled full time in these programs had many hours of unoccupied time as full-time participation entailed only 22.5 hours of instruction per week and there were no classes in the summer.[48]

The Impact on Administration

In recognition of the need for more adequate management information and long-term planning, Moran created a Division of Policy and Development in June 1985. For its first two years of operation, the new division was headed by Anthony Ventetuolo who doubled as Moran's executive assistant, but in 1987 the director was able to recruit A.T. Wall, a graduate of Yale Law School who had worked in the Vera Institute's Community Sentencing Project and had been most recently working as an aide to Governor DiPrete. During this time of massive population buildup, Wall was one of the few new faces to appear in the ranks of the ACI's middle management. Several of the old guard such as Sharkey retired and others, most notably Assistant Director Matt Gill, resigned from their positions, but all were replaced by promotions from below.

Between 1985 and 1989, increases in the total number of staff nearly kept pace with the increase in inmates, 51 percent v. 58 percent. These new positions, however, were mostly correctional officers and front-line medical staff such as nurses. During the same time period, the number of people in managerial positions increased by only 3 percent.[49] In just one year, from 1987 to 1988, as a result of court orders, the medical staff increased by 30, but at the same time, as already noted, there was neither a health program administrator nor a medical services director. Health services were thus directly supervised by the deputy assistant director for rehabilitative services, giving that office too great a span of control. Similarly, the chief of security—who at the time was responsible for the condition of all perimeter security devices, not to mention all locks and keys, security clocks and communication devices as well as all weapons, riot gear and restraints for seven different facilities—was working alone. Needless to say, he felt greatly overextended and stressed.[50]

In A.T. Wall's view, the overcrowding crisis might have averted, or at least abated, if the department had the capability to foresee the growth in population and develop creative alternatives. When he arrived in 1987 to head policy and planning, however, he found he was a "general without troops." Not only did he have no staff, but the only central repository of information on inmates was a file of 3x5 index cards maintained by a clerk in the classification unit.[51] Each separate unit within the department maintained its own file on each inmate, but there were no written policies defining what information was to be collected, how it was to be recorded or with whom it was to be exchanged. As a result, recordkeeping procedures were based on "'oral tradition' passed from one employee to another," as one section head informed the management consultants, and there was little, if any, exchange of information among the different units.[52]

The department was able to purchase some 60 computers in 1988 but funds to network them and begin the laborious job of data entry were not available until the following year. For some five years, then, the department, faced with explosive growth, was unable to ease the administrative burden or develop more effective population management strategies by use of sophisticated technological tools. Further, the lack of an adequate management information system quite probably contributed to the crush of numbers in the institutions. Without detailed information on the offender and programs in which she or he will be involved, judges were understandably reluctant to place offenders on probation. But the department probation officers, overwhelmed by caseloads twice the national average and with their files maintained on some 300,000 index cards, were forced to stop preparing presentence reports except in exceptional cases.[53]

Constant demands for information from the court, the legislature, the press and various interest groups meant that an already overextended management was being continually diverted from its routine but essential management activities to respond to some issue or crisis to the detriment of program development, communication and coordination, implementation and monitoring. The consultants noted, for example, that "unforeseen problems were occurring on almost every day during the period when this study was being conducted, and ACI managers acknowledged that responding to a crisis was the usual phenomenon, leaving little time to attend to routine, procedural management activities."[54]

The overall mission, goals and strategies to realize them had been set forth in an Administrative Policy Statement promulgated in 1981.

In the management consultants' view, this statement was "one of the most complete documents of its kind for any correctional agency in the country."[55] It was, moreover, only one of some 123 such policy statements contained in a manual with 25 separate sections, and there was a separate manual for policies and procedures dealing with medical services. But the department was "better, on the whole, at developing policy than at implementing and monitoring it."[56] New policies and procedures and revisions of old ones were continually developed but were not finding their way into the manuals maintained by middle managers nor becoming part of staff training programs. Oral directives and *ad hoc* memos addressed to immediate problems and often developed without regard to either policy statements or their impact on other activities, were more important in day-to-day operations than were formal policy and procedure.

Despite the tremendous growth in the size and complexity of the department over the previous decade, both vertical and horizontal communication remained largely informal. Policy prescribed twice-monthly staff meetings between managers and subordinates at all levels and that progress reports from each major unit be submitted quarterly. Formal staff meetings were rarely held, however, and quarterly progress reports seldom submitted. Managers did meet frequently with subordinates and other managers, but these meetings were most often addressed to a specific problem, usually a crisis of some sort, and included only the staff needed to solve it. Managers, moreover, tended to rely heavily on personal relations to accomplish tasks, bypassing the chain of command. This practice fueled personal resentments and undermined coordination and accountability. Misinformation and rumors were rampant, and with ill-informed mid-level administrators, various units charted their own courses independent of others or the department as a whole. The consultants, not unlike those of a decade before, concluded that the department, "to a fair degree . . . consists of separate aggregate components rather unified ones" and warned that "the consequences of continuing the current course of unregulated input and marginal increases in resources [is] risking a total collapse of the department under the weight of demands to do more with less."[57]

The Impact on Labor-Management Relations

Relations between labor and management, always tense, became strained nearly to the breaking point in the period from 1988 through 1990. Although he had completed a graduate degree in corrections, Don Ventetuolo, like his predecessor as assistant director, had no line experience in corrections prior to his appointment, having served as director of education. Correctional officers referred to him as "the principal" rather than "Director" or "Boss" just as they had with Gill. And, also like Gill, Ventetuolo was instructed by Moran to ride the correctional officers hard and began to micro-manage the division, becoming personally involved in such matters as uncovering tardiness, violations of uniform regulations and the abuse of sick leave and taking a hard line with respect to sanctions. Resentment built as many officers came to feel treated more harshly than inmates who violated rules. The number of grievances skyrocketed with over 100 pending action at any given time. It took months for most to come to a resolution and even then a large number went to arbitration outside the department.[58] The department lost the vast majority of those grievances going to arbitration, and in July 1988 the union overwhelmingly cast a vote of no confidence in Ventetuolo, calling upon the governor to appoint an independent labor mediator to avoid what they regarded as needless arbitration that was costly to all parties.[59]

One of the major points of tension concerned the number of lieutenants and captains, who are members of the union, and the amount of overtime they worked. In the opinions of Moran and Ventetuolo, many of the officers eligible for promotion at any given time were simply not qualified for the job. With the rapid expansion of the population, those scoring high on the civil service examination were quickly promoted. But as the exams were given infrequently, there were long periods of time in which those eligible for promotion were those who had barely passed the test. Adding to the dilemma was the fact the seniority system meant there was little staff development, and the department had been unable to get the union to agree to in-service training or specialized training for those to be promoted without additional overtime pay for the training time. Soon after his appointment, Ventetuolo, acting in concert with Donald Ellerthorpe, who was then in overall charge of both the HSC and Maximum, tried to circumvent the promotion process by giving temporary promotions, what they termed "battlefield promotions," to younger officers whom they saw as qualified. Clearly in violation of both the collective bargaining agreement and civil service regulations, this practice was short lived, and its abandonment left the administrators continually having to choose between promoting officers they regarded as unqualified or overextending the capacities of qualified supervisors. In either case, front-line supervision and morale suffered.[60]

Although exacerbated by Ventetuolo's personal style, conflict between management and labor would have intensified, no matter who else might have been in his position, due to the pressure of increased numbers along with the constraints imposed by the collective bargaining agreement. As hospital buildings were turned into prisons and space was converted from administrative and program usage to housing units, the number of posts for correctional officers proliferated, outstripping the department's ability to recruit and train new officers. Contractual provisions required that all posts be filled, by overtime if necessary, and as a result, overtime soared, crippling other activities such as programs and preventive maintenance.[61] Attempts to eliminate posts or even to limit the number of new posts created in an attempt to limit overtime met with resistance not only from anxious officers but also from facility managers who, not being responsible for a budget, had security and control as their sole concern. Then, when the overcrowding became so critical in 1988 and 1989, that officers who did not wish to work overtime were ordered to stay on the job, resistance to cutting overtime was converted, in an ironic twist, to anger at having to work overtime, further aggravating labor-management tension; on one occasion, some 250 officers demonstrated at the state capitol to protest working conditions and compulsory overtime.[62]

The Impact on Brutality and Disorder

Faced with the need to hire large numbers of correctional officers each year, the department was forced to be less selective than it had been earlier in the 80s. According to Warden Walt Whitman, some of those hired had only third- and fourth-grade educations and terrible work histories. Some even had minor criminal records, and it became a not uncommon occurrence for an officer to be absent from work because he was in a local lockup following a domestic disturbance or barroom brawl. In one incident, two probationary officers were fired after being charged with kidnapping a woman from a Providence nightspot; in another a probationary officer was discharged after being charged with offering an inmate $150 to assault another officer with a mop wringer.[63]

Moran's tough stance on brutality had seemingly reduced its incidence after 1978, yet isolated occurrences continued to come to light, although some of these seemed to proceed more from recklessness or negligence than specific intent. In one tragic incident in 1984, for example, an inmate was accidentally killed by an officer who was reenacting the game of "Russian Roulette" depicted in the movie *The Deer Hunter*.[64] As the population increased, however, so did allegations of more intentional brutality. In response Moran doubled the size of the investigative unit, and in the process replaced former correctional officers with retired police officers and federal agents. As a result, the proportion of allegations resulting in disciplinary action increased, and two notable cases ended in criminal convictions of officers.

In one of these incidents, an inmate mistakenly believed to be a child molester was beaten by several officers shortly after his arrival at ISC on November 17, 1989. Although the inmate was taken to a local hospital for treatment, no entry was made in the log concerning either the use of force or the run to the hospital and the incident did not come to light until three weeks later when the inmate's girlfriend called the press. During the internal investigation, the shift supervisors claimed ignorance but examination of the rolls and post assignments narrowed the focus to seven officers, two of whom then cooperated and gave evidence against three others. These three ultimately pleaded guilty in federal court to violating the inmate's civil rights and received jail sentences. The two cooperating officers also had to be placed on leave, however, due to threats and harassment from other officers.

Cartoons depicting them as rats were placed on bulletin boards; signs were put on their lockers proclaiming that "stool pigeons will die"; they were shunned on the job and were bombarded with anonymous verbal threats over the telephone at their posts. Despite repeated attempts over nearly a year, including a transfer to another unit, they were never able to return to their jobs. In the end the two accepted positions in other state agencies and sued the Brotherhood and several superior officers for damages. In the midst of the trial, the union agreed to a settlement, the terms of which were undisclosed.[65]

Two months after the officers in the above incident pleaded guilty in federal court, three others were held responsible for damages inflicted on an inmate in April 1988. When the inmate had refused to leave the shower when ordered, the officers had forcibly placed him in restraints and carried him out, inflicting serious injuries in the process. In ordering them to pay damages of $6500, Judge Ronald N. Lagueux, not one noted for his support of inmate rights, characterized their behavior as "brutal lawlessness."[66]

Reflecting both the lower quality of officers and the increased numbers of drug users in the prison, allegations against officers for transporting drugs into the prison increased along with the complaints of brutality. Some of these allegations proved false, and others, while cause to justify the arrest and firing of an officer, were not in of themselves serious, mainly involving small amounts of marijuana.[67] A few incidents, however, suggested widespread usage of hard drugs and an organized system of distribution and sales. In the case which received the most public attention, a guard was arrested entering Maximum Security and found to have in his possession 10 needles and syringes, an unspecified amount of cocaine and 85 "hits" of LSD. Although the guard pleaded no contest, testimony at the trial of the outside supplier revealed that the network had been operating for four years before it was discovered.[68]

As elsewhere in the United States, the war on drugs changed the composition of the prison population in Rhode Island. African Americans, who comprised just 20 percent of the population in 1980, occupied nearly one-third of the beds by the end of the decade, and Hispanics, who had been scarcely represented in the population in

1980, accounted for nearly 15 percent in 1990.[69] Although there were at this time no large gangs such as those in Texas, California and Illinois, inmates in Rhode Island as in most prisons tended to organize themselves into cliques sharply drawn along the lines of race and ethnicity; as the demographic profile of the population changed, periodic conflict broke out among these cliques over issues such as market shares in the drug trade, gambling debts and personal slights. One such period was in August and September of 1985 when five inmates were seriously stabbed, two were assaulted with pipes and officers were continually confronted with threatening groups of inmates as they attempted to break up fights or remove intoxicated inmates to the hospital or segregation. Virtually all of this activity was in Maximum Security, and to some it seemed a return to the chaos of the early '70s. However, prompt action in the form of an extended lockup and the transfer of nearly 20 inmates to other institutions had restored order by the end of October. Another similar flare-up during the summer of 1988 was quickly chilled by the same reaction.[70]

Other incidents were directly tied to overcrowding. In September 1988, a deputy warden was severely assaulted in the Maximum Security gym by an inmate body-builder infuriated by rumors that the gym was to be converted into a dormitory for 100 inmates. The melee spread to the yard where over 200 prisoners taking outside recreation refused to return to their cells until administrators promised to investigate ways to relax the restricted schedule which kept those without jobs in their cells nearly 18 hours per day.[71] A year later inmates at ISC and in Medium Security, supported by a vigil maintained by Justice Alliance, engaged in a week-long hunger strike to protest conditions in these two most overcrowded facilities. It was in response to this protest that Governor DiPrete ordered all administrative offices in the units to be converted into dormitories.[72]

Population pressures, administrative confusion, tension between management and labor, occasional brutality, drug smuggling and scattered warfare among cliques of inmates constituted continuing threats to the stability of the ACI in the period from 1985 through 1990. Despite these problems, however, the institutions, on the whole, remained orderly and secure. In a population three times larger than that in the mid-1970s, there was, for instance, only one homicide during these six years compared with seven in the five years prior to the court intervention brought about by *Palmigiano*.[73] Public fears were aroused in 1986 when, in separate incidents, two prisoners, one of whom was a five-time escapee who had killed a prominent physician in a 1970 escape, managed the first escapes from HSC. But both escapees were quickly re-captured without incident, and improvements to physical security prevented any recurrence.[74] Consultants in both 1985 and 1989 praised the staff's record in maintaining security and order under conditions that made inmate management extremely difficult.[75]

MONITORING AND INTERVENTION BY THE COURT

Overcrowding, as noted previously, was not an issue in the original litigation but became so as population growth impeded implementation and forced numerous modifications to the initial order, the renovation and continued use of the old maximum security building being the most prominent. The court's concern intensified as the numbers continued to grow, and the overall stability and security of the institutions in the face of the crushing numbers were in no small measure due to its continued monitoring and active intervention.

Monitoring, 1985-88

In his July 1985 report, Special Master Keating lauded the department's accomplishments and found it to be in substantial compliance with most of the provisions of the 1977 order. In his next breath, however, he had also expressed concern that the "rising population surge might undermine the considerable improvements accomplished by the defendants over the past eight years,"[76] set forth a list of tasks still to be accomplished, and recommended continued monitoring of efforts at compliance.

The defendants responded to Keating's report by seeking a modification of the order with respect to the two most overcrowded facilities, Medium Security and ISC. Given the improvements in conditions, they argued that they could operate constitutionally acceptable facilities with numbers in excess of the design capacities and that they should be allowed to do so in light of two decisions—*Bell v. Wolfish* and *Rhodes v. Chapman*—in which the U.S. Supreme Court had found that "double-bunking" inmates in cells built for one was not *per se* unconstitutional. In essence, they were arguing that the court no longer refer to its 1977 order but rather "independently determine whether conditions as they now exist meet constitutional standards."[77]

At a hearing in December 1985 Judge Pettine found that on a typical day some 260 prisoners were housed in Medium, about 40 more than had been determined to be the maximum number consistent with the APHA standards used in the 1977 order. Moreover, 40 percent of them were unemployed, and nearly half of those employed worked as porters, jobs that typically required less than an hour's work a day. Overcrowding in ISC was even worse. Shortly after the opening of the facility, the department had begun double-celling inmates; in July 1985, when the population rose to about 350, they had commenced triple-celling. Judge Pettine ordered an immediate end to this practice, but still conditions remained deplorable. Inmates were kept locked in their cells 19-20 hours per day, took meals there and were released for recreation into a room so small that it could accommodate only 10 to 12 at a time. Less than a third of the inmates held jobs and most of those were porters. In 20 months some 108 serious violations of health codes had been reported, and both the kitchen and medical resources were so severely overtaxed as to pose imminent dangers to the health of both inmates and staff.[78]

In his opinion, Judge Pettine held that both *Wolfish* and *Rhodes* had to be interpreted in terms of the particular facts of each case, and in neither case was there any evidence of adverse impact of overcrowding on the health or safety of inmates. The situation at the ACI was dramatically different; thus he rejected the defendants' motion, ordered them immediately to correct the medical, environmental health and safety deficiencies which had been identified and to develop plans to prevent their recurrence. He further ordered them to provide meaningful program opportunities for every inmate within 120 days. And finally, he imposed an immediate population cap of 268 in Medium Security and 250 in ISC. The population in Medium Security was to be reduced to 222 within a year and a schedule of progressively lower caps was set by which the population of ISC would be reduced to 168 by October 1, 1988.[79]

In anticipation of the order, which was five months in the making, Moran was able to secure a supplemental appropriation of $1.7 million dollars to hire additional staff and correct many of the deficiencies noted. Thus, in an October report to the court, Keating observed much progress had been made, especially with respect to medical care. Moreover, although there had been no success in reducing the numbers of prisoners, the populations of the two facilities had been kept under the caps. Despite the overcrowding and a continuing high level of idleness, he observed that Medium Security "appears to be a better run, more peaceful facility than at any time in the past ten years"[80] Tensions were higher at ISC, but he noted that efforts were underway to ease crowding there through projects to provide judges setting bail with more information on the community ties and prior records of defendants and to expedite the trials of pre-trial detainees.

There were, however, serious problems. Despite having been supplied by the plaintiffs with sample plans used in other systems, the department still had not been able to produce acceptable plans for correcting deficiencies and preventing their recurrence. Calling attention to the delays in the construction of the new medium security, Keating observed that "once again the fatuity of the defendant's construction projections have reduced the deadlines imposed by the court to a shambles" and suggested that while "the completion of the [new unit] recedes into the mists of the future . . . the defendants seem content to sit back and complacently await its completion to provide the relief they need."[81]

Over the next year, the population at Medium remained beneath the cap of 268 although it never approached the goal of 222. Medium, nonetheless, remained peaceful and attention came to focus on ISC where, as discussed above, the new initiatives failed to stem the tide of inmates. In May 1987 the department, finding itself in the words of Assistant Director A.T. Wall with "simply no place to stack the bodies,"[82] for a brief time refused admissions from local and state police while they agonized over whether to exceed the caps. With ISC

being the state's only jail, this tactic, used in many other states, was
scarcely a solution even in the short term, however, and would pose
even greater political difficulties for the governor than would
overcrowding. Nor was there any direct assistance to be had from the
other branches of government to whom the Republican governor, given
the separation of powers and partisan politics, was only a supplicant.
Meetings with the heads of other agencies did provide an
alternative, however. The corrections complex is on the same site with
the state's psychiatric hospitals, and the Department of Mental Health
had over the past 15 years operated one of the more successful
deinstitutionalization programs in the country, reducing the hospital
population from over 1500 to less than 400. Many of the buildings
were now vacant. After surveying them Director Moran was able to get
one transferred to Corrections and announced plans to renovate it to
house the lowest-risk prisoners awaiting trial. Moran hoped to complete
the renovations and be able to move some 30 detainees by July 1.[83]

Armed with this plan the state, in May 1987, requested the court
allow them to retain the population limit of 250 rather than the lower
caps to which the June 1986 order required. In an uncharacteristically
terse order, Judge Pettine permitted the cap of 250 to be continued until
August 1. To put teeth in the order, he imposed a $3000 fine for each
day the state might violate the 250 limit after that date.[84]

From the time of the original order in 1977, the *Providence
Journal-Bulletin* had been unwavering in its support of the court. Judge
Pettine believed this support had been essential to the success of the
intervention both by its effect on public opinion and by undermining
potential political opposition. Now, however, the newspaper broke with
this past pattern, and in very strong language attacked his order.
Asserting that judicial supervision "has long ceased to be necessary,"
and that "the people of Rhode Island . . . [are not] wards of the U.S.
District Court," the editors asked "Who's governor, Governor?"[85]

Fearing an appeal by the state during which time the situation
might worsen, Judge Pettine convened a chambers conference to
consider alternatives to population caps. Once again, the judge listened
to the defendant's argument that, despite the crowding, conditions in
the prisons passed constitutional muster and that actual conditions, not

numbers or technical compliance with arbitrary standards, should be the concern of the court. He also heard from the plaintiffs, however, that while conditions were much improved over 1985, there were still some serious deficiencies in medical services at ISC. On July 28 the judge entered an order lifting the population caps and substituting a complicated system of monitoring by a three-member team of neutral experts providing, first of all, that the state correct any medical deficiencies uncovered by a neutral expert who was to conduct an immediate review.[86]

Events over the next several months seemed to suggest that, although the population continued its explosive growth, the now ten-year-old case might draw to a conclusion. Medical deficiencies identified by the neutral expert were corrected by December. Construction of the new medium security prison was at long last begun that same month, and with the "fast track" construction methods employed by the PBA, the court was assured it would be completed by November 1989. Meanwhile, renovations to the former hospital building proceeded apace, and early in January the department was able to transfer nearly 100 inmates out of ISC to it, lowering the population in the main facility to 276. Early in January 1988, the panel of independent experts toured the facilities and concluded that, while there remained problems, both Medium Security and ISC met constitutional standards.

Following the receipt of these reports, Judge Pettine convened another chambers conference to explore the possibility of ending active monitoring. As he saw it, the conditions they were now dealing with were "refinements and high polish." Moreover, he was concerned about the cost to the state of continued evaluations by the special master and outside experts as well as criticism that the court was needlessly prolonging its involvement.[87] Plaintiffs' attorney Alvin Bronstein, citing some medical deficiencies still requiring remedy and the need to review the state's plan to deal with the continued increase in the pre-trial population, was uncomfortable with making a commitment but saw no reason that both problems could not be resolved by June 1. Assuming this was done, he thought the case could then be "put on the back burner," meaning that he would continue to monitor the prisons for serious deficiencies and attempt to deal with them informally before coming back into court.[88]

Active Intervention

In 1988 Rhode Island's prisoner population grew by 33.3 percent—faster than that of any other state in the country. This increase was concentrated among those being held without bail and those serving sentences of 1 year or less, stretching the capacity of ISC to its limit. Needless to say, the department was not able to meet the caps set in the court orders. Indeed in mid-May 1988, even with the added space in the renovated hospital building, the population at the Intake Center was in excess of 340. Not only was there double-bunking in all cells, but dozens of pre-trial detainees were bunked dormitory-style in multi-purpose rooms and the library. Program space was thus lost and all services and facilities were adversely affected by being forced to run at more than 250 percent of their design capacity. Bronstein, who earlier had thought the case might be put on the back-burner by June, petitioned the court to find the state in contempt for failing to maintain the population at or below the cap of 250 which all parties had previously agreed was to take effect on March 1.

At the Show Cause Hearing in July, the defendants argued that while they had made a good faith effort, the actions of other branches of government, actions beyond their control, had made it impossible for them to comply with the consent decree. Moreover, they argued that despite the numbers conditions still met constitutional standards, and as part of their good faith effort they had developed the court-ordered plan to deal with the crowding. Bronstein was quick to bring out, however, that many items in the plan—the hiring of a planner, contracting with a management consultant firm, and computerizing record-keeping—had no necessary relation to overcrowding. Others such as mandatory reviews of the cases of pre-trial detainees by the attorney general and the establishment of weekend courts at the ISC were dependent on other branches of government and were only under discussion. Still others, such as the recently instituted jail-based notification program seemed to have little impact. And, finally, most of the plan involved capital construction—three additional wings to the as-yet-to-be-built new medium security, the addition of two 96-bed wings to the ISC, renovation of another vacated building at the Institute of Mental Health to expand work-release and combining and enlarging the existing minimum and work release units. At best, these would take several years to complete during which time the population might expand at the same rate. Even worse, however, it appeared at this time that expansion might never become a reality as the City of Cranston had recently rescinded the local approval required by the Public Building Authority. In the meantime, between 25 and 40 percent of the pre-trial detainees were being held in lieu of surety bail of $5000 or less, and thus appeared to be good candidates for a diversion or pre-trial release program such as were available in many jurisdictions but not in Rhode Island.[89]

While not unsympathetic to the department's plight, Judge Pettine did not credit their defense. The issue was not the constitutionality of conditions but their lack of compliance with a court decree to which they had consented. Moreover, given their failure to implement any of the alternatives to incarceration recommended by the Governors' Task Force on Prison Overcrowding in 1984, the argument of factual impossibility seemed to him to be nothing more than "a blatant attempt to avoid responsibility for their own apathetic behavior. . . . "[90] Accordingly, he found Governor DiPrete and Director Moran in contempt of court and ordered them to file with the court by November 21, 1988 a detailed and specific plan that would end the dormitory-style housing of pre-trial detainees and the double-celling of any pre-trial detainee for more than thirty days and that would ensure the population at the Intake Center not exceed 250. The department was to implement said plan by February 20, 1989. By filing and implementing the plan by these dates, the governor and the director would purge themselves of contempt, but failure to meet either deadline would result in a fine of $50 per day for each detainee held in the ISC in excess of the 250 population limit. Subsequently, the date for filing the plan was extended until December 30, 1988, and in a letter to defendants, entered as an order, Judge Pettine required them to consider each of nine listed options being used in other states to reduce overcrowding: an emergency overcrowding release act, intensive probation supervision, home confinement, day fines and community service orders, halfway houses, accelerated good time, pre-trial release monitoring and services, and various prosecutorial options such as a diversionary programs. As part of their plan, the defendants were ordered to explain why they were unwilling or unable to implement each option they did not incorporate.[91]

In a conference call to discuss the state's need for additional time to prepare its plan, Judge Pettine forcefully informed the parties that "I'm not at all disposed to be flexible here. I would just as soon blow it high and wide at this point. Go on up on appeal if you want to . . . but so long as I have the authority here, we are going to move this time, make no mistake about it, and I'm not going to listen to a lot of long range plans. . . . "[92] Despite this admonition, the plan presented by the department on December 30 was essentially the same as that presented at the hearing in July.[93] There were a few new elements—the introduction of legislation to expand the director's discretion to include putting some inmates on home confinement, the possible introduction of early release legislation, additional meetings of the parole board—but these either were likely to have only marginal effects on the ISC or were dependent upon future legislation which might or might not be approved.

Home confinement and early release legislation had been two of the initiatives to which Judge Pettine had ordered the defendants to respond specifically. Another had been the development of a pre-trial release services unit. In his response to this latter option, Director Moran pointed to the Jail-Based Notification program and offered that this would be expanded into such a program but that the expansion would take two years. Intensive probation was rejected because of the high numbers already on probation and the likelihood that it would not reduce the prison population but actually widen the net of correctional supervision. Logistical problems made weekend bail hearings impossible, and the establishment of a bail fund would, the state argued, have little effect as 46 percent of the pre-trial detainees were being held without bail. Community service orders and day fines were possible under existing Rhode Island law but were at the discretion of the judiciary not the executive.[94]

The only initiative in the plan that gave hope of some immediate relief was the acquisition of another building from the state's psychiatric hospital and its renovation for use as an enlarged work release unit. To be financed with funds from the state's Asset Protection Fund, defendants estimated it would be completed by February 15, 1989 and would free space in other facilities for approximately 100 sentenced inmates currently held in the ISC. This would leave the Intake Center still above the cap, however, and the gain in bedspace seemed almost certainly to be wiped out as a result of the constitutional amendment approved in November giving the state's judges greater discretion to hold those accused of drug offenses without bail.

After reviewing the plan and the plaintiffs' response, Judge Pettine commended the department's efforts at long-term systemic planning but asserted that "at this stage of the crisis, nothing will suffice except an immediate reduction of the population at the Intake Services Center" and scheduled another conference to consider how this might be accomplished.[95] In this conference, Judge Pettine again made it known that he was not prepared to allow one man over the 250 limit at the ISC after February 20, 1989. Pointing to the fact that nearly 40 percent of those awaiting trail were being held for want of $5000 or less cash bail and that their release, together with the beds made available through enlarging the work release unit, would bring the Intake Center under the 250 cap, he tried to convince the defendants to establish a state-assisted bail program of some sort, and hinted that he might use the threatened fines for this purpose. The governor's legal counsel, who was present at the conference, objected that bail was a judicial function. To this, the judge pointedly argued that while setting bail was clearly a judicial function, many parties may post it; that being so there was no inherent reason the state could not do it.[96]

As expected, following the opening of the new work release unit, the population of the ISC remained at about 400 or some 60 percent above the limit set by the court. Judge Pettine thus found that Governor DiPrete and Director Moran had failed to purge themselves of contempt and imposed the threatened fine which was calculated to be $289,000. Further, drawing upon the equity powers of a court to use fines imposed as sanctions for civil contempt to remedy the problem underlying the finding, he ordered that $164,250 was to be used to establish an Emergency Overcrowding Relief Fund (EORF) to bail indigent defendants being held for $5000 or less cash bail; the remainder of the fine was suspended but could be imposed if the funds proved insufficient to achieve substantial compliance with the population cap. Having taken the hint given in the January conference and hoping to forestall this development, the governor had in the interim announced the formation of a privately financed bail fund—Project Bail. In his memorandum, the judge lauded this initiative and ordered that when Project Bail became operational, any funds remaining in the EORF be transferred to it. Moreover, implementation of the order was suspended for 30 days while the state filed an appeal.[97]

Echoing the sentiments expressed by his legal counsel at the January chamber's conference, Governor DiPrete indignantly declared his intent to appeal the decision. His action was widely and vocally supported by the state's judges, legislative leaders and the media, but the appeal was given only the most cursory consideration by the U.S. First Circuit Court of Appeals before it ordered the state to pay the fine.[98]

The bailing of inmates with state funds commenced in June 1989. Six months after it had begun, however, the population of the ISC stood at 526, 30 percent higher than it had been in March and 104 percent above the court-imposed limit of 250. The intake annex, moreover, was 160 percent over its capacity of 90.[99] The bail fund had merely offset two other new initiatives working in the opposite direction: the 1988 constitutional amendment providing judges discretion to deny bail to nearly all those accused of drug offenses and the attorney general's policy of seeking to hold all probation violators without bail. The state's trial judges were not of the mind that prison space is a scarce resource to be used only when necessary. When asked about the ACI's problems, for example, the Presiding Justice of the Superior Court could not recollect that "the guidelines for bail include overcrowding at the ACI" while the Chief Judge of the District Court put the responsibility on the legislators: "Citizens have cried 'We want these people off the street.' The politicians responded and when they responded they also had an obligation to make sure there were facilities."[100] Thus, judges making decisions about pre-trial detention used their new discretion with abandon with the result that in ten months, from December 1988 through October 1989, the percentage of pre-trial detainees being held without bail rose from 46 to 64 percent.[101] With 448 pre-trial detainees at the end of the year, the number being held without bail alone exceeded the cap of 250.

As is obvious from the numbers, the state's other initiatives were equally ineffective in controlling the jail population. Construction of the new medium security prison and the addition to the ISC, as we have seen, were held hostage by the City of Cranston for most of the year. That imbroglio was resolved in August 1989 but any relief from new construction was, even by the most optimistic estimates, at least one year away. Project Bail was unable to attract sufficient donations and abandoned. The home confinement legislation ran into significant opposition in the legislature, and when finally enacted set such stringent criteria that by year's end only three inmates, rather than the 100 to 150 which had been expected, had been released into the program.[102] Although funds were provided to establish a halfway house, efforts to locate a suitable site were given up after community pressure led Governor DiPrete to veto two possibilities and the funds were subsequently lost.[103]

The explosive growth in numbers, while concentrated at the Intake Center and its annex, was spreading to other units. By October 1989, for example, there were 224 inmates crammed into quarters designed for 125 at the Women's prison. In November some 300 prisoners in Medium Security and the ISC staged a hunger strike to protest the overcrowding, forcing Governor DiPrete to order 35 administrators to vacate their offices so that they could be converted to dormitories.[104]

Bronstein petitioned the court to impose an additional $2.6 million fine on the state for continued non-compliance and to consider other possible sanctions and remedies. Among those he suggested were that the state be required to remove all sentenced prisoners from the ISC, ease requirements for home confinement, suspend operation of the new law expanding judges' discretion to hold suspects in drug cases without bail, and award inmates grants of good time to accelerate their release.[105] Following a hearing on December 5, Judge Pettine ordered the defendants to advise the court by the end of the month of the expected impact of several options: fully and literally implementing the April 1989 order without restriction on who among the low bail population was eligible, expanding the numbers eligible by increasing the limit to $7500 cash bail or its equivalent, and accelerating the release dates of sentenced inmates by 30 and 60 days.[106] In their response, the department reported that modifications to the bail fund could not resolve the problem as the numbers being held without bail alone exceeded the population cap but, while their primitive management information system made any predictions extremely tentative, they estimated that accelerating release dates might immediately reduce the population by 2.8 to 5.7 percent. With construction of the new facilities now proceeding apace and occupancy expected in November 1990, however, they did not think such measures were necessary and requested temporary modifications to previous orders. These modifications included raising the cap at the ISC from 250 to 416, allowing the housing of pre-trial and sentenced inmates together and permitting dormitory housing of detainees.[107]

The weeks following the December 1989 hearing were difficult ones for Judge Pettine. The situation was grave, and the state's record in prison construction inspired little confidence in the current schedule. But the recommendations before him would be extremely unpopular and might be no more effective than had been the bail fund. Even before he had taken any action, the *Journal-Bulletin* labelled him a "leading local enthusiast of the ACLU" and accused him of "state-bashing" and contemplating measures that would "ease prisoner discomfort, giving that concern priority over the public' protection."[108] Privately, even Special Master Michael Keating, who had been his long-term confidant and who shared the judge's view of the situation's urgency, was nonetheless adamantly opposed to measures such as accelerated releases without review.[109] Keating suggested the court seek the views of a third party, and on February 5 Judge Pettine named Vincent M. Nathan, an attorney with vast experience as a special master, as a court-appointed expert to determine if the court could safely modify its previous orders as the state had requested and, if not, to evaluate the sanctions and remedies suggested by the plaintiffs and recommend a course of action.

Nathan had often been the center of controversy during his masterships in Georgia and Texas,[110] and the 92-page report he submitted to the court in April showed why. At the time of his visit there were 563 inmates in the Intake Center and 234 housed in the annex. In blunt and graphic language, he described how these prisoners were living in every nook and cranny of these facilities, overwhelming staff and defeating all efforts to maintain a safe and healthy environment. Idleness was pervasive, and classification had completely broken down so that pre-trial and sentenced prisoners were mixed randomly, thereby vastly increasing the possibility for violence. Surveillance by staff was made immeasurably more difficult by double-celling and bunking people dormitory-style in hallways and in rooms designed to be offices and libraries. Assaults against both prisoners and staff were very high and the disciplinary process had broken down as there were an insufficient number of isolation cells available for this purpose. Although some staff were forced to work five to eight consecutive shifts, more staff could not be easily added as there was no physical space available in which they could work. Forty to fifty inmates shared each toilet causing serious plumbing problems. The ventilating system was overworked, and the lack of fresh air was probably a major factor contributing to the seemingly high incidence of bronchitis, conjunctivitis, sinus infections, sore throats and headaches experienced by inmates and staff alike.[111]

In Nathan's view, the Intake Center was, by any conceivable standard, "a correctional disaster," and he recommended that immediate and drastic steps be taken to reduce its population to 250 and that of the annex to 90 within 3 months. To accomplish these reductions, he recommended that additional fines of at least $1 million be made available to continue the bail program, that the criterion for eligibility for the bail program be raised to $10,000 cash bail or its equivalent, and that, with the exception of certain narrow classes of inmates, the court order 90 days of good time be awarded to all sentenced inmates to accelerate their release and that this award be made every 60 days until all sentenced inmates were removed from the ISC and the annex. Failure to achieve the caps within 3 months, he recommended, should be met with daily fines of $100 per inmate over the limit.[112]

Nathan's report was accepted into evidence at a hearing in early May; three experts for the plaintiffs echoed its findings. Most unexpected, however, was the testimony of the one expert witness for the state, Major John D. Case. Although he believed that, given certain repairs and improvements, the facilities could be operated safely for several more months, he nonetheless admitted that he thought an accelerated release program such as suggested by Nathan should also be put into effect immediately. To Judge Pettine, this testimony was "the final, quintessential blow to defendants' request that this Court stay its hand until November. . . . "[113] Within a week, he entered an order which required the state to maintain a bail fund of $200,000 or its equivalent for indigent defendants, increase eligibility to those with bails set at $10,000 or less, award all sentenced prisoners 90 days of good time immediately to be credited toward their eligibility for release, and make such awards every 30 days until all sentenced prisoners were removed from the ISC. It was further ordered that within 30 days, there were to be no more than 450 prisoners housed in the ISC and no more than 184 in the annex; goals for additional reductions would be established at the end of the thirty day period. Finally, the defendants were ordered to make extensive repairs and improvements in both facilities.[114]

The early releases began on May 23. Several of those released were re-arrested for new crimes soon thereafter. Most often the offenses were minor, but one of those released was arraigned in a homicide and three were charged with sexual assault. Another was found in the trunk of his car, executed gangland-style.[115] All re-arrests received extensive coverage in the *Journal-Bulletin*, but did not ignite a storm of criticism; indeed, public reaction was surprisingly mild. The results of Nathan's study had been released to the press at the time of its delivery to the court in April and had made headline news. It followed by only one month the department's management study that had come to similar conclusions and had received even more fanfare. The two studies, together with the testimony of the state's own expert, seems to have muted any significant opposition. This is not to say the crimes were without effect, however. Judge Pettine was painfully aware of them as over several months he continually modified the order striving for the most narrow yet effective solution.[116]

The impact of the order on the population was immediate. Within two weeks Keating reported that the cap of 184 had been reached at the annex and the ISC was within striking distance of 450; by the end of the month, the population of both units was below its cap, 403 at the Intake Center and 163 in the annex.[117] On June 28, Judge Pettine personally toured the facilities. Even with the reduced numbers, however, he found conditions that "arguably violate the Constitution" and characterized life in some domiciles as "the equivalent of life on a subway or bus from which one may not exit."[118] He thus lowered the cap at the ISC to 380 and that at the annex to 134. Mindful of the likely short-term nature of the overcrowding, however, he also suspended early releases once those caps were reached and for so long as population remained below the new limits. If the population went above the caps, accelerated releases were to be given to only so many as needed to bring the population back below them. At the same time he tightened the eligibility for the bail program, reducing the limit to $1000 cash bail or $10,000 surety, and excluded from both programs people accused or convicted of a wide range of violent crimes and sex offenses.[119]

Once again the population started growing. By the end of July it was in excess of the new caps at both facilities due, in part, to the aforesaid modifications to the May order. Another reason, however, was that about one-third of those bailed or released early were immediately re-arrested on pending warrants and thus never left the ACI. There were also delays in the effects of the early releases: grants of good time disproportionately resulted in the release of inmates in the least restrictive custody levels while sentenced inmates in the Intake Center awaiting placement, more often than not, required space in the more secure facilities. And, of course, there was the new policy of the attorney general regarding probation violators and the action of the state's judges under the new laws: by August about 75 percent of those detained awaiting trial were being held without bail.

On August 3, Judge Pettine raised the caps slightly but at the same time ordered that the department not accept for admission until November 15 any convicted offenders who remained free on bail or personal recognizance pending imposition of their sentence provided that the offender was able to obtain new bail in the same amount and form. He also ordered that persons committed to the ACI by the Family Court for contempt not commence serving their sentences until the same date, and he directed the special master to investigate the feasibility of releasing pre-trial detainees held without bail into home confinement.[120] At what Keating later described as a "wild and raucous session," however, the state court judges outrightly refused to cooperate with their colleague on the federal bench on any of these measures. Faced with such obstinacy, Judge Pettine might have invoked the superior powers of the federal court under the Supremacy Clause, but as construction remained on schedule and additional space would be available in November, he simply suspended those portions of the August 3 order rather than engage in a needless confrontation.[121]

Once ground had been broken in August 1989 for the new Medium Security prison, the state had, for the first time in the long history of the case, been able to keep the construction on track and on time by using a construction manager and prefabricated construction techniques. In the meantime, the facility had grown to encompass six 96-bed modules, space for 576 inmates. By mid-November 1990, four of the planned modules were ready for occupancy, two being reserved for administrative and programmatic purposes until the entire facility was completed. The first 96 inmates moved into the new prison and were followed by an additional 288 over the next few weeks. Construction of the 800 bed addition to the ISC had begun in March 1990, and using the same procedures and techniques, was ready for occupancy in January 1991.[122] Thus, in the short space of three months the state had added 1376 beds, increasing the design capacity of the institutions by some 75 percent. Prison overcrowding in Rhode Island was, for a time at least, relieved.

NOTES

1. *The New York Times*, January 23, 1985, p. A1.
2. *The New York Times*, December 16, 1990, p. D1.
3. *The New York Times*, June 4, 1987, p. D1.
4. *The Truly Disadvantaged: The Inner City, the Underclass and Public Policy* (Chicago: University of Chicago Press, 1987).
5. *Rethinking Social Policy: Race, Poverty and the Underclass* (New York: HarperPerennial, 1993), p. 14.
6. Diana R. Gordon, *The Return of the Dangerous Classes: Drug Prohibition and Policy Politics* (New York: W. W. Norton and Co., 1994), esp. ch. 10.
7. *The New York Times*, October 10, 1986, p. B19.
8. *The New York Times*, September 6, 1989, p. A1.
9. Kathleen Maguire, Ann L. Pastore and Timothy J. Flanagan, eds., *Sourcebook of Criminal Justice Statistics 1992* (U.S. Department of Justice, Bureau of Justice Statistics. Washington, DC :USGPO, 1993), Table 4.8 p. 433; Kathleen Maguire and Ann L. Pastore eds., *Sourcebook of Criminal Justice Statistics 1994* (U.S. Department of Justice, Bureau of Justice Statistics. Washington, DC :USGPO, 1995), Table 4.7 p. 383.
10. Gordon, p. 33.
11. Maguire and Pastore, *Sourcebook 1994*, Tables 1.2, p. 3; 6.11, p. 533; 6.19, p. 540.
12. Criminal Justice Institute and Carter Goble Associates, *A Management Study of the Rhode Island Department of Corrections* (Cranston, RI: Rhode Island Department of Corrections, 1989), pp. 225-27; *Palmigiano v. DiPrete*, C.A. 74-172, "Report of the Court-Appointed Expert," prepared by Vincent M. Nathan, (D. R.I., April 24, 1990) at 20, hereinafter referred to as the Nathan Report.
13. *Journal*, August 16, 1988, p. A3.
14. *Sunday Journal,* November 29, 1987, p. A1.
15. Criminal Justice Institute and Carter Goble Associates, p. 255.
16. RIGL 21-28-4.01.1. and *Constitution of the State of Rhode Island and Providence Plantations*, Article 1, Section 9.
17. Nathan Report at 17-18.
18. Task Force on Prison Overcrowding, *Rhode Island's Overcrowded Prisons*, Judge Anthony A. Giannini, chairman (Providence, RI: Governor's Justice Commission, 1984), pp. 13-27, 30-39.
19. *Journal-Bulletin*, June 28, 1985, p. A8. At the time of this announcement, the use of the PBA was roundly criticized by the local ACLU

chapter as a subversion of the democratic process. Five years later, legislative and media investigations uncovered evidence of widespread corruption in the awarding of PBA contracts leading to the indictment of Governor DiPrete and to requiring legislative approval of PBA bonds. *Journal*, July 1, 1990, p. A1.

20. Personal interview with John Moran, July 7, 1992.

21. *Journal*, September 27, 1988, p. B1; September 29, 1989, p. C1. The final agreement included a $900,000 annual reimbursement to the city, the transfer of 60 acres of prison property to the RI Port Authority which would lease it to private enterprise, state police patrols on the prisons' grounds, and city membership on panels to plan any further expansion.

22. *Journal*, August 11, 1989, p. A12.

23. Personal interview with Elena Natalizia, November 2, 1992.

24. Personal interview with Roberta Richman, September 15, 1992.

25. Personal interview with John Moran, June 10, 1992.

26. *Journal*, June 25, 1988, p. A16.

27. *Journal-Bulletin*, June 7, 1986, p.A1; *Journal*, May 24, 1989, p. A17.

28. *Journal-Bulletin*, March 5, 1988, p. A5; *Journal*, January 10, 1989, p. A3; January 19, 1989, p. A3; June 29, 1989, p. D10.

29. Criminal Justice Institute and Carter Goble Associates, p. 154.

30. Moran interview, July 7, 1992.

31. Criminal Justice Institute and Carter Goble Associates, pp. 250-52.

32. *Palmigiano v. DiPrete*, C. A. 74-172, "State of Rhode Island Initiatives to Reduce the Inmate Population at the Intake Service Center" (D. R.I., December 30, 1988) at 20-22.

33. Wall interview, August 23, 1992.

34. George M. and Camille G. Camp, *Corrections Yearbook 1985* (South Salem, NY: Criminal Justice Institute, Inc., 1985), pp. 49-52.; George M. and Camille G. Camp, "Probation and Parole," *The Corrections Yearbook 1990* (South Salem, NY: Criminal Justice Institute, Inc., 1990), pp. 13-14.

35. *Journal*, February 4, 1990, p. A1.

36. Criminal Justice Institute and Carter Goble Associates, p. 234.

37. British Broadcasting Corporation, *Prisons for Profit*, 1985.

38. J. J. Clark, "Security Inspection and Recommendations for Corrective Action" (Cranston, RI: RI Department of Corrections, September, 26, 1985), pp. 3 and 6.

39. *Palmigiano v. Garrahy*, C. A. 74-172, "Special Master's Findings and Recommendations" (D. R.I., July 22, 1985) at 10-24.

40. Criminal Justice Institute and Carter Goble Associates, p. 212.

41. *Ibid.*, p. 175.

42. *Ibid.*, pp. 171-80.

43. Personal interview with Jeffrey Laurie, October 16, 1992; Natalizia interview; *Journal-Bulletin*, August 12, 1989, p. A3; *Journal*, February 28, 1990, p. B7.

44. Criminal Justice Institute and Carter Goble Associates, pp. 185-92.

45. *Ibid.*, pp. 192-98; Natalizia interview.

46. Criminal Justice Institute and Carter Goble Associates, Table 10, pp. 118-120.

47. *Ibid.*, pp. 123, 142-44.

48. *Ibid.*, pp. 122, 130; Personal interview with Joseph DiNitto, Director of Classification, September 30, 1992; Richman interview.

49. Criminal Justice Institute and Carter Goble Associates, p. 50.

50. *Ibid.*, pp. 101-103, 170-71.

51. Personal interview with A.T. Wall, September 2, 1992.

52. Criminal Justice Institute and Carter Goble Associates, p. 38.

53. *Ibid.*, pp. 232-35.

54. *Ibid.*, p. 78.

55. Criminal Justice Institute and Carter Goble Associates, p. 16.

56. *Ibid.*, p. 17.

57. *Ibid.*, pp. 33-35.

58. *Ibid.*, p. 64.

59. *Journal*, July 19, 1988, p. C9.

60. Moran interview, July 7, 1992; Personal interviews with Donald Ventetuolo, September 9, 1992; Lt. Kenneth Rivard, Grievance Officer for the RI Brotherhood of Correctional Officers, August 26, 1992; Warden Donald Ellerthorpe, October 7, 1992.

61. Criminal Justice Institute and Carter Goble Associates, pp. 113-114; Richman interview.

62. Personal interview with Warden Walt Whitman, September 23, 1992; *Journal*, September 21, 1988, G1.

63. Whitman interview; *Journal*, March 4, 1986, p. A6; July 1, 1989, p. A3.

64. *Journal*, November 11, 1986, p. A1. The officer was acquitted of manslaughter in state court but later convicted of violating the inmate's civil rights in federal court and sentenced to five years in federal prison.

65. Ventetuolo and Rivard interviews; *Journal*, July 25, 1990, p. B4; February 12, 1991, p. B3; March 17, 1993, p. C17.

The other incident involved an inmate who had been placed in segregation on the morning of April 26, 1989 and was later that day found in his cell, beaten severely. An investigation revealed the assailant was an officer. He was fired, but insufficient evidence prevented action being taken against several other officers who were implicated. Moran interview, July 7, 1992; Ventetuolo interview; *Journal*, July 10, 1986, p. A10.

66. *Journal*, April 8, 1991, p. A3.

67. In one incident investigators provided $2000 in "buy" money to an inmate who had targeted an officer against whom he had a grudge. The inmate then used the money to pay off debts to other inmates. *Journal*, March 1, 1990. p. A1.

68. *Journal*, May 25, 1988, p. A1; February 10, 1990, p. B10; February 14, 1990, p. D5.

69. George M. and Camille G. Camp, "Adult Corrections," *The Corrections Yearbook, 1991* (South Salem, NY: Criminal Justice Institute, 1991), pp. 4-5.

70. Ventetuolo and Rivard interviews; Personal interview with Thomas DeFusco, an inmate in 1985, November 23, 1992; *Journal*, August 17, 1985, p. A1; August 21, 1985, p. A12; August 28, 1985, p. C3; September 27, 1985, p. C6; September 30, 1985, p. D4; October 1, 1985, p. A1; July 30, 1988, p. A14.

71. Ventetuolo interview; *Journal*, September 3, 1988, p. A1.

72. *Journal*, November 2, 1989, p. A1; November 7, 1989, p. A3; *Journal-Bulletin*, November 14, 1989, p. B3.

73. See Table 4, Appendix B.

74. *Journal*, March 10, 1986, p. A1; September 5, 1986, p. A1.

75. Clark, "Security Inspection," p. 14; Criminal Justice Institute and Carter Goble Associates, p. 88.

76. "Special Master's Findings," July 22, 1985, at 3.

77. *Palmigiano v. Garrahy* 639 F. Supp. 244 (D. R.I., 1986), at 254-256.

78. *Ibid.*, pp. 248-54.

79. *Ibid.*, pp. 258-60 as modified by *Palmigiano v. Garrahy*, C. A. 74-172, (D. R.I., June 26, 1986).

80. *Palmigiano v. Garrahy*, C. A. 74-172, "Special Master's Tentative Findings and Recommendations" (D. R.I., October 3, 1986) at 7, 11-13.

81. *Ibid.*, pp. 3-6, 28.

82. Wall interview, September 2, 1992.

83. *Ibid.*; *Journal*, May 13, 1987, p. A3.

84. *Palmigiano v. Garrahy*, C. A. 74-172, (D. R.I., June 9, 1987).

85. *Journal*, June 16, 1987, p. A16.

86. *Palmigiano v. Garrahy*, C. A. 74-172, (D. R.I., July 28, 1987).

87. *Palmigiano v. Garrahy*, C. A. 74-172, "Transcript of Chambers Conference" (D. R.I., January 28, 1988) at 3-5.

88. *Ibid.* at 10.

89. *Palmigiano v. DiPrete*, 700 F. Supp. 1180 (D. R.I., 1988), at 1189-90, 1194-98; *Palmigiano v. DiPrete*, C. A. 74-172, "Transcript of the Testimony of Lindsay Hayes, Assistant Director of the National Center on Institutions and Alternatives" (D. R.I., July 21, 1988).

90. *Palmigiano v. DiPrete*, 700 F. Supp. 1180 (D. R.I., 1988) at 1197.

91. *Ibid.* at 1199; *Palmigiano v. DiPrete*, C. A. 74-172, (D. R.I., December 14, 1988).

92. *Palmigiano v. DiPrete*, C. A. 74-172, "Transcript of Conference Call," (D. R.I., November 30, 1988)at 20, 23.

93. "State of Rhode Island Initiatives to Reduce the Inmate Population," December 30, 1988.

94. *Ibid.* at 27-36.

95. *Palmigiano v. DiPrete*, C. A. 74-172, "Memo from Judge Raymond J. Pettine to Director of Corrections John Moran" (D. R.I., January 23, 1989).

96. *Palmigiano v. DiPrete*, C. A. 74-172, "Transcript of Chambers Conference," (D. R.I., January 31, 1989) at 15-33, 69.

97. *Palmigiano v. DiPrete*, 710 F. Supp. 875 (D. R.I. 1989) at 888-890.

98. *DiPrete v. Palmigiano*, 887 F.2d 258 (1st Cir).

99. *Journal*, December 5, 1989, p. A3.

100. *Journal*, November 4, 1989, p. A1.

101. *Journal*, November 1, 1989, p. D5.

102. *Journal*, December 6, 1989, P. A3. RIGL 42-56-20.2 excluded anybody convicted, either in the instant offense or in past 5 years, of a violent or capital offense, breaking and entering, or sale or possession of drugs and anybody who was sentenced to more than two years. Those eligible had also to have a home and employment, and the release had to be approved by a judge.

103. Wall interview, September 2, 1992; Ventetuolo interview, September 30, 1992.

104. *Journal*, October 3, 1989, p. A1; November 3, 1989, p. A3.

105. *Palmigiano v. DiPrete*, 737 F. Supp. 1257 (D. R.I., 1990) at 1259.

106. *Palmigiano v. DiPrete*, C. A. 74-172, (D. R.I., December 12, 1989). The provision regarding fully implementing provisions of the April order stemmed from later modifications to that order which permitted the attorney general several days to review the records of those eligible to be

bailed and to exclude those with outstanding warrants on other charges, detainers, etc.

107. *Palmigiano v. DiPrete*, C. A. 74-172, "Defendants' Post-Hearing Submission and Memorandum"(D. R.I., December 31, 1989)at 3-10; *Palmigiano v. DiPrete*, 737 F. Supp. 1257 (D. R.I., 1990) at 1259.

108. *Journal*, December 12, 1989, p. A12.

109. Keating interview, June 22, 1992.

110. Bradley S. Chilton, *Prisons Under the Gavel: The Federal Court Takeover of Georgia Prisons* (Columbus, OH: Ohio State University Press, 1991), pp. 58-69, 79-80; Steve J. Martin and Sheldon Ekland-Olson, *Texas Prisons: The Walls Came Tumbling Down* (Austin, TX: Texas Monthly Press, 1987), pp. 183-202.

111. Nathan Report, *passim*.

112. *Ibid.* at 91-92.

113. *Palmigiano v. DiPrete*, 737 F. Supp. 1257 (D. R.I., 1990), p. 1262.

114. *Ibid.*, pp. 1262-63.

115. *Journal*, May 29, 1990, p. A1; June 14, 1990, p. A3; August 3, 1990, p. C5; September 11, 1990, p. A3; October 3, 1990, p. A12.

116. Personal interview with Judge Raymond J. Pettine, October 21, 1992.

117. *Palmigiano v. DiPrete*, C. A. 74-172, "Special Master's Interim Findings of Fact" (D. R.I., June 13, 1990) at 2.

118. *Palmigiano v. DiPrete*, C. A. 74-172, (D. R.I., July 3, 1990) at 4.

119. *Ibid.*, pp. 6-8.

120. *Palmigiano v. DiPrete*, C. A. 74-172, (D. R.I., August 3, 1990).

121. Keating interview, June 22, 1992; *Palmigiano v. DiPrete*, C. A. 74-172, (D. R.I., August 22, 1990).

122. *Journal*, November 11, 1990, p. B5; January 11, 1991, p. A1.

CHAPTER 7

Consolidation

In July 1990, the national economy fell into a recession. Officially, it lasted only through March of the following year, but the recovery was so anemic and marked by periodic flame-outs that nine months into it polls revealed that 8 in 10 Americans still believed the economy to be in very bad shape.[1] Not until 1994, nearly a year after Bill Clinton rode the tide of economic "doom and gloom" to victory over George Bush in the 1992 Presidential election, did the economy experience marked improvement. Even then public anxiety remained high. At the end of 1995, one of the strongest boom years in the post-World War II era, a poll conducted by *The New York Times* found that more than half the respondents believed they were not as well off as they had expected to be at this point in their lives and that 28 percent felt they had fallen behind in the past couple of years.[2]

The slow recovery and lingering anxiety were the result of several trends which had been evident during the 1980s but which became even more pronounced with the recession. On the one hand, huge budget deficits inherited from the Reagan administration severely restricted the ability of the federal government to stimulate the economy through spending on public works. On the other hand, attempts to reduce federal spending by turning over responsibility for many domestic programs to state and local governments drove up their deficits, serving to aggravate and lengthen the recession in some areas of the country, notably the Northeast. Corporate debt was also high as a result of the conglomeration in the economy. Rather than invest in expansion, many large corporations began to "outsource" activities previously performed in-house and to "downsize" their staffs to both increase profits and position themselves to adapt more quickly to the next recession. It was not until the number of jobs created in small- and medium-sized businesses, the recipients of "outsourced" activities, began to outdistance those eliminated in large corporations late in 1993, that the recovery became robust. Expansion continued through the next two years but its benefits were unevenly distributed. The newly created jobs offered neither the salaries nor the benefits of those they replaced. Moreover, created as a buffer to recession, they held no promise of security. The share of the national income earned by the top five percent of households increased at an even-faster rate than it had during the Reagan years while the share earned by the poor declined,[3] and the low level of official unemployment masked the fact that millions who had lost their jobs during the recession never returned to the labor force. Economist Lester Thurow concluded that no country had ever had as rapid or as widespread increase in inequality without experiencing a revolution or military defeat and occupation.[4]

Public fear and anxiety continued to express itself in retributive attitudes and policies toward drugs and crime. As evidence mounted that costly efforts at interdiction produced only temporary delays in the flow of drugs and that crackdowns on drug cartels resulted only in the replacement of one by another, the Bush administration had come under criticism for attempting to solve the problem by international showmanship while ignoring prevention and treatment programs that might decrease demand. Nonetheless, the war on drugs continued to be fought albeit with somewhat less intensity. Under Clinton, federal expenditures on the drug war declined and a larger proportion of resources were allocated to treatment, but the clear emphasis remained on enforcement.

From 1990 through 1994, rates of serious crime dropped significantly but this was largely due to declines in property crime. Rates of violent crime remained at an all-time high, kept there primarily by a sharp upturn in violence among juveniles; the number of arrests of persons under age eighteen for murder and non-negligent manslaughter, for example, increased by 167 percent between 1984 and 1993.[5] As polls registered a sharp rise in fear and a widespread sense of vulnerability and helplessness,[6] politicians scrambled to appear tough on crime. Throughout the country, states passed laws allowing or requiring juveniles accused of violent crimes be treated as adults. Congress in 1994 passed a comprehensive anti-crime bill that, among other things, aimed to put 100,000 new police officers on the streets over five years and extended the death penalty to more than 50 crimes. The anti-crime bill was followed just several months later by "truth-in-sentencing" legislation that restricted federal funds for prison construction to states that require violent offenders to serve 85 percent of their sentences before being eligible for release.[7] In 1994 the California legislature adopted a "three-strikes-and-you're-out law" that required judges to impose a 25 year-to-life sentence upon anyone convicted of a third felony. Twenty-three states passed similar legislation over the next several months, and others increased the severity of enhanced sentences for second and third offenses.[8]

The number of inmates in federal and state prisons continued to increase at rates of between seven to nine percent per year taxing the capacities of institutions across the country. By year's end in 1994, there were, for the first time, over 1 million sentenced prisoners and the incarceration rate stood at 387 per 100,000, 30 percent higher than in 1990.[9] A massive construction program that added over 200,000 beds to institutional capacity between 1990 and 1994 barely kept pace with the growth in population so that at the end of 1994 the nation's correctional system was operating at about 25 percent above capacity, slightly higher than it had been in 1990.[10] As the numbers in prisons mounted, retributive urges blended with utilitarian concerns to cut costs. Alabama re-introduced chain gangs in mid-1995, a step soon taken by Arizona and Florida as well, while other states banned "frills"such as weight-lifting equipment, televisions, stereos and free college courses, and some sought to make prisoners or their families pay a portion of the costs of medical care.[11]

Rhode Island's General Assembly between 1990 and 1995 enacted over 50 laws that increased the length of criminal sentences and a number of other measures that symbolized a growing toughness on violent crime. Among the latter measures were a bill that increased the time a "lifer" must serve before becoming eligible for parole from 15 to 20 years, one that required that seventeen-year-olds accused of

murder or rape be tried as adults and another that allowed the transfer
of juveniles who present a danger to the staff or inmates at the state's
Training School for juvenile offenders to the Adult Correctional
Institutions (ACI).[12]

The state's prison population continued to increase, although it did
so at a slower pace than experienced by other states and much slower
than in the late 1980s. From 1990 through July 1995, the average
annual population at the ACI grew by 22 percent from 2,495 to
3,050.[13] Virtually all growth was in the sentenced population; the
awaiting trial population, which had exploded in 1988 and 1989,
remained steady at about 500. Two factors account for this difference.
The first was the Emergency Overcrowding Relief Fund (EORF)
established, as we have seen, by court order in 1989 to provide bail to
eligible indigent detainees. The second was a decision by the Rhode
Island Supreme Court in 1990 that limited the impact of the 1988
constitutional amendment that had allowed those charged with drug
offenses to be held without bail. The decision required judges first to
make a finding of fact relating to the individual defendant's
dangerousness before denying bail.[14]

Additional breathing room came from the expansion of prison
capacity. As we have seen, portions of the long-awaited medium
security prison opened late in 1990, and an addition to the Intake
Services Center (ISC) was ready for occupancy early in 1991. As these
new units were fully completed during 1992, Rhode Island became one
of only seven systems in the country operating under capacity, and by
some measures was the least crowded system in the country at the end
of 1994.[15] The unused space permitted the department to supplement its
budget by renting beds to North Carolina in 1994 for use by medium
security prisoners for whom that state had no space. However, renting
space to other states could never solve what had come to replace
overcrowding as the major challenge facing the department: budget
shortfalls as a result of the poor fiscal condition of the state.

The "1990 recession" began in 1989 in the Northeast and lasted
longer than in the rest of the nation. In Rhode Island, the economic
situation was aggravated by the worst banking crisis in the state since
the 1930s Depression and the end of the Cold War. The embezzlement

of some \$20 million by the head of a credit union triggered the bankruptcy of a private insurer and necessitated the closing of 45 financial institutions in January 1991.[16] And cutbacks in defense spending following the end of the Cold War had a severe impact in a small state where thousands of the most highly paid jobs were dependent, directly or indirectly, on the manufacture of nuclear submarines. The population of the state, which had grown past 1 million in 1990, fell below that number in 1994. As late as mid-1995, at a time when the national economy was booming and employment was finally increasing in the other New England states, employment in Rhode Island was still declining.[17]

Faced with huge deficits, the state attempted to balance its books by involuntary furloughs without pay, lay-offs, and cutting back on all but essential services. Between 1991 and 1995, Rhode Island led the nation in the downsizing of state government, reducing the number of full-time equivalent positions by about 6 percent.[18] Corrections was immune to some of these cuts but fiscal problems nonetheless had a significant impact on the department as it struggled to recover from the overcrowding crisis and remove itself from the supervision of the federal court.

A CORPORATE ADMINISTRATION

In an effort to cope with the burgeoning fiscal problem of the state, the DiPrete administration offered an attractive early retirement package to state employees in 1990. One of the many administrators to take advantage of this plan was Corrections Director John Moran, whose 12-year tenure came to an end in August of that year. A search was begun immediately but it fell to DiPrete's successor, Governor Bruce G. Sundlun, to name the new director. A wealthy business executive and liberal Democrat, Sundlun chose George A. Vose, Jr., who had served as commissioner of corrections in Massachusetts in the Dukakis administration to fill the position.

Only thirty-nine years old at the time of his appointment, Vose nonetheless had substantial administrative experience. He had started work in the Massachusetts system as a classification counselor just after he had graduated from college 17 years before and had worked his way up the administrative hierarchy serving as a deputy superintendent of the state's maximum security prison at Walpole, superintendent of its largest prison at Norfolk and then as deputy commissioner for three years prior to becoming commissioner in 1989. The newly-elected governor, William Weld, had wanted him to stay on in Massachusetts but Vose was attracted to the opportunity he saw in Rhode Island where, unlike Massachusetts, he would answer directly to the governor and have control over an entire correctional system including probation and parole.[19]

Vose's philosophy of corrections and management style are close to those articulated in a recent book by Kevin Wright.[20] He views offenders primarily as individuals who have failed in their obligations as citizens, often because they have derived fewer benefits from citizenship than do most of us. If they are to become responsible citizens, Vose believes it is essential that they be treated civilly by correctional authorities who ought to model good citizenship by protecting and providing for certain fundamental rights. Included among these rights are the right to safety, adequate care, personal dignity, meaningful activity, ample opportunity for self-improvement and hope for the future. Political rights of self-determination are not included among those to be provided and protected.[21] Nor is the recognition of rights a recipe for permissiveness. Responsibility for the development of policies and the operation of programs must remain squarely with the correctional staff. Inmates might be permitted to have limited input in areas where it may be deemed of value, but should this be done it should be accomplished only through focus groups established for a short time and with a clear agenda. Moreover, the recognition of rights implies reciprocity. To enjoy their rights, inmates must act responsibly and respect the rights of others; those who do not are to be held accountable through firm, consistent and lawful enforcement of rules and regulations.

With respect to staff, Vose advocates a decentralized and participative management style that seeks to generate commitment to the organization's central values. Central to the process is the development of a vision or mission statement on which there is widespread agreement and the translation of that vision, through strategic planning, into a prioritized set of goals and measurable objectives. Responsibility for achieving measurable objectives is clearly assigned and authority is extensively delegated. To ensure proficiency, training is given a high priority; to monitor performance and identify problems on an on-going basis, management information systems are highly developed, and to coordinate activities, there are extensive channels of communication and the widespread use of *ad hoc* task-oriented teams.[22]

Reorganization and Decentralization

Soon after he arrived, Vose took his senior staff to a bucolic setting for what he hoped would be a two-day strategic planning session. What he encountered, however, was a bitter, dispirited and hostile group who were feeling overwhelmed just trying to do what they had to do every day. It quickly became clear to him and the consultants he had retained that pushing long-term goals would only lower morale further and increase resistance. What the staff needed was to be reenergized, to begin working together to solve some immediate problems that would begin to build a sense of pride and accomplishment. Thus, although progress was made on a mission statement for the department and a team assigned the responsibility for completing a draft of it, most of the two-day session was spent identifying short-term problems and assigning teams to develop action plans to meet them. Three years later, Vose could not recall the substantive problems addressed but offered that the specific problems addressed were far less important than was the process itself and its impact on the organizational culture.[23]

For his part, Vose established a team to work with him in reorganizing the department along lines that would better align structure with function and thus produce greater coherence. In July 1991, the department was reduced from five divisions to three: Institutions and Operations, Rehabilitative Services and Administration. Each division was headed by an assistant director, and these positions were removed from the state's civil service thus giving the director greater control over his immediate subordinates. The assistant director for institutions and operations was responsible for the management of the five prisons, the ISC, and essential institutional support services such as food and maintenance. Rehabilitative services included all institutional services such as medical, dental and mental health treatment; correctional industries and vocational education; transitional programs such as the furlough program and work release; and community-based programs such as home confinement and adult probation and parole. The administration division was responsible for all general administrative functions such as human and financial resources, management information systems, planning and research, and policy development. Later, as the department sought to increase inmate activity as part of its effort to negotiate an end to the *Palmigiano* case, a fourth division was created and given responsibility for correctional industries and construction.

A.T. Wall and Jeffrey Laurie, both key figures under Moran, were picked to head administration and rehabilitative services, respectively, and Donald Ventetuolo was placed in charge of industries and special projects. Thus, despite the reorganization, only one new person joined Vose's inner circle in 1991. This was Joe Ponte whom he named assistant director for institutions and operations. Ponte had worked closely with Vose in Massachusetts where he had risen through the ranks to head the four facilities at its Bridgewater complex. Along the way he had played a vital role in the restoration of control at Walpole after the disorder of the 1970s and had served a stint as director of that department's training academy. He had become a controversial figure in Massachusetts when he was found liable for authorizing the use of excessive force in putting down a disturbance. Vose thought the allegation baseless, however, and believed that Ponte, "although cold and tough, possessed excellent instincts for security and control and was a great teacher."[24] He seemed the ideal choice in light of what Vose saw as his top priorities: getting the unit managers to take more responsibility for their institutions and regaining control of Maximum Security.

Vose firmly believes that "prisons run best when they are run on

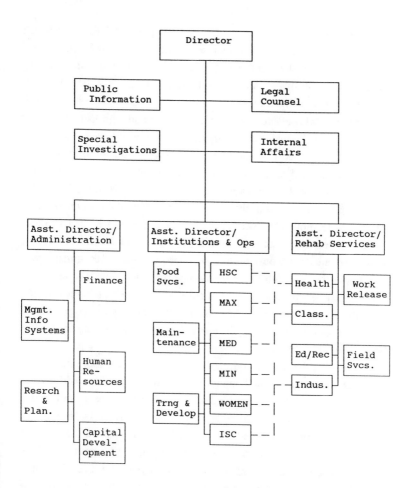

Figure 7.1 Table of Organization, 1991

site, not from a central office."[25] The small size of Rhode Island's system and the location of all its institutions in one complex, however, had led to the development of an organization in which decision making was highly centralized. As Vose saw it, the deputy assistant directors and associate directors were merely "checkers," super shift commanders whose sole concern was custody and who had neither the authority to make major decisions nor the responsibility for managing the full range of activities in their institutions.[26] Full responsibility for the scheduling and staffing of classification boards, for example, rested with the director of classification, and all classification counsellors were accountable to him. Similarly, teachers were accountable to the director of education, not to the warden of the unit(s) in which they worked. Although permitting some economies, this structure which had its roots in a department with only three institutions and some 500 inmates was unsuitable for one with twice the number of institutions and six times the number of inmates. The bifurcation engendered endemic conflict over matters such as scheduling making the delivery of programs and services uncertain and left a vacuum at a point where strong leadership was essential.

As part of the reorganization, Vose returned to the more traditional designations of warden and deputy warden and was able to add several new positions at that level. Under the new scheme each unit had a warden and a deputy warden and the two largest units, Maximum Security and the new medium security prison—named the Moran unit—were given deputy wardens for programs. Beginning in July 1991, Vose and Ponte commenced working closely with the wardens, preparing them to assume responsibility for everything that goes on within the four walls of their institution while incrementally pushing everything, from the classification and discipline of inmates through the rationing of toilet paper, down to the unit level.

Decentralization necessitated that virtually every policy in the department had to be rewritten and many new policies developed. The new units, for example, meant that the disorder management policies and procedures were outdated. Anticipating problems in his first year, Vose assigned a high priority to rewriting these and personally spent a considerable amount of time on it. Soon after the reorganization, however, a policy development unit was created and a system for the development and distribution of policy put into place. With this system in place, all major policies and procedures were rewritten, and increasingly policies came to be developed in anticipation of problems rather than in reaction to them. For example, the development of problems with gangs in the prisons of a neighboring state prompted the department to develop a policy to identify and track inmates thought to be members of a security risk group although at the time there was not a problem with gangs in Rhode Island.

New policies and procedures, in turn, required the retraining of staff. Not only were the disorder management policies outdated, for example, but training and practice in disorder management had lapsed due to overcrowding and staff shortages. Over the course of several years, the full-time staff of the department's training academy was increased from two to eight, and its orientation switched from an almost exclusive emphasis on pre-service training to include in-service training and a 40-hour curriculum for first-line supervisors. Middle managers came to be regular attendees at training sessions run by the National Institute of Corrections in Colorado and participants at national and regional conferences.

For the first year, Vose and Ponte met almost daily with the wardens, "spoon-feeding them change," and spent countless hours inspecting the units, monitoring implementation and correcting deficiencies.[27] By July 1992, however, all the pieces seemed to be in place, and the wardens were provided with a budget that was prorated on the basis of past use, given the responsibility for managing it and given operational control of all activities within their facility. Under the new scheme, central office units such as industries, medical services or education were made responsible for securing contracts or grants, hiring personnel and providing them with technical supervision. The personnel were assigned to the units, however, and the scheduling and coordination of their activities became the responsibility of the warden and his or her deputies. Moreover, the units were encouraged to develop programs of their own, and this led, as we shall discuss more fully below, to some creative entrepreneurship and use of volunteers from the community, reminiscent of the 1970s but far more controlled.

As wardens began to exercise authority in areas that had previously been the exclusive domain of a central office, disputes inevitably arose. Where formerly the head of maintenance had set the priorities for his own division, for example, these now were set in consultation with the wardens. With classification boards now run by each institution, wardens in the Moran unit and Minimum Security felt freer to challenge the decisions of the director of classification to place inmates coming from the Intake Center in their units. The wardens of Maximum and the Moran unit decided that representatives of the program staff should be present in the dining hall at lunch so that inmates might easily contact them with problems and concerns; the affected staff resented the additional duty and enlisted the support of their supervisors in the central office in an unsuccessful appeal.[28]

Early in the process, Vose and Ponte thus found themselves continually fighting brush fires. With time, however, the frequency of such flare-ups declined as precedents were set, new policies developed, old policies modified and a consensus on the boundaries of authority developed. Ponte resigned in 1993 and his successor stayed on the job only a year. Partly for budgetary reasons and partly as a symbolic statement to mute labor-management conflict over post cuts, Vose has decided to leave the position open spreading its duties among himself and the assistant directors and making widespread use of task forces to address issues as they arise. Rarely did he receive a call from a warden asking for his help in settling a problem.[29]

The rarity of calls for assistance reflected in part the relative absence of crises, on the one hand, and the frequency of staff meetings and improved communications, on the other. Managers at all levels were required to meet with their immediate subordinates weekly, and minutes of these meetings periodically monitored to check the flow of information. As another check, Vose established bi-weekly focus groups to serve as a conduit of information from the front-line staff to the director, unfiltered by layers of middle management. Moreover, the flow of information has been enhanced by computer networking. The Criminal Justice Institute Report of 1989 had made a strong case for upgrading the department's computer technology, and each year since then funds were set aside and consultants retained for that purpose. By

1995, the department was able to analyze trends and make projections that in the recent past were beyond its capability, middle managers at all levels had ready access to information previously unavailable even at the top, and all could communicate with each other speedily.

Despite the effort to move authority and responsibility down the hierarchy, middle managers tended to see the department as remaining highly centralized.[30] The nature and cost of some services, medical for example, when considered in the context of the compact nature of the department's institutional complex, made decentralization impractical. Moreover, the state's financial woes led Vose to keep a tight rein on the budget, reviewing appropriations and expenditures regularly. Budget constraints also prevented the addition of sufficient staff for each unit to be fully autonomous, and because support staff were spread so thinly, temporary assignments to other units to cover unforeseen situations became common, leaving wardens with the impression that their hold on their staff was tenuous. Finally, direct professional and technical supervision was not pushed down to the unit level but remained with the central office, at too great a distance to be truly effective. There were no education or counselling supervisors in the different prisons, for example. The same was true of training which could be made more effective by having training officers in each unit. Nonetheless, there was by 1995, in the words of Assistant Director Jeffrey Laurie, "for the first time a feeling that the place is being managed."[31]

Labor-Management Relations

Over the twenty years since its establishment in 1971, the Brotherhood of Correctional Officers (RIBCO) had developed into a shadow government at the ACI, exerting a profound influence upon the organizational culture and day-to-day events. Director Moran, as we have seen, first attacked the union and then entered into an uneasy accommodation with it. That accommodation was upset by the overcrowding of the later 1980s. Vose, upon assuming office, attempted to develop a more cooperative arrangement, giving the union a greater role in decision making; that attempt foundered as a result of financial pressures.

Among the first directives Vose received from Governor Sundlun was an order to cut the department's expenditures by $5.9 million dollars, about 6 percent of its budget. At the time the department, as it had for some years, was spending about $350,000 per week in overtime. Cutting overtime thus emerged yet again as a top priority. While the contract with the officers' union prohibited management from changing tours of duty or hours of work solely for the purpose of avoiding payment of overtime, it gave the director full and sole responsibility for the creation and abolition of posts.[32] Previous directors had been reluctant to exercise this authority, but from his initial tours of the prisons, Vose was convinced that many posts were "featherbedding," and he decided to seek permanent savings by abolishing unnecessary posts altogether.[33]

Working with the wardens, Vose developed a list of over 100 posts slated for abolition, brought in knowledgeable consultants to review the list and made adjustments based on their recommendations. Union officials were consulted during the two-month process, and the final list was presented to the leadership of the Brotherhood and modified further in light of their concerns before 98 posts were eliminated.[34] Vose was taken aback, then, when nearly three-quarters of the officers scheduled to work on the first day of the post cuts called in sick. Lt. Ken Rivard, speaking for the union, asserted that the cuts jeopardized the safety of the officers but denied that the union had organized the sick-out. Vose clearly did not believe him and publicly branded the job action as "unprofessional, irresponsible and illegal" and something that "I'm not going to forget."[35]

Despite the tension, dialogue continued. For the first time since the formation of the Brotherhood in 1971, management and labor began holding regularly scheduled meetings to discuss matters of mutual interest, and for a time relations between the two groups were characterized by an unprecedented degree of harmony and cooperation. In response to allegations of discrimination and harassment from minority officers, a joint management-labor racial and cultural sensitivity committee was established to develop and implement a training curriculum that is now required for all employees. Vose agreed to increase from three to five the number of union officials who could be released from their posts on a daily basis to conduct full-time union business; union officials agreed to the creation of a team of investigators (Special Investigation Unit) composed of correctional officers who would be selected on the basis of merit rather than seniority, the first non-supervisory positions to be filled without regard to seniority.[36]

The harmonious relations were in no small part due to the fact that Vose served a liberal Democratic governor who had exempted the correctional officers from the involuntary furloughs and layoffs that had been imposed on other state workers in 1991. In negotiating the 1992 contract with the union, however, the Sundlun administration sought concessions that would assist them in balancing the state's budget. After protracted negotiations, the union ratified a contract that made a further incursion upon seniority rights in granting to the administration the right to transfer correctional officers from one unit to another temporarily to avoid having to call in officers on overtime. The contract also stipulated that the first three days of sick leave would be paid at 60 percent. Many officers, already disgruntled by the loss of overtime pay due to the post cuts, were upset, and, although the contract was ratified, there was significant opposition to it, with a good number choosing not to vote.[37]

Dissatisfaction turned to anger several months later when for budgetary reasons, Vose ordered the closing of the Special Needs Facility (SNF)—the old medium security prison. The protective custody inmates housed there were to be transferred to other units, and it was rumored that most of the staff would be laid off. In response, the union organized a demonstration of about 500 officers at Vose's office. In the end no officers were let go, but many had to accept transfers to posts and shifts they did not want. At the next election, the entire slate of union leaders was voted out presumably because they were perceived as "being in bed with management." In negotiating the 1994 contract, the new leadership steadfastly refused to renew the provisions regarding transfers and sick leave.[38] Thereafter, tension between labor and management intensified.

Under Ponte, the wardens were exhorted to crack down on officer misbehavior such as being late, being out of uniform, engaging in inappropriate behavior with inmates, and being rude to superiors or visitors. Not surprisingly, cracking down led to highly charged confrontations over interpretations of what constitutes misbehavior. For example, a female officer who is a single mother was recommended for a one-day suspension without pay for being belligerent to her shift commander. She had been caught between the gates during roll call and gone into his office to protest being reported as late for work; her protest erupted into a shouting match.[39]

In an effort to specify behavioral expectations, the department promulgated a *Code of Ethics and Conduct* early in 1994 and sought to have all personnel sign that they had read and understood it. The union, however, viewed much of the *Code* as changes in working conditions that required negotiation and urged its members not to sign for it. Subsequently, the administration made a number of modifications in light of the union's concerns, but the Brotherhood remained steadfast in their position citing provisions such as one that required personnel to report any arrest to the department within 24 hours. Nonetheless, the department has used the *Code* to justify disciplinary action in many cases, and this, in turn, has caused an increase in tension and grievances.[40]

Tension was also fed by administrative proposals to provide training to one or a few officers in specialized areas such as in handling dogs doing drug searches, the operation of urinalysis machines or to qualification as an armorer. Management viewed such training as being in the interests of the organization as a whole; the union saw it as a subtle attack on the seniority system, the next step being the creation of posts or positions for which only a select few are qualified. At one point, the civil service list for promotion to lieutenant expired and a new test was being developed but had not yet been administered. The administration requested volunteers to apply for a temporary promotion to remain in effect only until a new exam was given. About 50 applied but most withdrew when the union sent out a letter telling its members not to apply. When the temporary lieutenants were appointed, many of their subordinates refused their orders. The car tires of one of the temporary lieutenants were slashed and another's was spray-painted while they were at work.[41]

The latter incident occurred in mid-1995 and symbolized the sharper edge to labor-management relations that followed the election of Republican Lincoln Almond to the governorship in 1994. Shortly after taking office, the new governor called public attention to the fact that officials of public employees' unions were working full time on union business while being paid by the state and issued an executive order detailing the kinds of activities for which officials could be granted time off with pay and the procedures they need follow to secure it. As soon as the department attempted to implement this order, the union filed for arbitration, arguing that the order violated its contract that explicitly granted time off for activities prohibited in the governor's order and which contained a maintenance of benefits clause by which long-established, mutually acceptable practices attain contractual status. In support of the latter contention, RIBCO introduced a 1994 letter from Vose limiting the paid time off taken by union officers for union business to 160 hours per week but that, in so doing, recognized that having some officers employed full-time on union business was a long-established practice. RIBCO's position was upheld both in arbitration and in a subsequent suit brought by the state.[42]

In May 1995 Governor Almond ordered his department heads to find ways to cut 15 percent from their fiscal 1996 budgets. For several months Vose and his staff considered a number of options. One of these was closing the labor-intensive High Security Center (HSC) and placing its occupants in segregation at Maximum or in the Moran unit. As soon as word leaked that the HSC might be closed there was intense resistance. The move was decried in near-hysterical calls to radio talk shows causing Vose and the union president, Richard Loud, to trade accusations of irresponsibility in the press.[43] As before, the idea was abandoned in favor of closing the work release unit, moving its occupants into Minimum Security, and cutting more posts throughout the other units.

In deciding which posts were to be cut, Vose followed the same format as he had in 1991— having plans drawn up by the wardens and reviewed by two highly experienced and well respected consultants—but he did consult with RIBCO. In their report, the consultants recommended cutting 95.75 posts, resulting in an estimated annual savings of nearly $4 million. Vose and his staff were uncomfortable with many of the recommendations, however, and ultimately decided to eliminate 66 while seeking a supplemental appropriation from the legislature to make up the difference.[44]

Vose did not inform the union leadership of his decision until just prior to the press conference at which he announced it publicly. A group of angry correctional officers crashed the press conference and sat sullenly listening to the director. Later, union officials presented reporters with proposals to achieve savings by cutting inmate activities and services and criticized the department for being top heavy with administrators while "balancing the budget on the backs of correctional officers."[45] Their proposals, which had previously been shared with the consultants and were rejected in their report as unrealistic and a threat to overall security, attracted no support.[46]

Subsequently, RIBCO filed for arbitration arguing that a large number of the post cuts were in reality changes in work conditions that should have been negotiated. In their view, management's contractual right to abolish posts meant precisely that, a post is no longer to be manned and its duties no longer performed.[47] Management on its own might decide to close the work release unit, as it did, or no longer man a guard tower on the 7AM to 3PM shift. Many of the cuts, however, were not of this nature but involved eliminating posts and redistributing their work load. For instance, at the ISC there were four utility posts to assist the officers in the eight modules, one utility post for two modules. These four posts were eliminated and the work redistributed among two new utility posts, one for every four modules. This, the union argues, was not post elimination but redefinition, a change in work conditions that required negotiation.

Whether management was within its rights in making the posts cuts remained to be decided. What was clear in 1995, however, was that despite a more professional management and more open lines of communication, labor-management relations had again become intensely adversarial, and the chronic mistrust between the two parties, dormant for a while, was once again much in evidence.

MANAGEMENT AND OPERATIONS

From 1986 through his departure in 1990, the attention and energy of Moran and his small staff had been focused on dealing with overcrowding at the Intake Center, constructing the new medium security prison and sparring with the federal court. Maximum Security, itself the focus of attention from 1977 through 1985, was ignored and those in charge of it left to their own devices. Those in charge included a warden, Gordon Zelez, who had been recruited after his retirement from the military but who by all accounts remained in retirement, seldom entering the facilities, and a deputy warden, Stafford Quick, who, although a loyal and conscientious administrator, was temperamentally unsuited to manage a unit of this sort. Moreover, relatively unnoticed amid the crises besetting the department had been the return of many of the inmates who had been leaders in the NPRA and transferred to federal prisons in the late 1970s. Gradually, over the years an indulgency pattern by which the compliance of inmates was purchased through the corruption of authority,[48] rather than secured by its lawful exercise, had once again come to characterize relations between inmates and their keepers in Maximum.

Custody and Control

On a tour of Maximum during his job interview, Vose had been amazed to find the inmates in street clothes not to mention the amount of personal property in their cells, many of which had been made completely private by blankets hung on the bars. He was, moreover, offended by the arrogant demeanor of certain inmates and the insolent tone with which they addressed him and those guiding him. Writing to Governor Sundlun after his visit, he advised him of the problem and warned that there would probably be a disturbance as he set about reestablishing custody and control. He received the governor's assurance of support.[49]

Shortly after the reorganization was approved by the legislature and Ponte was named assistant director for operations and institutions, Warden Zelez resigned and Deputy Warden Quick was made warden of Minimum Security. They were replaced by Walter Whitman, who was named warden of Maximum Security, and Thomas Partridge who became the deputy warden for operations. Both men had begun their careers as officers in the mid-1970s and were highly respected among the officers for their leadership ability and their toughness. Whitman and Partridge were also well known among the inmates, and Ponte's reputation as a hard-nosed administrator who was unafraid to use force when he thought it necessary spread quickly after his arrival from Massachusetts. The three were still planning the operational changes they would make when the disturbance anticipated by Vose broke out. On the afternoon of September 30, nearly 300 of the 440 inmates in Maximum Security went on a rampage, destroying a greenhouse and a supply shed, trashing the kitchen and setting some 21 fires that severely damaged the industrial building. Confronted by 100 officers in riot gear and armed with shot guns and tear gas, inmate leaders eventually agreed to return to their cells voluntarily if the tactical team were withdrawn and officials met with them to discuss their grievances. In the meeting, Ponte let it be known that they "were not going to let inmates dictate to them how to run the facilities" and stubbornly insisted that changes to increase custody and control were going to be made; the defiant inmates made it clear that they would resist any and all such changes. Having reached no accommodation, officials kept the institution locked up until 38 inmates were transferred to other states and then imposed all at once a series of changes they had been planning to make over several months.[50]

The restoration of order in Maximum was based on the model Ponte had used successfully at Walpole in the early 1980s. Cells, which had been an assortment of colors, were painted bright white and the bars painted black. A short list of allowable personal property was developed, and everything not on the list removed from the cells. A system of random cell searches and urine tests was implemented. Televisions and radios were fitted with earphones to cut down on noise. Inmates were put in khaki uniforms, required to walk along the exterior walls of the cell blocks and within lines painted on the floor. Movement between buildings was limited to ten-minute periods several times per day. Video cameras were placed in the visiting room, and inmates strip-searched after every visit. Many of these policies were put into effect in the other securities as well.

Correctional officers were encouraged to enforce all rules and assured that their reports would be supported. Moreover, they were given a role in the decision-making process. Before implementation, major changes in rules and procedures were discussed with the entire staff at "town meetings" in the dining hall and modified in light of the discussion. Focus groups consisting of two members from each shift, with membership changing every six months, were established to meet with the warden every month with the intent of identifying problems and proposing solutions.[51]

Staff were also empowered by the introduction of an internal system of classification developed by Herbert Quay in the early 1980s.[52] As with other internal classification systems, the intent of the Quay system is to reduce the incidence of violence and disorder by separating potential predators from potential victims. Unlike other systems, however, Quay's scheme is not based on verbal or written responses from inmates but on staff observations of inmate behavior. Inmates newly classified to Maximum were housed in a separate cell block for several weeks to be observed by counsellors and correctional officers. Both then complete standardized forms that, in turn, are used to classify the prisoners into one of several groups. The group to which they are assigned determines in which cell block they are to be housed.

As had been the case in the mid-1970s, the indulgency pattern in Maximum had made many inmates unwilling to move to lower custody. Reestablishing control of that institution together with the development of greater program opportunities in the new medium security prison paved the way for the development of an elaborate system of inmate management. Under the "Morris Rules" established in 1970 and later modified, inmates could be placed into four categories, A through D, with "A" being the general prison population and "B" through "D" being inmates whose misconduct necessitates close supervision and control on either a temporary ("B") or permanent ("C" and "D")

basis.[53] Until 1991, however, these powers had been used only
sparingly, and except for a few notorious inmates housed in the HSC,
all prisoners were categorized into "A" status. Beginning early in 1992,
downgrades to "B" and "C" status became a common part of the
disciplinary process and were tied to placement in the different units.
Only inmates with "A" status were permitted in the Moran unit or
Minimum/Work Release; minimum and medium security inmates
reduced to "B" or "C" status are transferred to Maximum or High
Security, usually after a period in disciplinary segregation.[54]

The administration also became more proactive with respect to
inmate misconduct. Up until the 1991 riot, all investigations work had
been done by a four-person unit made up of ex-law enforcement
officers. This unit also handled investigations of staff misconduct and
thus was overloaded with work and somewhat alienated from the line
correctional officers. Shortly after the riot, as noted above, Vose
negotiated with the union to create a five member Special Investigation
Unit (SIU) composed of selected correctional officers. This mission of
this unit was to investigate major crimes among inmates and, more
importantly, to cultivate informants, gather information about on-going
conspiracies and inmates moving into leadership positions and to place
suspects under surveillance. In its first year of operation, it presented
evidence to the state police resulting in no fewer than a dozen major
arrests.[55]

Early in 1994, the SIU was given major responsibility for
identifying and monitoring inmates designated as members of a Security
Risk Group (SRG). Although developed primarily in anticipation of the
development of a gang problem similar to one that had engulfed
Connecticut's prisons, inmates may be tagged as SRG for a variety of
reasons other than gang membership: the sophisticated nature of their
crime or their membership in a large-scale criminal enterprise, the
notoriety of the crime or the victim, or prior status as a public official.
Once an inmate is designated as an SRG member, that designation is
entered after his or her name on the computerized inmate tracking
system along with a risk level that indicates the degree of monitoring
and special precautions to be taken. A separate file is established and
updated by the SIU.[56]

Investigation to determine membership in an SRG is begun at the initial classification screening. The steps to be taken in this investigation were carefully outlined in a comprehensive manual that governs the classification process.[57] Two years in the making, the manual includes the objective custody classification form based on a study conducted for the department by the National Council of Crime and Delinquency, lists the precise tests to be administered to each inmate during admission and orientation as well as the special needs and/or problems to be identified and specifies the procedures to be followed at both the initial and subsequent reclassification hearings. Counselors now complete the required forms on a computer screen as they interview inmates or review written material, and a summary of every classification board's deliberation on each inmate, together with its recommendation, is entered into the computerized file during the meeting.

Since the riot in 1991, the ACI has been safe and secure. There was another moderate disturbance in Maximum in July 1992 but none since then. Moreover, in a population averaging nearly 3000 per year, there was only one homicide and one escape from a close custody institution in the six years from 1990 through 1995 (see Appendix, Table 4). In the Moran unit, with an average inmate population of 850 and a staff of about 250, there were about four assaults on staff per year and some 20 assaults on inmates.[58] No comparable data are available for the other securities but data from other sources and numerous observations suggest a similarly low level of disorder. For instance, although caches of drugs are occasionally found, fewer than three percent of the nearly 12,000 urine samples taken each year tested positive.[59] Touring Maximum in 1995 was like taking a trip back in time to the Big House. Cell block floors were highly polished; inmates were either at work, in a program, at recreation or in their cell; there was an eerie silence in the cell blocks during the day and three times a day a long line of men in khaki moved quietly into the dining hall, walking up against the outer walls within white lines painted on the floor and sitting where directed by one of five or six burly correctional officers spaced evenly along and facing the line.

The dominance of the custodians is clearly reflected in the results of the disciplinary process. Despite the due process guarantees of the "Morris Rules," few inmates charged with an offense are acquitted. From July through September 1995, there were 251 disciplinary reports written on inmates in Maximum Security. All of these inmates were found guilty at the disciplinary board, and of 155 appeals, only two were upheld. Similar results are found at the Moran unit. Of 152 hearings from July through September, 137 resulted in findings of guilt, six were dismissed and nine were not processed for some reason. Of 92 appeals, only four were approved.[60]

Officials offer two general explanations for the relative lack of acquittals and successful appeals. Some, such as Warden Brule who quipped that "in the case of a tie, the officer wins," cite the need to maintain the authority of the officers. Others such as Warden Whitman argue that the process presents such hassles for correctional officers that they only write reports when there is clear evidence of guilt.[61] Not surprisingly inmates express another view. Long-term inmates Tony Souza and Freddie Bishop think the disciplinary boards merely rubber-stamp the decisions of officers, which are at times incorrect and sometimes even malicious. Pointing to the permanency of identification as a member of a security threat group and the inability of inmates to appeal this, they believe the due process guarantees of *Morris* are a farce. As further evidence they argue that the use of unidentified but supposedly reliable informants at disciplinary hearings has increased since the formation of the SIU and has turned the disciplinary process into an elaborate snitch system that is widely abused by inmates seeking to get revenge on others, curry favor with the administration or eliminate competitors.[62]

Brutality and Corruption

Two-thirds of the correctional officers working at the ACI in 1995 were hired between 1988 and 1990 to meet the need created by the rapid growth in the inmate population and the opening of the new facilities. For most of that time, unemployment in the state was very low thus limiting the pool of eligibles and resulting in a cohort of officers who, in the eyes of most administrators, are of lower than average caliber. Once when he spoke to a group of young officers taking a community college course, Vose could scarcely believe his ears when they claimed they had every right to "cold cock" an inmate who got out of line, that it was the only way to teach him a lesson.[63] Attitudes such as this had apparently not been effectively countered during the pre-service training which, due to the crowding, was minimal as new recruits were rushed onto the job. They may also have been reinforced by young officers misinterpreting Ponte's hard-nosed approach or simply from seeing their increased power as an opportunity to take revenge upon inmates who had intimidated them.

Complaints of brutality and harassment, especially from minority inmates and community groups advocating for minority rights, increased dramatically in the months following the restoration of custodial control after the 1991 riot, and anger at perceived brutality provoked another disturbance in July 1992. When a black inmate refused to enter his cell following dinner, a six-member tactical team—the cell extraction team—was summoned, forcibly placed him in restraints and removed him to segregation amid a chorus of threats from other inmates. An hour later when the cell block was released for recreation, some 45 inmates assaulted six officers on duty in the yard, one of whom had to be hospitalized, and then entered the abandoned industrial building where they barricaded themselves for several hours until being forced out with tear gas.[64]

Vose and Ponte required that all actions of the cell extraction team be videotaped. Thus, Vose was able to provide credible assurances to community groups that, despite the allegations of the inmates, the actions of the team had been highly professional, in accord with departmental policy and that the inmate had not been injured. Moreover, he had already launched a full-scale investigation of complaints lodged by a coalition of advocacy groups and held a meeting with all minority officers and staff in which they were brutally frank with him about racism they encountered on the job. It was at this point that Vose and the union established a racial and cultural training committee that developed a curriculum required of all staff. Vose also established an affirmative action committee that designed a policy to increase the recruitment and retention of minority staff and promoted several minority officers into key positions of authority and high visibility.[65]

More immediate and dramatic in its impact on brutality was the placement on administrative leave of a deputy warden, a senior captain and five officers suspected of beating an inmate who had assaulted an officer. Ultimately, investigations by the state police and the FBI failed to uncover sufficient evidence to press charges against any of the seven men and all were reinstated, but during the year it took to complete the investigations, complaints dropped off sharply. At the same time, training in the proper use of force was increased. There continue to be complaints of brutality, to be sure, and some are undoubtedly well founded. In January 1993, an inmate in Minimum Security was found handcuffed to a metal pole in a vacant visiting room with his trousers around his ankles, and in March 1994 an officer at the ISC stood by and watched while four inmates assaulted another by rubbing Ben-Gay on his genitals and anus. Such incidents appear to be scattered and isolated, however, rather than part of a deeply entrenched pattern of control and are met with quick action. The officers involved in the first incident, for example, received a week's suspension without pay, and the officer in the latter incident was fired and later convicted on charges of aiding and abetting an assault.[66]

In his first five years as director, Vose fired or permitted to resign between 80 and 100 staff.[67] Some of these actions, as in the above incident, followed upon allegations of brutality. More commonly, however, the administrative action has been brought on by other forms of misconduct ranging from sex with inmates through bookmaking to conveying drugs to prisoners. In one case, an affair between an officer and an inmate was discovered when the inmate was found using the officer's phone card to call her while she was in Florida on vacation. In another case, an officer assaulted another while both were on duty. The dispute, as it turned out, was over a gambling debt; the officer who was the object of the assault was a "bookie" in the employ of a major organized crime figure.[68]

As suggested by the small percentage of positive urine tests, the amount of drugs in the prisons does not seem to be great, and most of it is brought in by visitors. Nonetheless, the number of staff who have been arrested for drug use and/or conveying controlled substances into the prison over the past several years is so large that Vose sometimes thinks that small-time dealers have sought to work at the ACI in order to have access to the large market in prison. In the first two months of 1996 alone, two officers were arrested for smuggling heroin into the prison; one was arrested for bookmaking and possession of a needle and syringe, and a fourth was arrested for possession of marihuana.[69]

There are no data to compare the incidence of staff misconduct in the 1990s with that of a decade before. Most administrators think misconduct increased, however, and attribute the increase to the lower quality of officers hired during the late 1980s when the war on drugs was raging and the population exploding. Three of the four officers arrested in 1996, for instance, had been hired in 1990 and the fourth hired in 1987. Be that as it may, there were other factors that contributed to the increase in misconduct; some of these reasons suggest that it was a real increase while others suggest that was only perceived. On the one hand, the sexual integration of the correctional officer staff during the 1980s, while expanding opportunities for female staff, also created greater opportunities for sexual relationships between staff and inmates and placed female inmates, especially, at a greater risk of exploitation. Moreover, the greater use of drugs in the community and the incarceration of large numbers of substance abusers both created a greater demand for drugs in the prison and increased the likelihood that staff had access to drugs and/or a vulnerability that could be exploited.

On the other hand, some of the increase was undoubtedly due to increased efforts at detection. As noted above, the number of investigators employed by the department doubled between 1991 and 1995, going from four to eight, and the tools available to them became much more extensive and elaborate ranging from drug-sniffing dogs to video cameras in the visiting rooms. Moreover, there were now two new specialized units doing investigations: one (SIU) focused on inmates and cultivated informants; the other, Internal Affairs, focused on staff, was manned by ex-police officers and worked closely with the state police. Thus, an inmate caught in a major violation by the SIU might have provided them with information leading to the surveillance of a staff member by Internal Affairs. Conversely, information gleaned from the state police by Internal Affairs may have led to surveillance of a particular inmate or group of inmates by the SIU.

In response to the perception of widespread staff misconduct, the administration developed the *Code of Ethics and Conduct*, the express purpose of which was to provide all employees "a clear understanding of the conduct expected of them. . . ."[70] In point of fact, the *Code* consists of 40 regulations, 12 of which concern nepotism and favoritism among staff, personal relationships with clients and contact with law enforcement agencies. As previously discussed, the union views portions of the *Code* as changes in working conditions that should have been negotiated and has filed for arbitration in a number of cases in which contested provisions of the *Code* have been used to justify disciplinary action. However, the union gave its strong support to legislation recently enacted on behalf of the department that criminalizes even seemingly consensual sexual relationships between staff members and inmates, making such a felony punishable by up to five years in prison or a fine up to $10,000.[71]

The era of electronic surveillance began at the ACI in the early 1980s with the opening of the High Security Center and the Intake Services Center. At that time, it was used almost exclusively to enhance security with video cameras sited so as to cover the perimeter of both units and all interior gateways. More recently, as we have noted, electronic surveillance has spread to the other units and turned inward. In the close custody facilities cameras are discreetly placed in the visiting areas in such a manner as to permit easy and close-in monitoring of all visits, and the rooms where inmates are strip-searched after visits are electronically monitored to ensure that officers assigned this onerous task carry it out properly. Because of the large number of complaints of staff misconduct in the Women's division, all common living areas in the close custody branch of that unit are now covered by cameras so powerful that one can read a paperback being read by an officer sitting at a table.

Programs and Services

The rapid increase in the inmate census between 1985 and 1989 swamped institutional programs and services, wiping out many of the gains made in previous years. By 1989, the strain placed on medical services was so severe that consultants retained by the department thought the state vulnerable to a lawsuit in this area, and Doctor Lambert King, an expert witness for the plaintiffs in *Palmigiano*, believed the medical shortcomings at the ISC so great that they represented a serious and present danger to the inmates. Prodded by the federal court the department increased its medical resources significantly in the following years, nearly doubling the number of full-time physicians and nurses, and contracted with a private physicians' group to provide specialized care for chronically ill inmates. With the increase in resources, all of the specific deficiencies cited by Dr. King in 1989 were corrected so that by mid-1993, the health program administrator believed that "...the department is in substantial compliance with all court orders."[72] In another inspection in 1994, Dr. King agreed that the provision of health services by the department was much improved and took particular notice of the care provided to HIV+ prisoners through a program run in conjunction with the Brown University Medical School. He still had serious concerns, however, about the lack of formal training and board certification in internal medicine of most of the salaried medical staff, the quality of the medical records, the tracking of patients with chronic diseases and the adequacy of the quality assurance system.[73]

A clinical psychologist and a psychiatrist, Doctors Joel Haycock and Bernard Katz, retained to review the provision of mental health services in 1994 found there was much "creative work" being done by a group of "dedicated mental health professionals with enviable experience."[74] They were especially lavish in praising the Lifeline program which trains and uses inmates to identify others showing signs of depression and encourage them to seek treatment. Modeled on one developed by the Samaritans and used in the Suffolk County (MA) Jail, the program at the ACI was in their view "the best-organized one that

we have seen, superior in several respects to the prototype" on which
it was modeled. Nonetheless, such programs are not a substitute for an
adequate number of staff, and the number of mental health staff at the
ACI remained significantly below national norms, having stayed at
about the same level as in 1987 while the population to be served
increased by 120 percent. Perhaps because the staff growth was not
proportional to the number of clients, Haycock and Katz found
screening for mental health problems to be "thin and perfunctory" and
the system for tracking inmates with chronic mental illness to be
inadequate.

For years the department had argued that lack of space was the
major factor contributing to the high rate of inmate unemployment and
idleness. That situation began to change in 1990 with the construction
of a new correctional industries building in Maximum Security, and
each year for the next several years saw significant additions to
program space without a concomitant rise in the population. Following
the riot in September 1991, the old industries building in Maximum
was razed and two new buildings—one for industries and the other for
education and recreation—opened. Like the 1990 industries building,
these were constructed outside the walls of the old facility to protect
them from damage in any future disturbances. Meanwhile, thousands
of square feet of space for industries and programs was being added in
the Moran unit.

By 1994 the department operated 15 industries in the various
institutions and marketed their products through a four-color catalog,
a showroom and the salesmanship of shop supervisors who were put on
the road part-time. Moreover, business had received a significant boost
in 1993 with the establishment of a program to purchase, recondition
and sell surplus federal government property. Gross sales of
correctional industries rose from $1.4 million in 1990-91 to $2.5
million in 1994-95.[75] Despite this growth, Bronstein, in an evaluation
conducted in mid-1994, found that "none of the facilities are able to
provide meaningful work opportunities for all prisoners at this time"
and "that only small numbers of people have the opportunity to be in
meaningful jobs."[76] Figures developed by the department in response
to Bronstein's report confirmed his conclusions. In the largest unit and

the one with the most the most developed industries program, the
Moran unit, there were only 382 jobs for 692 prisoners. Moreover,
many of the employed were "sub-employed" as some two-thirds of the
382 jobs were in institutional support activities, about the same
proportion consultants, five years earlier, had found department-wide
and judged to be too high.[77]

Outside the institutions, the services of Minimum Security inmates
were offered to other state agencies and non-profit organizations at a
rate of $3.00 per inmate per day. This operation met with great success
initially: over 200 inmates were put to work cleaning streets and
highways, removing graffiti from public buildings, painting and
repairing windows in state and municipal offices, etc. However, the
program quickly encountered significant opposition from organized
labor, who argued that the agencies used inmate labor to displace
government workers in an effort to reduce their budgets. A number of
grievances and suits were filed, several of which were successful,
stalling the program and causing some retrenchment.[78] Moreover, the
controversy led to media investigations of inmate employment in
non-profit organizations. These investigations in turn led to public
outcries in several communities that the inmate/workers either be
supervised by correctional officers or removed. Given its budgetary
constraints, the department had little choice but to remove them.[79]

The department also had difficulties in developing an adequate
level of programming in other areas. In a June 1993 assessment, A.T.
Wall observed that "the numbers of program staff have not in any
sense kept pace with the rising inmate census" and concluded that the
department fell far short of the requirements of the 1977 court order.[80]
At the time, the department was attempting to take advantage of the lull
in population growth to bring programming into line with the size of
the population. A year later, however, Bronstein still had serious
concerns about the level of programming although he noted that "the
women's facility comes fairly close to adequate programming and
medium security [the Moran unit] is making a very serious effort in
that regard but is not near substantial compliance."[81]

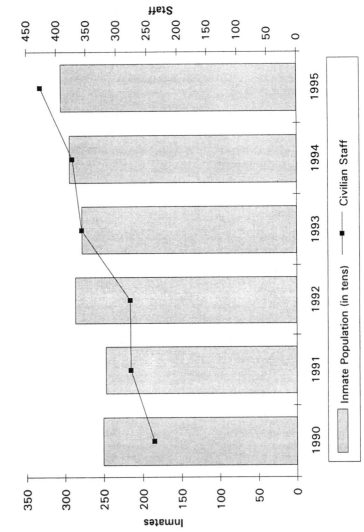

Figure 7.2 Inmate Population and Civilian Staff, 1990–1995

Inmate Population (in tens) —■— Civilian Staff

Being the largest of the state's prisons, the Moran unit was planned to be the center for programming. As soon as space became available, the department contracted with a local organization well known for its substance abuse programs to operate a therapeutic community in one of the modules. The same organization offered an eight-week drug and alcohol education program. Also under contract with a private vendor, an extensive treatment program for sex offenders was developed, involving 50 participants at a time. Other programs were offered by volunteers from groups such as the Literacy Volunteers of America, Alcoholics Anonymous and Narcotics Anonymous. Thus, on a typical weekday morning, there were approximately 150 inmates actively involved in some form of educational or therapeutic activity in addition to the nearly 400 prisoners who were working.

Taking its much smaller population into account, program development in the women's division was greater than that in the men's medium security; it has also been less dependent upon state funds. Warden Roberta Richman retained the notion that criminality, lack of skills, a poor work ethic and substance abuse are all symptoms of deeper problems and that time in prison is best spent dealing with these deeper issues than working in correctional industries. To deal with these underlying issues most efficiently, Warden Richman involved a network of community agencies in providing the services to offenders both while they are incarcerated and after their release.[82]

Soon after her appointment in 1991, Warden Richman began searching for innovative ways to finance programs linking the prison with the community and was the first to begin using the Inmate Welfare Fund for treatment programs not funded by the state. She contracted with several agencies to provide education and counseling with respect to drug and alcohol abuse, domestic violence and sexual abuse, parenting and life skills, and to do discharge planning. Representatives from the agencies were organized into an advisory board and with their help funding was secured from the state's Department of Economic Development to establish a mentoring program that matched women about to be released with women in the community who could advise and assist them. Additional grants were secured from private sources to add case managers, a job developer and an instructor in job interview skills to the mentoring program. A three-year federal grant allowed the department to contract with a local agency to establish a 24-bed residential drug treatment unit female substance abusers. By the end of 1994, most female offenders met with a discharge planner soon after they were sentenced and could then be involved with a variety educational and counseling programs during their incarceration and move into a support network in their community upon release.

Though the other units all provided basic education and recreation programs, supplemented in most by some groups funded through the Inmate Welfare Fund, they lacked the program development seen in the Moran unit and the women's division. In part this was because financial pressures prevented the department from duplicating the state-funded programs offered in the men's medium security. It was also due in part to the nature of the other facilities and their populations. At any given time, half the population of the High Security Center, for example, was on "C" status or in segregation making them ineligible to participate. The population at the Intake Service Center, as is the case with all jails, was transient and in constant movement to and from court, which made organized programming difficult and frustrated any attempt at sustained treatment. Finally, the lack of programs was in part a reflection of the emphasis placed on competing goals. In Minimum Security, the emphasis upon working under minimal supervision both to test readiness for release and to subsidize the department's operation relegated most programming to the evening, a time when most inmate/workers would rather take recreation. In contrast to the situation in Minimum, the paramount emphasis in Maximum was on maintaining security in a century-old building. Moreover, given the nature of the population, Warden Walt Whitman thought little of significance could be done for them with the available resources. Programming there was more or less an attempt "to fill in with things that don't cost a lot of money just to give them something to do."[83]

AUTONOMY

Judge Pettine scheduled a status conference in *Palmigiano* for January 10, 1991 to evaluate the department's progress in occupying the new medium security prison. Progress had been such, however, that the conference became the occasion for the judge to announce his recusal and turn the case over to Judge Ronald Lagueux. To almost everyone's surprise, Governor Bruce Sundlun, who had become a named party in the suit only 10 days previously when he had taken office, attended the conference along with his new director of corrections, George Vose, and pledged that the "administration of this state will do everything it possibly can to comply with the court's orders."[84] Bronstein, impressed by this first personal appearance of a governor in the judge's chambers in the 15-year history of the case, likewise offered his hope that the parties could proceed to end the case in a "cooperative, non-adversarial fashion." But, having been made wary by the false hope that had existed in 1988, he felt compelled to make clear that the case was not yet over.[85] His caution proved to be prophetic: it was to be more than four years before the case was settled.

Negotiating a Settlement Agreement

Although the parties met several times in 1991, little progress was made toward an agreement until the end of the year. Vose, as we have seen, was reorganizing the department, opening two new facilities and trying to improve the morale of his staff while dealing with a major budget crisis. Sensing that it was not a good time to be pushing the new director for a settlement, Bronstein devoted his attention to other cases that were more immediately threatened by impending changes in the law.

Early in 1992 the U.S. Supreme Court, in *Rufo v. Inmates of the Suffolk County Jail*, clarified the standards to be used in determining whether consent decrees may be modified. Prior to this decision, lower courts had required "a clear showing of a grievous wrong evoked by new and unforseen circumstances" before modifying a consent decree[86] In *Rufo*, however, the Court held that lower courts had misinterpreted earlier cases and developed a more flexible standard. Henceforth, a consent decree could be modified whenever it is established that "a significant change in facts or law warrants revision . . . and that the proposed modification is suitably tailored to the changed circumstances."[87]

The *Rufo* decision had been signalled in earlier cases. Several of Bronstein's cases, notably New Mexico and Hawaii, involved consent decrees, and these early warnings prompted him to seek settlement agreements that would insulate the cases from its effects. *Palmigiano*, of course, was initially a remedial decree but, in Bronstein's view, through the innumerable amendments and modifications it had evolved over the years into a consent decree, and at a meeting with Rhode Island's officials in December 1991 he presented them with the products of his labors in New Mexico and Hawaii, suggesting them as frameworks for a possible settlement in Rhode Island.[88]

Vose and his colleagues approached that meeting in a similar frame of mind. At Governor Sundlun's direction, Vose and Wall earlier in the year had prepared a paper outlining their vision for the correctional system. That vision was the development of a full and balanced correctional system featuring an array of alternative sanctions between incarceration and traditional probation. A week before the meeting with Bronstein, the department had presented this concept, along with supporting data such as population projections and alternative construction plans, to most of the influential people in the criminal justice system at an all-day meeting called by the governor. At the conclusion of the meeting, a committee was formed to study the issue further and eventually prepared legislation easing restrictions on placement in home confinement. That bill was passed in the 1992 legislative session, and over the next year the number on home confinement went from 55 to over 180.[89] Thus, the department came to the meeting with Bronstein able to make a credible claim that the governor and key leaders were willing to take the steps necessary to lay the foundation for a comprehensive solution to *Palmigiano*.

The department also came to the meeting with an immediate problem. Population projections prepared by the National Council on Crime and Delinquency predicted that, even with all the additional beds added, the number of inmates would exceed capacity by the end of 1992. Additional space was sorely needed in several units—the older wing of the Intake Center, the Special Needs Facility, and the Women's

Division—but this meant raising the court-imposed caps; for this, Vose needed Bronstein's approval. Impressed by the department's efforts to develop alternative sanctions, Bronstein agreed to raise the caps contingent upon an environmental assessment to determine the maximum capacities of the units and the completion of any renovations necessary to support those capacities.[90] It was in the course of this discussion that Bronstein presented the department with drafts of the proposed settlements in Hawaii and New Mexico. The parties agreed to work toward a comprehensive settlement along the lines of what Bronstein was crafting in Hawaii. That process was to take over two years, however, and somewhat ironically the agreement finally reached in Rhode Island became the model for a new agreement in Hawaii.[91]

Some delay was caused by the inevitable linguistic nit-picking, but for the most part the protracted negotiations were due to the complexity of the issues involved. These included the establishment of mutually agreeable population caps for each facility, a definition of substantial compliance and a mechanism for its determination and, most importantly, a means to prevent future overcrowding. Furthermore, the agreement had to be acceptable not only to the plaintiffs and the department but also to the governor's office and the attorney-general, all of whom took an active role in the process.

Additional tension and delay arose from the same political context that had inclined Bronstein toward settlement. Following the *Rufo* decision and leading into the 1992 Presidential campaign, U.S. Attorney General William Barr began offering the assistance of his office to states in litigation to release them from consent decrees and the strictures of prison population caps. This presented the department with an alternative to settlement and raised the possibility that entering into a settlement agreement might lock them into permanent population caps at a time when the changing law would make it unnecessary. Vose attended a seminar to learn more about the assistance being offered and the likelihood of success while the department's legal counsel, Anthony Cipriano, set about the task of reviewing the entire case in light of the legal changes.[92]

The tension came to a head in 1992 when the department was forced to close the Special Needs Facility for budgetary reasons.

Cipriano requested that Bronstein permit them to double-cell in the Moran unit independent of any settlement agreement.[93] Bronstein had always had grave concerns about the old facility and thought it particularly unsuited for protective custody; he would be glad to see it closed. Nonetheless, he refused to consent to any double-celling "in isolation from a larger agreement."[94] Thus, the department was forced to balance their immediate and pressing need for cell space against the advantages of litigation which were long term, uncertain and expensive. The issue was decided in favor of continued negotiation as it "became clear," in the words of A.T. Wall, that "any capacity we would agree to would be one that we, in our professional correctional judgement, thought should be the limit at which the facility should be run even in the absence of court-ordered capacities."[95]

For Bronstein, the *sine qua non* of an agreement was the development of a mechanism by which the state would itself enforce the agreed upon caps so as to provide lasting protection against overcrowding. This had become the pet project of the governor's legal counsel, Judith Savage, who was excited by being involved in a case on the "cutting edge of correctional law" and especially interested in "finding a middle path between the Bush approach of shoe-horning inmates into prisons if necessary and the libertarian approach of allowing consent decrees to remain in effect indefinitely."[96] Sometime in the Fall of 1992, Savage proposed the establishment of a criminal justice oversight committee to be composed of the heads of the major criminal justice agencies and authorized to take action to maintain the prison population within capacity on an ongoing basis. This proposal became the basis for a Governor's Commission to Avoid Future Prison Overcrowding and Terminate Federal Court Supervision over the Adult Correctional Institutions that Governor Sundlun established by executive order in December. Chaired by the former Special Master, J. Michael Keating, Jr., the commission, like the committee established to study alternative sanctions the previous year, was composed of the heads of the major criminal justice agencies and charged with developing a plan comprised of specific initiatives to guarantee that the prison population will not exceed capacity.[97]

The commission delivered its report together with three pieces of proposed legislation on February 15, 1993, just 70 days after it was established. The centerpiece of the report was the recommendation to create a Criminal Justice Oversight Committee. This committee would adopt the population caps set for each facility and function to keep the populations below those limits. Comprised of the heads of each of the criminal justice agencies, several judges, two legislators and a representative of the governor, the committee was to be granted enforcement powers ranging from encouraging innovations to expedite the processing of offenders, establishing temporary bail funds, directing the parole board to expedite the paroles of nonviolent offenders and recommending grants of emergency good time to the governor. The second bill authorized judges to sentence convicted offenders to a range of punishments from unsupervised probation through placement in a minimum security reintegration unit, and the third piece of proposed legislation raised the number of parole board members from six to seven, made the chairmanship a full time position and empowered the board to meet in subcommittees of three to consider the parole of all but those serving life sentences.[98]

Throughout the preceding year the department had campaigned for intermediate sanctions by publicizing success stories and the experience of other states, cultivating key legislators, and by hosting another conference for criminal justice officials at which their counterparts from Delaware explained their highly regarded system. With this groundwork, the backing of the governor, the widespread support of criminal justice officialdom, and the endorsement of the *Providence Journal-Bulletin*[99] the legislation proposed by the commission met with virtually no resistance and the foundation for a settlement agreement was laid.

After nine more months of negotiations over matters such as timetables for the accomplishment of certain tasks, the payment of expenses and fees and the finer points of language, a settlement agreement was signed on March 18, 1994. In exchange for dismissal of the case against it, the state pledged to operate a constitutionally adequate system in which environmental conditions, the quality of health care and the level of activity for inmates meet national correctional standards. The agreement set capacities for each facility and required the Criminal Justice Oversight Committee to exercise its powers if the caps are exceeded for more than five consecutive days in a non-emergency situation. In the event the committee fails to exercise its authority to enforce the population limits, the plaintiffs retained the right to seek enforcement through the court.[100]

The agreement further required that external monitors assess the state of compliance with its terms, make findings and recommendations to bring about compliance and conduct periodic inspections until such time as they could certify that the defendants had generally fulfilled the remedial provisions of the original order and all subsequent orders of the court. Temporary, isolated or sporadic incidents of non-compliance would not prevent a finding of substantial compliance, and in certain situations the agreement also allowed a finding of substantial compliance on the basis of detailed written plans approved by counsel for the plaintiffs in lieu of actual completion of the work.[101] Given the previous history of missed deadlines by the defendants, the latter provision was a testament to the credibility the department had established with Bronstein over the past several years.

When all of the monitors had certified that the defendants were in substantial compliance, the state was to file a motion for such a finding by the court. Following such a determination, there was then to be a four-month period of self-monitoring. If the department remained in substantial compliance through this period, the parties were to file a stipulation dismissing the lawsuit and dissolving any outstanding decrees in the case except those pertaining to the overcrowding restrictions set forth in the settlement agreement.

Finally, the agreement was insulated from modification under the ruling in *Rufo* by incorporating language to the effect that a wide range of circumstances ranging from crime rates to construction costs and delays are "within the contemplation of the parties" and that "a condition or eventuality within the contemplation of the parties does not constitute a changed circumstance."[102]

Notice of the proposed settlement agreement was posted throughout the various prisons, copies of it were deposited in each law library and inmates were given three months to file objections with the court.

Throughout the thirty months of negotiations, Bronstein had met with selected inmates to apprise them of what was transpiring and to solicit their advice and recommendations, but except for an occasional slip the negotiations had not been publicized. Thus, most members of the plaintiff class remained unaware of the impending end to the lawsuit; indeed, many prisoners were totally unaware of the case which had begun when they were young children. Bronstein and several of his staff spent a week touring the prisons, meeting with groups of inmates to explain the case and their reasons for wanting to settle it, answering their questions and listening to their objections. In their efforts to convince doubters that settlement was in their best interests, they were assisted by the few prisoners who recalled what conditions had been in the 1970s and who welcomed the opportunity to inform their fellow captives what they had survived.[103] Nonetheless, some 27 objections were filed with the court. Most, however, were requests for an enlargement of time in which to file an objection which Judge Lagueux summarily denied, and the majority of the others did not pertain to *Palmigiano*. Those objections relevant to *Palmigiano* concerned matters under review by the monitors and subject to remedy before a finding of substantial compliance. Following a brief hearing on June 30, Judge Lagueux placed the imprimatur of the court on the settlement agreement.[104]

Monitoring, Compliance and Dismissal

At the department's request Bronstein himself took on the responsibility for evaluating and monitoring programming. He conducted his initial assessments in May and June 1994. As noted above, he found that, with the possible exception of the women's prison, none of the facilities was in substantial compliance but concluded his report by noting the difficulty in meeting substantial compliance in this area and making it known that he was "prepared to discuss some possible modifications of the existing court orders . . . so that we can achieve realistic goals for compliance."[105]

Regarding programming, Bronstein had always believed that Judge Pettine had "gone way overboard" in the original order which was interpreted as requiring six to eight hours per day of meaningful activity for each inmate. The growth in the size of the population, the costs involved in establishing and operating programs, public opinion, the mood of the legislature not to mention the state's fiscal plight conspired to make compliance with such a mandate unfeasible. Moreover, changes in the law since 1977 offered him little hope of success should he seek to coerce the state to meet the requirement. And if he chose to litigate it, he would not argue his case before Judge Pettine but before Judge Lagueux, "a very different judge."[106]

Thus, rather than attempt to pressure the department for an across-the-board increase in the level of programming Bronstein elected instead to accept a statement of the department's intent "to work diligently in the future to expand vocational training and industries..." as evidence of substantial compliance.[107] He did, however, push hard for selected improvements in certain areas. One area was the relative lack of vocational training despite the space designed for such in the Moran unit. In response, the department agreed to utilize monies from the Inmate Welfare Fund to contract with a local technical school for a course in automotive electronics to be offered to 70 inmates per year. An even greater concern was the lack of programming for those in protective custody who, Bronstein found, were being treated worse in every way than prisoners in the general population. The department agreed to develop jobs for these prisoners, expand the sex offender and substance abuse treatment programs to include them and hire two teachers specifically for those in protective custody. By December 1994, the educational program was underway, and contracts were being reviewed for the other programs.[108]

Dr. Lambert King, Medical Director of New York's St. Vincent Hospital and Medical Center, was selected to assess the state of compliance in medical care. Dr. King had been a witness for the plaintiffs in the original litigation and had inspected conditions on several occasions over the years, most recently in 1989. As noted above, he was impressed with the progress made over the five years since his last visit but found conditions were as yet not in compliance with the relevant standards. Citing a case in which a physician had missed obvious symptoms of bacterial endocarditis with the result that the inmate/patient had to have a double-valve replacement, he expressed concern about "the relative lack of training and board certification in internal medicine among the current salaried staff."[109] He also found the quality of documentation in medical records to be deficient and the quality assurance program to be superficial and inadequate. Except for the clinic in the women's prison, he thought the medical facilities met standards but that the amount and quality of care provided to chronically ill prisoners was not up to par.

Both parties knew the plaintiffs were on firmer legal ground with respect to medical care than in the area of programming, and the defendants moved quickly to resolve the issues raised by Dr. King. Within four months of his report, they had transformed a vacant room into another clinic for women, contracted with a private vendor for the services of an internist to provide an additional 20 hours of medical care per week for the chronically ill and contracted with a nationally recognized expert recommended by Dr. King to assist them in developing an adequate quality assurance program and to evaluate its operation periodically thereafter. Moreover, they had persuaded the state to create a position for a medical program director to be filled by a board certified internist and were in the process of recruiting a qualified individual.[110]

Drs. Bernard Katz and Joel Haycock, both affiliated with the Forensic Training Program of the University of Massachusetts Medical Center, evaluated mental health services. In their joint report they expressed a number of concerns, as indicated above. Many of the concerns about staffing had been anticipated, and two clinical psychologists were hired before the report was submitted. At that time the department was already rewriting policies governing the treatment of inmates in crisis management status and the length of stay in psychiatric observation cells. In response to other concerns, the department agreed to increase the number of hours of psychiatric service available and to add two psychiatric social workers to the staff in the next fiscal year and deploy them according to a schedule that would ensure mental health coverage at most intake screenings.[111]

Probably the most vexing report to deal with, and certainly the most expensive in terms of immediate outlays, was that of Dr. Robert

W. Powitz, an environmental health and safety consultant with particular expertise in such matters as they pertain to prisons. Powitz completed his initial inspection in early April 1994 and submitted several drafts of his assessment between then and his final report in July. Although he found the various units to be "sanitary and well maintained," in the initial report he listed approximately 20 administrative issues and some 57 different deficiencies with the physical plant that required remedy before he could certify that conditions were in compliance with American Public Health Association Standards for correctional institutions.[112] The administrative issues ranged from the simple development of a policy prohibiting inmates from blocking air ducts to the completion of a comprehensive occupational safety and industrial hygiene inspection. Similarly the repairs to the physical plant ranged from the replacement of a toilet with trough urinal to the complete redesign and rebalancing of the heating, ventilation and air conditioning system (HVAC) in the High Security Center.

Within six months of Powitz's first inspection most of the minor issues had been resolved, and plans had been developed and contracts signed for the major work that had to be done. Following a reinspection in mid-October, he reported to both parties that in his opinion "substantial compliance on all environmental health and safety issues has been met."[113]

At the compliance hearing on December 6, 1994, Bronstein was able to report to the court that defendants had generally fulfilled the provisions of the 1977 order as amended. Necessary changes to meet the relevant standards had either been made or, as defined in the settlement agreement, sufficiently detailed plans inclusive of funding sources and timelines for completion had been prepared and met with his approval. Thus, he recommended that the defendants be determined to be in substantial compliance.[114]

Nonetheless a substantial amount of work remained to be completed: the hiring of a medical director and additional mental health staff, the development of a quality assurance program, repairs to the ventilation system in the women's prison, the redesign and rebalancing of the HVAC system in High Security and a host of other projects. As he had done for the past year, A.T. Wall broke each project down to specific components, assigned responsibility for each task to a staff member, directed others to work with him or her, and required weekly reports with documentation. Each month his report to Bronstein, summarizing actions taken with respect to each issue, grew thicker, going from 8 to 36 pages between December 1994 and June 1995. By the end of June, all of the work was completed or well underway towards completion, and on July 10, Judge Lagueux issued an order dismissing the 18-year-old lawsuit.[115]

For the first time since constitutional standards were thought to apply to prisons, Rhode Island's correctional institutions were a lawful order. And even the system's fiercest antagonist over the years, Alvin Bronstein, believed that those managing it had so thoroughly internalized constitutional values that it will remain so despite the threats and dangers now looming about and growing within it.[116]

NOTES

1. *The New York Times*, January 10, 1992, p. A1. The recovery was so weak that it took the Dating Committee of the National Bureau of Economic Research nearly 2 years to decide when it ended. *The New York Times*, December 23, 1992, p. D1.

2. *Journal*, April 2, 1996, p. A6.

3. *Ibid.*, June 20, 1996, p. A1.

4. Lester C. Thurow, *The Future of Capitalism: How Today's Economic Forces Shape Tomorrow's World* (New York: William Morrow and Co. 1996), p. 42. Thurow thinks that were there an alternative economic system, the stage might be set for revolution in the United States and western Europe. The collapse of communism has left no alternatives, however. He believes this could lead to stagnation and eventual decline similar to what occurred in the Dark Ages. Cf. pp. 261-70.

5. Kathleen Maguire and Ann L. Pastore, eds., *Sourcebook of Criminal Justice Statistics 1994* (U.S. Department of Justice. Bureau of Justice Statistics. Washington, DC: USGPO, 1995), Tables 3.94, 4.7 and Figure 3.1.

6. *The New York Sunday Times*, January 23, 1994, Section I, p.1.

7. *The New York Times*, August 26, 1994, p. A1; *The New York Sunday Times*, February 11, 1995, Section I, p. 1.

8. *Journal*, June 26, 1996, p. A19. On June 20, 1996 the California Supreme Court ruled that judges who think a 25-year to life sentence is too harsh may impose a lighter sentence.

9. "Prisoners in 1994," *Bureau of Justice Statistics Bulletin* (Washington, DC: U. S. Department of Justice, August 1995), Tables 1 and 11.

10. *Ibid.*, Table 8; Kathleen Maguire and Ann L. Pastore, eds., *Sourcebook of Criminal Statistics 1993* (U.S. Department of Justice. Bureau of Justice Statistics. Washington, DC: USGPO, 1994), Table 6.39.

11. *Journal*, May 4, 1995, p. A8; *The New York Times*, July 10, 1995, p. B7.

12. *Journal*, January 8, 1993, p. A13; June 30, 1994, p. D19; April 1, 1995, p. A9.

13. R.I. Department of Corrections, Planning Unit, "Statistics and Trends: Quarterly Report" (Cranston, RI: RI Department of Corrections, January 1996), pp. 4-5.

14. *Witt v. Moran*, 572 A.2d 261 (R.I. 1990).

15. "Prisoners in 1994," Table 8.

16. *The New York Times*, January 2, 1991, p. A1.

17. *Journal*, August 22, 1995, p. E1.

18. *Ibid.*, February 26, 1996, p. A1.

19. Personal interview, George A. Vose, November 30, 1994.

20. *Ibid.*; Kevin N. Wright, *Effective Prison Leadership* (Binghamton, NY: William Neil Publishing, 1994), esp. pp. 93-96.

21. In this respect, the citizenship model advocated by Wright and endorsed by Vose is quite different from that which was found in many states, including Rhode Island, during the 1960s and 1970s. See Chapters 2 and 3. For an incisive criticism of this model, see Bert Useem and Peter Kimball, *States of Siege: U.S. Prison Riots 1971-1986* (New York: Oxford University Press, 1991), ch. 2.

22. Wright, *passim.*

23. Vose interview, November 30, 1994.

24. *Ibid.*

25. Personal interview, June 25, 1996.

26. *Ibid.*

27. *Ibid.*

28. Vose interview, June 25, 1996; Personal interview, Ronald Brule, retired Warden, July 8, 1996.

29. Vose interview, June 25, 1996.

30. *Ibid.*; Brule interview, July 8, 1996; Personal interviews with Jeffrey Laurie, Assistant Director for Rehabilitative Services, June 26, 1996, and Roberta Richman, Warden of the Women's Division, July 10, 1996.

31. Personal interview, June 26, 1996.

32. *Agreement Between State of Rhode Island and Rhode Island Brotherhood of Correctional Officers,1989-1991*, Articles 5.9 and 9.1.

33. Vose interview, June 25, 1996.

34. *Ibid.*; Personal interview, Lt. Kenneth Rivard, Grievance Chairman, R.I. Brotherhood of Correctional Officers, June 3, 1996.

35. *Journal*, March 27, 1991, p. A1; March 28, 1991, p. A3.

36. Rivard interview; Personal interview, George Vose, July 10, 1996. Since 1972 the collective bargaining agreement has contained an article granting union officials time off with pay to conduct union business, and the amount of time made available had increased gradually over the years with increases in membership and the number of grievances. The increase agreed to by Vose, however, was still substantial.

37. Rivard interview. In exchange for these concessions, the officers received what amounted to, on average, a 6 percent increase in salary by spreading what was then 5 longevity pay raises into 15 steps.

38. *Ibid.*

39. Personal interview with Roberta Richman, Warden of the Women's Division, September 13, 1995.

40. Rivard interview.

41. *Ibid.*; Personal interview, George Vose, July 25, 1995; *Journal*, June 13, 1995, p. B4.

42. *Correctional Officers v. Department of Corrections*, C. A. No. PM 95-4859, 1996 R.I. Superior 348.

43. *Bulletin*, August 30, 1995, p. A1.

44. James D. Henderson and Jerry A. O'Brien, "Report on Technical Assistance Project" (Cranston, RI: R.I. Department of Corrections, September 11-15, 1995); *Journal*, December 5, 1995, p. A1.

45. *Bulletin*, August 30, 1995, p. A1.

46. Henderson and O'Brien, p. 3 and pp. 5-9, 15.

47. Rivard interview.

48. The concept "indulgency pattern" was first used by Alvin Gouldner in his study of a gypsum plant; "corruption of authority" was coined by Gresham Sykes to describe a pattern of control frequently found in prisons. See Alvin W. Gouldner, *Patterns of Industrial Bureaucracy* (New York: The Free

Press, 1954) and Gresham M. Sykes, *The Society of Captives: A Study of a Maximum Security Prison* (Princeton, NJ: Princeton University Press, 1958).

49. Vose interview, June 25, 1996.

50. *Ibid.*; *Journal*, October 1, 1991, p. A1.

51. Personal interview with Walter Whitman, Warden of Maximum Security, July 31, 1996.

52. Herbert Quay, *Managing Adult Inmates: Classification for Housing and Program Assignments* (College Park, MD: American Correctional Association, 1984). The Quay or Adult Internal Management System, as it is called, classifies inmates into five groups: asocial aggressive, immature dependent, neurotic anxious, manipulator and situational. A recent evaluation finds that these classifications correlate well with a number of measures of treatment needs, institutional behavior as well as with classification based on other systems. See Patricia Van Voorhis, *Psychological Classification of the Adult Male Prison Inmate* (Albany, NY: State University of New York Press, 1994).

53. *Morris v. Travisono*, 499 F. Supp 149 (D. R.I., 1980).

54. Brule interview; Whitman interview. The use of "B" status, in the eyes of Warden Whitman, has been particularly successful for reasons that were unforeseen at the time it was begun. Most inmates in "B" status—an indefinite confinement to their cells in a general population cell block—suffer extreme relative deprivation. Where those in segregated living areas have only others in the same situation with whom to compare themselves, those on "B" status every day must endure the pain of seeing others with privileges they cannot enjoy, being able to watch a game on television or play a game of basketball in the yard. This motivates most to take full advantage of the opportunity to go to school or to participate in programs in an effort to return to the general population.

55. *Journal*, January 4, 1993, p. A1.

56. R.I. Department of Corrections, "Security Risk Group Members," Operational Memorandum N0. 8.13.08, March 25, 1994.

57. R.I. Department of Corrections, *Classification Policy and Procedures* (Cranston, RI, March 1995).

58. R.I. Department of Corrections, "Medium Security Quarterly Report for the Second Quarter, 1995-96" (Cranston, RI, January 1996), p. 40.

59. Vose interview, July 10, 1996.

60. R.I. Department of Corrections, "Maximum Security Quarterly Report for the First Quarter, 1995-96" (Cranston, RI, November 1995), p. 13;

"Medium Security Quarterly Report for the First Quarter, 1995-96"(Cranston, RI: November 1995), pp. 23-25.

61. Brule interview; Whitman interview.

62. Personal interviews with Anthony Souza and Alfred Bishop, August 15, 1996.

63. Vose interview, November 30, 1994.

64. *Journal*, July 20, 1992, p. A1.

65. Vose interview, July 10, 1996; Rivard interview.

66. Vose interview, July 10, 1996.

67. *Ibid.*

68. *Journal*, January 21, 1993, p. B8; February 7, 1996, p. B5.

69. Vose interview, July 10, 1996; *Journal*, January 18, 1996, p. A1; February 24, 1996, p. A10.

70. R.I. Department of Corrections, "Code of Ethics and Conduct," Administrative Policy Statement No. 1.00.02-2, January 1, 1994, p. 1.

71. Rivard interview; *Journal*, June 15, 1994, p. B5.

72. Memo from Joseph R. Marocco to Jeffrey J. Laurie, August 4, 1993 (Cranston, RI: R.I. Department of Corrections).

73. Letter from Dr. Lambert N. King to Alvin J. Bronstein, August 4, 1994 (Cranston, RI: R. I. Department of Corrections).

74. Letter from Drs. Joel Haycock and Bernard Katz to Anthony A. Cipriano, Legal Counsel for the Department of Corrections, and Alvin J. Bronstein, November 25, 1994 (Cranston, RI: R.I. Department of Corrections).

75. Memo from Paul Petit, Associate Director, to A.T. Wall, July 31, 1996 (Cranston, RI: R.I. Department of Corrections).

76. Letter from Alvin J. Bronstein to A.T. Wall, August 11, 1994 (Cranston, RI: R.I. Department of Corrections).

77. Memo from Warden Ronald R. Brule to George Vose, September 9, 1994 (Cranston, RI: R.I. Department of Corrections).

78. Ultimately, the court ruled in favor of the state, concluding that the term "employee" is not an apt description of the relationship between the state and its convicted prisoners. *Rhode Island Council 94, AFSCME, AFL-CIO v. State of Rhode Island*, C. A. No. PC 96-0307, July 31, 1996.

79. *Journal*, December 26, 1994, p. C5; May 28, 1995, p. B2.

80. Memo from A.T. Wall to George Vose, June 28, 1993 (Cranston, RI: R.I. Department of Corrections).

81. Bronstein letter to Wall, August 11, 1994.

82. Richman interviews, September 13, 1995; June 10, 1996.

83. Whitman interview.

84. *Palmigiano v. Sundlun*, C.A. 74-172, "Transcript of Chambers Conference"

(D. R.I., January 10, 1991) at 5.

85. *Ibid.*; Telephone interview with Alvin J. Bronstein, August 21, 1996.

86. This interpretation by the lower courts arose out of the standard used in *United States v. Swift*, U.S. 106 (1932) at 119.

87. *Rufo v. Inmates of Suffolk County Jail*, 112 S. Ct. 748 (1992) at 765.

88. Bronstein interview; Personal interview with Anthony Cipriano, Chief Legal Counsel for the Department of Corrections, July 19, 1996.

89. Personal interview with A.T. Wall, July 30, 1996; *Journal*, May 2, 1993, p. A1.

90. Bronstein interview; Personal interview with George Vose, July 31, 1996.

91. Bronstein interview.

92. Cipriano interview; Vose interview, July 31, 1996.

93. Letter from Anthony Cipriano to Alvin J. Bronstein, May 13, 1992.

94. Letter from Alvin J. Bronstein to Anthony Cipriano, May 19, 1992; Bronstein interview.

95. Wall interview, July 30, 1996.

96. Letter from Judith Savage to George Vose, April 19, 1992.

97. *Report of the Governor's Commission to Avoid Future Prison Overcrowding and Terminate Federal Court Supervision over the Adult Correctional Institutions*, J. Michael Keating, chairman, (Providence, R.I.: Governor's Justice Commission, February 15, 1993), p. iv.

98. *Ibid.*, especially Appendices A, B and C.

99. *Journal*, February 21, 1993, p. A8.

100. *Palmigiano v.Sundlun*, C.A. 74-0172, "Settlement Agreement" (D. R.I., March 18, 1994).

101. *Ibid.*, at 6.

102. *Ibid.*, at 13.

103. Bronstein interview; Souza interview. Mr. Souza was one of the original plaintiffs and has remained in the ACI, except for several years when he was transferred to the federal system, since the petition was filed in 1974.

104. *Palmigiano v. Sundlun*, C.A. 74-0172, "Transcript of Hearing" (D. R.I., June 30, 1994) at 9-11.

105. Bronstein letter to Wall, August 11, 1994.

106. Bronstein interview.

107. *Palmigiano v. Sundlun*, C.A. 74-0172, "Memorandum in Support of Motion for Determination of Compliance, Exhibit A"(D. R.I., December 6, 1994) at 8.

108. *Ibid.*, p. 7.

109. Letter from King to Bronstein, August 4, 1994. The physician was an obstetrician/gynecologist who had been in private practice for 20 years before taking the job at the prison in 1990 where he provided primary care mostly to male inmates. The state medical board subsequently restricted his practice to obstetrics/gynecology until he completed additional training in primary care medicine. (*Journal*, February 20, 1996, p. B3).

110. "Memorandum in Support of Motion for Determination of Compliance, Exhibit A," at 5.

111. *Ibid.*, at 6.

112. Memo from Dr. Robert W. Powitz to R.I. Department of Corrections and ACLU National Prison Project, July 5, 1994 (Cranston, RI: R.I. Department of Corrections).

113. Memo from Dr. Robert W. Powitz to R.I. Department of Corrections and ACLU National Prison Project, November 7, 1994 (Cranston, RI: R.I. Department of Corrections).

114. "Memorandum in support of Motion for Determination of Compliance."

115. *Palmigiano v. Almond*, C. A. 74-172, (D. R.I., July 10, 1995).

116. Bronstein interview.

CHAPTER 8

Conclusion

The foregoing chapters have charted the history of Rhode Island's Adult Correctional Institutions over the past forty years, a period in which the institutions underwent a radical transformation in response to changes in their external environment. Looking back over this transformation, it can be seen as having proceeded through five distinct stages: patriarchy, anarchy, restoration, threat and consolidation.

THE COURSE OF ORGANIZATIONAL CHANGE

In 1956, the Rhode Island State Prison was renamed the Adult Correctional Institutions. This change symbolized the renewed faith in rehabilitation that had developed amid the affluence and optimism of the post-World War II period. There was, however, no certain technology by which offenders could be rehabilitated, much less a model of how such technology could be incorporated within the structure of the prison. Larger states, California in particular, launched major treatment programs and a large-scale research effort to evaluate their effectiveness. In Rhode Island, as perhaps in most states, however, the commitment to rehabilitation remained largely symbolic, involving no substantial commitment in funds, staffing or programs. Nonetheless, the prison was transformed by a wave of reforms introduced under the umbrella of legitimacy extended by the rehabilitative ideal.

Harold Langlois, who became warden in 1957, operated the small system as a large family with himself as *paterfamilias*. Traditional social orders such as this were common in prisons at the time. Joseph Ragen, for example, was a virtual dictator at the Stateville Penitentiary and his disciple, George Beto, introduced a similar regimen to Texas.[1] In comparison to these better-known contemporaries, Langlois's style was a more benign form of paternalism that reflected the prevailing liberal reform ideology. Far from emphasizing obedience, conformity and control, he eliminated the more onerous symbols and practices of custodial regimes and gradually empowered inmates through programs that increased their contacts with the community and gave them a voice in establishing prison policies and practices. Introduced haphazardly, with little planning or concern with their wider impacts, these reforms also raised inmate expectations to unrealistic levels and alienated and demoralized the correctional officers. Moreover, the reforms brought the institutions under public scrutiny to a greater degree than had ever been the case.

In the late 1960s, the weakened regime proved unable to contain a wave of disorder triggered by racial conflict that spilled over the prison walls from the surrounding society. Charges of racial discrimination and demands for separate organizations by politically conscious black prisoners touched off a series of disturbances. Crude attempts to repress the conflict, in turn, led to the first intervention by the federal court. In *Morris v. Travisono*, the administration and inmate plaintiffs consented to a decree that established, for the first time, a formal classification and disciplinary process. The impact of this first intrusion of judicial norms extended far beyond policy and procedures, however. It redefined the status of inmates, marking them as citizens who retained constitutional rights, and it ended the traditional paternalistic order by demanding that decision making be formalized and based on universalistic criteria.

The Rhode Island Department of Corrections was formed in 1972 in an attempt to restore order by centralizing authority and increasing resources. Ironically, the department's creation marked the beginning of a period of anarchy. Under Anthony Travisono, the first director, the citizenship model initiated in the 1960s was extended even further. Inmates were permitted to form what was, in effect, a prisoners' union and developed alliances with liberal legislators and various reformist groups in the community. The top administration aligned itself with the inmates and their allies, bringing them into a consultive relationship on both long-range planning and day-to-day operations. Any concern with security or internal order was likely to be branded obsessive, and embittered correctional officers retreated to the walls in the face of intimidation by inmates. In 1971, the officers had formed a wildcat union and set about the task of building their own base of support in the community and legislature. As violence and disorder escalated in the ensuing years, the officers' union seized upon it to dramatize their demands for better pay and benefits, participation in management and a return to a more custodial regime.

Little attention was given to internal management processes and lines of authority became hopelessly blurred. In 1973, Governor Philip Noel, whose hard-nosed public stance symbolized the change in public sentiments regarding offenders, displaced Travisono by appointing a state police captain, James Mullen, as warden of the ACI and giving him *carte blanche* to run the prison as he saw fit. Warden Mullen, however, had neither administrative experience nor operational knowledge of prisons, and soon abandoned his attempt to run the prison by coercion and the force of his personality. But rather than training staff and bureaucratizing the institutions, he reverted to a "con boss" system that extended privileges and immunities to a number of organized crime figures in exchange for their cooperation in maintaining order. This attempt at accommodation also failed, however. Other powerful cliques were angered and challenged the coopted inmate leaders, and the correctional officers were demoralized and alienated even further. Physical conditions continued to deteriorate and violence continued its upward spiral.

Restoration began in 1978 following the decision in *Palmigiano v. Garrahy.* That decision, in which conditions in the prisons were found to constitute cruel and unusual punishment in violation of the Eighth Amendment, imposed upon the department a comprehensive decree mandating improvement in all phases of prison operations and appointed a special master to oversee implementation. When the administration proved incapable of implementing the decree, the court orchestrated the ouster of the director and his replacement with a seasoned professional from outside the state, John Moran.

Following the near-fatal stabbing of an officer in September 1978, Moran transferred 15 inmate leaders, several of whom were named plaintiffs in *Palmigiano*, into the federal system and abolished the prisoners' union. In a seemingly ironic twist, the court, which had earlier sanctioned the union, openly supported this move and later ruled against inmates who challenged their transfer. Subsequent decisions by the U.S. Supreme Court had made it clear that inmate unions had no constitutional protection, and nine months of all-out war between the union-led inmates and the administration had convinced the court that the organization and its leaders were frustrating the administration's sincere attempts to implement the decree the inmates had won.

Moran also took a strong stand with the officers. Officers accused of brutality were suspended and indictments sought. Job actions by the union met with court injunctions, and violations of the injunctions resulted in findings of contempt against the union and its officers. Later, something of an accommodation between the administration and union was reached through the creation of an employee relations office. Although continuing to be tense, labor-management relations were for a time stabilized.

The court decree provided the department with something it had not before had: a clear statement of concrete objectives by which to set priorities and order decision-making. Attainment of constitutionality, rather than the more emotionally charged and ambiguous goals of rehabilitation or incapacitation, became the operative goal. With order restored and under continuous pressure from the court, the administration in 1979 began the task of bringing conditions and practices into line with constitutional standards. Achievement of these objectives required attention to the long-neglected internal management processes. Moran reorganized the department to clarify lines of authority and areas of responsibility, and recruited a small number of talented mid-level administrators from both inside and outside the organization. Staff training was increased, formalized policies and procedures were put into place, old facilities were completely renovated and long-delayed new facilities constructed and brought on line. This process was slow and at times painful, marked by a kind of antagonistic cooperation between the court and the department, but by 1985 it appeared that the prisons would soon be in compliance with the court order.

Just as the department seemed about to wrap itself in the mantle of constitutionality, however, the nation declared war on drugs. The number of prisoners, which had been growing steadily since 1979, suddenly skyrocketed and the crush of numbers threatened to undo all that had been accomplished. As in most jurisdictions, Rhode Island first attempted to meet this rapid increase in numbers by expanding capacity rather than by developing alternative sanctions. When the new facilities were delayed by local community opposition, the resultant overcrowding swamped existing programs and services and nearly overwhelmed the staff. However, the foundation of sound practice that had been laid in the preceding years plus constant pressure and emergency action by the court prevented disaster. Nonetheless, physical conditions again deteriorated, polices and procedures were not updated and ignored as they became irrelevant, and communication and coordination declined while labor-management tensions once again intensified.

Beginning in 1991, the department entered a fifth stage, one of consolidation. The opening of new facilities eased overcrowding, at least temporarily, and a new corrections director, George Vose, set about repairing the damage and rebuilding the organization. Programs and services were expanded to meet the demands of the increased population and the mandates of the court; a sophisticated management information system was developed; formal polices and procedures were updated and elaborated; training was reemphasized. Formalization and increased training permitted a decentralization of authority and responsibility dictated by the increased size and structural differentiation of the department. Moreover, lateral communication and coordination were strengthened by the widespread use of task forces and project teams in the successful effort to terminate judicial oversight. The *Palmigiano* case was at long last dismissed in June 1995. Where twenty years before, there had been anarchy, there was now a highly sophisticated and complex organization.

The management style of the Vose administration is one that emphasizes a rational, emotionally detached approach to problem-solving and a cost-effective allocation of resources among the department's multiple tasks. In line with changes in the wider culture, the department is more likely today to ground its claims to legitimacy upon its incapacitative mission—the protection of society through the provision of safe, secure and humane control of offenders—than upon rehabilitation. Nonetheless, rehabilitation survives as a strong secondary goal that exerts an important influence on decision making. Ironically, although the level of programming remains well below what is desirable from a strictly treatment standpoint, the department offers far more today by way of treatment program and services than it did twenty years ago when it trumpeted rehabilitation as its primary mission. Moreover, because of the concern with internal management processes, those programs and services are offered in a more stable, safer and healthier environment than were those in the past. Whether this level of services can be continued without the leverage provided by the federal court, however, is an open question.

The process of organizational change in Rhode Island has followed a course similar to that charted by Crouch and Marquart in their analysis of judicial intervention in Texas.[2] Unlike Texas, however, Rhode Island's prison system was not brought within the ambit of the federal court because it constituted a separate and autonomous moral order at odds with the Constitution, but because conditions deteriorated as a result of flawed attempts to implement mainstream ideas of rehabilitation and because of emotional reactions to the symbolism of court intervention in behalf of prisoners' rights. In this sense, the destabilization of the traditional order in Rhode Island parallels closely the breakup of that at Illinois's Stateville Penitentiary under the reform regimes of the early 1970s and the process of administrative breakdown found by Useem and Kimball to characterize riot-prone prisons.[3] Unlike Stateville, however, which today continues to be plagued with disorder and violence, Rhode Island's prisons appear remarkably safe and secure. Although certainly not the only factor, a key influence in the process of organizational development in Rhode Island was the role played by the federal court from 1977 through 1995. Both because of its fundamental importance and the fact that it differed markedly from that documented in other, more dramatic cases, the process of intervention warrants more detailed consideration.

JUDICIAL INTERVENTION AND INSTITUTION BUILDING

The federal court has been a constant feature in the operating environment of Rhode Island's correctional system since 1969. A large number of cases concerned with a variety of issues have come before the court during that time, as we have seen. Two of these, however, have by far had the greatest impact: *Morris* and *Palmigiano*. The former signified the dissolution of the patriarchal order and contributed to a period of anarchy from 1972 through 1977; the latter was the instrument by which the state was able to constitute a department founded upon principles of organizational rationality and institutionalizing constitutional values.[4]

The court in *Morris* redefined the meaning of incarceration. By extending minimal due process protection to prisoners facing disciplinary action, it recognized them as citizens who retained constitutional rights while at the same time it circumscribed and limited the discretionary powers of correctional authorities. It thus negated the taken-for-granted assumptions underlying the traditional regime of Harold Langlois in much the same way as the order in *Ruiz* prohibiting the use of "building tenders" to supervise other inmates ten years later negated that which had developed in Texas prisons under George Beto and Jim Estelle. And, as in Texas, the order in *Morris* was resisted though in Rhode Island that resistance took a considerably different form reflecting differences in regional culture.

Unlike *Ruiz*, the decree in *Morris* received little publicity and generated no public reaction. Although it was a consent decree, neither Corrections Director Anthony Travisono nor his assistant, John Sharkey, felt a strong commitment to implement the negotiated settlement. Neither administrator had much input in the negotiations, which had been conducted largely by attorneys, and both thought the court was overstepping its bounds, that formalized disciplinary and classification procedures unduly infringed upon their rightful and necessary discretionary powers. Travisono believed that such regulations would interfere with decisions about appropriate treatment, where Sharkey was concerned that they would undermine security.

Even if they had felt a strong commitment to the agreement, the administrators probably lacked the power to implement the regulations successfully. The custodial staff, from the lowest ranking correctional officer to the deputy wardens in charge of units, had already been alienated from the top administrators by the wave of humanitarian reforms initiated by Warden Langlois which, they felt, threatened their status and authority. The *Morris* decree left them feeling betrayed by the court, sold out by their superiors and endangered by inmates empowered by the court's action. The demoralized officers withdrew their allegiance from the organization, retreated from job performance and banded together in a wildcat union. Over the next several years, the officers' union vied with both the administration and the prisoners' union for power within the organization.

Later events demonstrate that there was nothing in the "Morris Rules" that prevented the maintenance of security and internal order. Indeed a proper reading and interpretation of them by a more detached and professional administration today finds the rules grant correctional authorities extensive powers to control unruly inmates, and officials who once were adamantly opposed to them now strongly endorse them. At the time, however, the new regulations, in prescribing universalistic standards and due process protection, challenged the conventional understanding of how prisons operated. In so doing, the decree delegitimated the traditional system in much the same way as the intrusion of judicial norms did in correctional systems around the country. It was not until a new order was established, one rooted in different premises, that the *Morris* reforms could be successfully implemented; the creation of that new order was the work of *Palmigiano*.

Disturbances, riots, escapes of dangerous convicts, murders and job actions by correctional officers kept the ACI in the headlines during the seven years between *Morris* and *Palmigiano*. The trial in the latter case, with its judicial tour of the facilities and train of correctional experts declaring Rhode Island's institutions to be the worst in the country, further dramatized just how bad conditions had become. The highly publicized turmoil generated widespread public support for the remedial decree and Governor J. Joseph Garrahy, only eight months into his first term at the time, greeted it by announcing that improving conditions in the state's prisons was a goal he shared with Judge Pettine. Implementation of the *Palmigiano* decree thus began in a decidedly different atmosphere than had been the case in Alabama and Texas where public officials vilified the judges and action was delayed by extended appeals. That gesture of acceptance and good faith by the state set a tone which persisted over the long history of the case despite significant strains and tensions and occasional moments of high drama.

The *Palmigiano* decision, as are all legal decisions, is couched in the language of individual rights. The real problem confronting the court, however, was one of organizational development, and his prior experience in *Morris* and other cases had convinced Judge Pettine that accomplishment of this task would require a strong judicial presence. If he had been faced with intense opposition to his order as was Judge Justice in Texas and Judge Johnson in Alabama, Judge Pettine may have assumed a commanding or directorial role, issuing ever more detailed and specific orders and perhaps even assuming responsibility for implementation by placing the institution in receivership.[5] The spirit of cooperation in Rhode Island, however, permitted the judge to fashion a more moderate approach: establishing channels for participation by correctional officials and using traditional judicial sanctions both to induce their participation in the process of remedy formulation and then to implement them.[6] The court also used its informal powers to secure for them necessary resources and expertise and it closely monitored their progress.

The role played by the special master was crucial to the approach fashioned by the court in *Palmigiano*. Given the demonstrated incapacity of the department's administration and the apparent receptivity of the governor to the intervention, the master was charged not only with monitoring compliance and implementation for the court but also with advising and assisting the department to the fullest extent possible. In fact, the role expanded even beyond what was spelled out in the order of appointment with the master, in addition to being a fact-finder and adviser, coming to function also as an intermediary and mediator.

Such a multifaceted role contains a high potential for conflict.[7] To provide effective advice and assistance to the department, for example, requires a degree of familiarity and confidence that is at odds with impartial fact-finding and the imposition of sanctions for non-compliance. Critics of intervention have argued that as a result of such conflicts courts are emboldened to enter areas where they best not tread, and administrators are seduced into accepting and implementing remedies that are unworkable. As a result, conditions frequently worsen and the credibility of the court is undermined.[8]

However true the critics' allegations may be with respect to other cases, there is no evidence of such in the history of *Palmigiano*. Two factors seem to account for this. First, the potentially most serious conflict was that between advising and assisting the department, on the one hand, and monitoring its efforts on the other. This dual responsibility certainly stressed Allen Breed, the first special master, as he agonized over whether he should assume a directive role or let the department continue in crisis while he documented the failure of the administration to deal with it constructively. It later resulted in public conflict between his successor, J. Michael Keating, and Corrections Director John Moran over projected growth and the need for new facilities. Such conflicts occurred early in the case, however, and as the latter example suggests once the department had competent leadership, the advising and assisting role of the master waned.

Second, the master was not charged with arbitrating disputes or imposing penalties. Although it was well known that Special Master Keating and Judge Pettine were usually of one mind, the formal resolution of disputes and the imposition of sanctions remained in the hands of the judge. This left Keating free to fashion his role along less judicial lines and more consistent with his background in alternative dispute resolution. As obstacles to implementation arose, he negotiated compromise solutions which, as the record clearly shows, frequently meant persuading the plaintiffs that, due to political and fiscal realities, that they should accept less than the original order had given them. Seldom, if ever, did the court insist on the implementation of a remedy that the administration deemed unworkable. Indeed, the realization that the court would not require of the department anything that professional administrators themselves would not insist upon was a major factor in clearing the way for a settlement agreement.

Early in the remedial process, the mastership formed a bridge connecting the system to the wider professional world of corrections from which it had become isolated. Over that bridge flowed much needed leadership, expertise and resources. Breed, as we saw, convinced Governor Garrahy to replace an ineffectual director who had been a political appointee and used his network to find a competent and experienced professional administrator. Experts in all aspects of prison operations from heating and ventilation through classification and security to medical services were retained by the special master to identify problems, assist in the development of remedies and to evaluate progress in implementation. Contact with these experts exposed those in the system to new approaches, provided them with technical assistance, and recommendations by the consultants led to the infusion of expertise in areas that were lacking. Equally as important, contact with these experts and the agencies they represented—the Federal Bureau of Prisons, the National Institute of Corrections, the American Correctional Association, the National Commission on Correctional Health Care etc.— provided the Rhode Island system with sources of policies and procedures by which the organization could be reconstituted and its operations rationalized.

The master was also instrumental in securing needed funds. Keating, at one point, went so far as to locate federal funding for court-ordered renovations and to assist the department in preparing its application. More generally, the threat of court sanctions was used by officials to gain increases in legislative appropriations and public support for bond issues, and pressure from the court was a key factor in the use, if not the development, of a new funding mechanism for the construction of state buildings.

After 1985 the focus of the case shifted from prison conditions to jail overcrowding. With this shift in focus, the role of the court changed from monitoring progress to designing tactics to prevent the erosion of the gains that had been made. Population caps were set and reset. When these were exceeded, experts were brought in to determine if conditions remained within acceptable limits despite the overcrowding. Finally, as the situation reached crisis proportions, the court took the unpopular step of fining the state, using the funds to bail indigent offenders, and then awarding good time to convicted offenders to accelerate their releases.

The crush of numbers was alleviated when new facilities came on line but buffering the system from overcrowding in the future remained a major concern of both parties as they moved toward termination of the suit. From this shared concern came the creation of a new agency, a federation of the state's criminal justice organizations, empowered by statute to take action to keep the prison population within the limits set by the court. Thus, the impact of the intervention into the ACI has extended beyond corrections to the entire criminal justice system, establishing a vehicle with the potential to develop an awareness of a common mission among the various agencies and to fashion more coordinated policies. Whether the commission will, in fact, operate this way or indeed take any action at all, however, remains to be seen.

The flexible approach fashioned by the court succeeded in maintaining a spirit of fundamental cooperation between the adversaries despite periods of tension, strain and occasional high conflict. Although the court chastised the defendants and threatened severe sanctions for non-compliance on numerous occasions, the aforementioned fine was the only substantial penalty imposed during the 18-year history of the case. Typically, negative sanctions were converted to inducements by offering the defendants a period in which to purge themselves of contempt, and their efforts at compliance drew public recognition and praise from the bench. On occasion, moreover, the court gave strong public support to administrative actions even in cases where the judge and master privately had doubts such as Moran's efforts to restore order. Most importantly, the decree was never treated as if carved in stone. Judge and master remained sensitive to the fact that failure to comply was often the result of factors beyond the control of the department and that changing circumstances might require tailoring the order to meet those changes. Thus, the defendants, although having a judgement against them, always had something to win by continuing to participate in the deliberative process. Nor, as the record shows, were they without power. As a result of bargaining and negotiation deadlines were continuously extended, and every aspect of the order amended and modified. The fact that the old maximum security prison, ordered closed by 1978, was incrementally renovated and remains in use today is only the most obvious example of the court's flexibility.

One of the long-standing criticisms of judicial efforts to reform social institutions is the argument that courts lack the competence and capacity for such a task. A recent and powerful critique along this line has been advanced by Gerald Rosenberg in *The Hollow Hope: Can Courts Bring About Social Change?*[9] The main title suggests Rosenberg's answer to the question he poses. He maintains that the capacity of the courts to produce "significant social reform" is limited by three structural constraints integral to the American political system: the limited nature of constitutional rights, the lack of judicial independence and the judiciary's lack of powers of implementation. For courts to produce significant reform, according to Rosenberg, there must be ample legal precedent, substantial support for change in the legislature and the executive, and either support from some of the citizenry or at least little opposition. In addition, Rosenberg contends that at least one of the following conditions must be present: other actors offering incentives or imposing costs to induce compliance, a market mechanism for implementing the reforms or officials crucial to implementation who are willing to act and able to use the court order to leverage resources or as a shield for their actions.

Viewed in the light of the history of *Palmigiano,* Rosenberg's theory appears to underestimate the ability of the court to win the support of key officials, to create effective incentives and sanctions, and to empower officials. As we have seen, the court was able to orchestrate the replacement of the director of corrections with one who was more professional. Administrative succession of this sort appears to be common following major interventions and seems usually to bring into power officials who are attuned to implementing the court's directives, as it did in this case. Moreover, the court was able to retain the cooperation of corrections officials by engaging them in an extended process of bargaining and negotiation during which the original decree was continuously amended and modified, often to their advantage. Further, the court was the gateway through which flowed expertise that was indispensable to the organization's development. Finally, although the financial penalties threatened by the court were never huge and seldom imposed, they were effective in spurring action where there had been inertia. Equally if not more important than the financial penalties, however, was the apparent sensitivity of elected officials and professional administrators to the stigma of being publicly chastised and found in contempt of court as well as to the opportunity to bask in the glow of constitutionality when compliance with any part of the order was achieved.

Both the sting of sanctions and the satisfactions of compliance were greatly enhanced by the widespread media coverage accorded all court proceedings. Moreover, the editorial board of the state's leading newspaper, one with statewide circulation and virtually no competition, played a crucial role. All political actors in the state view the editorial pages as a barometer of public opinion. Early in the case strong backing of the court's order by the editors helped to undercut political opposition. Later as public attitudes toward crime and criminals hardened, however, that editorial support turned to sharp criticism, and in the face of this the court seemed to stumble and stall. Nonetheless, in the end the court was itself able to neutralize this criticism and dampen opposition to its emergency actions by retaining its own expert, one who had not been previously involved in the litigation, to evaluate conditions. The report and subsequent testimony of this expert, which received front-page coverage for several days, described conditions in such dramatic terms and recommended such drastic action that the actions actually taken by the court were made to seem mild by comparison.

Rosenberg never clearly defines what he means by "significant social reform" nor does he present a standard by which it can be measured. However, by virtually any standard one might employ—be it the capacity to incarcerate inmates safely and provide for their basic human needs, opportunities for meaningful activity and self-improvement, or operation in accordance with the rule of law—Rhode Island's prisons are significantly better today than they were twenty years ago. In this case, at least, the intervention of the federal court has resulted in the institutionalization of constitutional values and practices. One concrete measure of this success may be seen in the fact that a prison system that was once the focal point of almost continual litigation now has among the lowest rates of civil rights actions filed against it of any state prison system in the country.[10]

CONCLUDING REMARKS

Histories of complex organization, prisons in particular, suggest that entropy rather than stability may be the more natural state.[11] Certainly, current events in Rhode Island suggest that the Vose administration, for all its improved managerial capability, will be sorely challenged to maintain the current equilibrium and prevent a process of deinstitutionalization. For one thing, America's great punishment experiment continues apace with the number of prisoners continuing to climb in Rhode Island as elsewhere. Although the legislature enacted intermediate sentencing alternatives into law as a condition of terminating the *Palmigiano* suit, funds to implement intermediate sanctions other than home confinement have not been appropriated. Along this same line, the concentration on improving institutions and expanding their capacity has resulted in proportionately fewer resources for non-institutional services such as probation which remains very understaffed and underfunded. Thus, there is little within the system to buffer the institutions from overcrowding, and without such buffers it seems doubtful if the Criminal Justice Oversight Committee will have sufficient options available to it to avert a crisis should the numbers continue to increase.

A related challenge is the question of cost. Efforts to maintain constitutionally acceptable prisons may founder on the principle of less eligibility.[12] The utilitarian logic of this principle, born at the same time as the prisons, holds that the maintenance of social order requires that the standard of living accorded inmates be kept lower than that of the poorest workers in the free world. At a time when the income level of those workers, in real dollars, is declining, economic inequality growing, and welfare benefits are being slashed, it will be difficult to maintain prison programs and services at their current level. The operation of the "less eligibility principle" amid these circumstances is fueling the movement "to make time tougher," which has seen the resurrection of chain gangs in some states, the removal of various amenities such as televisions and air conditioners in others, co-payment plans for inmate health care and the discontinuance of long-standing college education programs in prisons.

There has as yet been no such pressure in Rhode Island, but the increased obligations being shifted from the federal government to the states combined with Rhode Island's narrow economic base suggest that the fiscal constraints which the department has faced in the past few years will continue for some time into the future. Budget considerations, as we have seen, necessitated the elimination of posts and the closing of two facilities inflaming labor-management tensions in the process. More recently, start-up costs have delayed the development of a reintegration unit, the centerpiece of the intermediate sanctions legislation, leaving the institutions more vulnerable to the specter of overcrowding than had been planned at the time the suit was dismissed. Further, the costs of bringing facilities up to the level of American Correctional Association's accreditation standards have led the department, at least temporarily, to abandon that effort, one which was highly valued for its symbolism and as a means of maintaining the *esprit de corps* and the momentum developed in the course of bringing to an end the nearly eighteen years of judicial oversight.

One alternative certain to be considered seriously by the administration as it attempts to deal with its financial problems is privatization, either of the entire operation or at least of some programs and services. A corporation recently proposed such to the department, promising a savings of at least 15 percent in operational costs. No decision on that proposal has been reached, nor is it clear that it is being seriously considered, but any attempt to privatize is likely to be defined as a survival issue by the union and resisted fiercely. The resulting struggle could be of such proportions as to significantly disrupt the new order. Moreover, although prisons run for profit are becoming more common, they have not been the subject of extensive evaluation and there remain major unanswered questions about their ability of private enterprises to operate cost-effective facilities that comport with constitutional criteria.[13]

Finally, the intercession of the federal court seems less likely in the future. The court may become re-involved if the Criminal Justice Oversight Committee fails to execute its responsibility to maintain and enforce the population caps placed on each facility. However, allegations of other violations would necessitate a new trial. Standards adopted by the U.S. Supreme Court in recent years will make it more difficult for plaintiffs to prevail in future litigation. Moreover, the recently enacted Prison Litigation Reform Act (PLRA) will make it more difficult for prisoners to bring suits in the future and will limit the relief to which they may be entitled even if they do prevail. Among its many provisions, this far-reaching law requires prisoners to pay filing fees; bars prisoners with three prior frivolous lawsuits from most future filings; limits preliminary injunctions to 90 days; requires a court to terminate relief, on the motion of either party, two years after issuance of an order unless the court holds a new trial and finds an on-going violation of law; and greatly restricts the role of special masters. Under the PLRA, the powers of special masters are limited to making findings based on the record. They are prohibited from any *ex parte* communications with the parties and therefore from the very assistance and mediation functions found to be vital to the successful resolution of *Palmigiano*.[14]

Thus, the key question for the future is not whether courts have the capacity to reform institutions but whether the state can maintain the institutions in their now-reformed condition. The pressure of managing large numbers of people with diminishing resources will continue to place a premium on organizational rationality, and there are now significant institutional supports for such both in and outside of corrections. Thus, it seems unlikely that the institutions will devolve to the anarchy of earlier times. However, a scenario such as that outlined by Feeley and Simon in which the sole purpose of corrections becomes the cost-effective management of a class of people perceived to be permanent offenders, "a kind of waste-management function" involving the recycling of the underclass, seems quite possible given current trends.[15]

Some observers, however, see the possibility of an alternative paradigm developing, one rooted in a logic of inclusion and hence more hospitable to democratic values. In particular, these scholars argue that the convergence of a number of factors may result in the reemergence of rehabilitation as a public idea, one which "resonates with Americans' personal fears and shared hopes for a better society" and which points the way to the realization of those hopes.[16] Among the factors they see as converging to produce this new paradigm are the costs of continuing the expansion of penal harm and its ineffectiveness in reducing crime, the continued widespread support for rehabilitation among the general public and corrections officials, research demonstrating the effectiveness of treatment programs and redefinitions of treatment in ways that emphasize the acceptance of personal responsibility by offenders as part of the treatment process.

In and of itself, the rehabilitative paradigm is not sufficiently broad to provide a plausible basis on which to reshape the political economy. It is, however, compatible with a more encompassing ideology that emphasizes both the primacy of the person and the primacy of each person's responsibility to the common good, that defines citizenship not merely as rights and interests but also as obligations and duties. This communitarian ideology, once found only in conversations among the nation's cultural elite, has come recently to inform an emergent social movement that seeks to restore civil society by fostering both corporate and individual responsibility for rebuilding and maintaining shattered communities.[17] To the extent this movement gathers strength, it will provide a cultural context unfavorable to the further expansion of penal harm.[18] To the extent that it is actually successful in reconstructing communities, it will provide an environment favorable to the continued institutionalization of constitutional values in prisons.

NOTES

1. James B. Jacobs, *Stateville: The Penitentiary in Mass Society* (Chicago: The University of Chicago Press, 1977); Ben M. Crouch and James W. Marquart, *An Appeal to Justice: Litigated Reform of Texas Prisons* (Austin, TX: University of Texas Press, 1989).

2. Crouch and Marquart, 1989, especially ch. 8.

3. Jacobs, 1977, especially ch. 8; Bert Useem and Peter Kimball, *States of Siege: U.S. Prison Riots, 1971-1986* (New York: Oxford University Press, 1991), ch. 10.

4. The terms "institution" and "institutionalization" have been defined in a variety of ways. Recently, W. Richard Scott has offered a definition that incorporates most of these meanings. By his definition "institutions consist of cognitive, normative and regulative structures and activities that provide stability and meaning to social behavior." The cognitive structure refers to taken for granted assumptions and understandings; the normative structure consists of related values and norms that are internalized as felt moral obligations; and the regulative structure refers to formal rule-making and the monitoring and sanctioning of behavior with respect to them. See W. Richard Scott, *Institutions and Organizations* (Thousand Oaks, CA: Sage Publications, 1995), pp. 33-44, quote from p. 33.

5. Steve J. Martin and Sheldon Ekland-Olson, *Texas Prisons: The Walls Came Tumbling Down* (Austin, TX: Texas Monthly Press, 1987), ch. 6; Larry W. Yackle, *Reform and Regret: The Story of Federal Judicial Involvement in the Alabama Prison System* (New York: Oxford University Press, 1989), esp. pp. 105-107 and ch. 5.

6. Susan Sturm, "Resolving the Remedial Dilemma: Strategies of Judicial Intervention in Prisons," *University of Pennsylvania Law Review* 138 (1990): 856-860.

7. Note, "Mastering Intervention in Prisons," *Yale Law Journal* 88 (1979): 1082-85.

8. Roy H. Reynolds, "The Role of Special Masters in Federal Judicial Supervision of State Prisons: The Need for Limitations," *American Criminal Law Review* 26 (1988): 491-511.

9. Gerald Rosenberg, *The Hollow Hope: Can Courts Bring About Social Change?* (Chicago: The University of Chicago Press, 1991), ch. 1 and pp. 305-314.

10. Kathleen Maguire and Ann L. Pastore, eds., *Sourcebook of Criminal Justice Statistics 1994* (United States Department of Justice. Bureau of Justice Statistics. Washington, DC: USGPO, 1995), Table 6.42, p. 564.

11. Scott, p. 79.

12. Georg Rusche and Otto Kirchheimer, *Punishment and Social Structure* (New York: Russell and Russell, 1968. Originally published in 1933), p. 94; Dario Melossi, "Gazette of Morality and Social Whip: Punishment, Hegemony and the Case of the USA, 1970-92," *Social and Legal Studies* 2 (1993): 259-279.

13. Charles H. Logan, *Private Prisons—Cons and Pros* (New York: Oxford University Press, 1990); Alexis M. Durham III, *Crisis and Reform: Current Issues in American Punishment* (Boston: Little Brown and Co., 1994), ch. 10; David Shichor, *Punishment for Profit: Private Prisons/Public Concerns* (Thousand Oaks, CA: Sage, 1995).

14. *Prison Litigation Reform Act of 1995.* S 1279, 104th Congress, 1st Session.

15. Malcolm M. Feeley and Jonathan Simon, "The New Penology: Notes on the Emerging Strategy of Corrections and Its Implications," *Criminology* 30 (1992): 449-474.

16. Frank T. Cullen and John P. Wright, "Two Futures for American Corrections," in *The Past, Present and Future of American Criminal Justice*, eds. Brendan Maguire and Polly F. Radosh (Dix Hills, NY: General Hall, 1996), pp. 209-215, quote on p. 211.

17. Robert N. Bellah et al., *The Good Society* (New York: Alfred A. Knopf, 1991); Amitai Etzioni, *The Spirit of Community: Rights, Responsibilities and the Communitarian Agenda* (New York: Crown, 1993); "Boston-based Institute To Help Push for Civility," *The Providence (RI) Journal-Bulletin*, December 16, 1996, p. A5.

18. Todd R. Clear, *Harm in American Penology: Offenders, Victims and Their Communities* (Albany, NY: State University of New York Press, 1994).

Statistics

Table 1. Inmate Population and Full-time Staff Positions, 1956-1995

FY Ending	Inmate Population	Staff Uniformed	Staff Civilian	Total
1956	513	134	18	152
1957	468	135	18	153
1958	438	135	33	168
1959	499	140	31	171
1960	474	142	32	174
1961	477	152	38	190
1962	483	164	47	211
1963	487	162	39	201
1964	523	171	44	215
1965	493	168	46	214
1966	497	163	47	210
1967	477	163	47	210
1968	439	NA	NA	NA
1969	442	163	52	215
1970	473	162	55	217
1971	477	157	53	210
1972	485	166	49	215
1973	488	164	49	213[a]
1974	559	187	69	256
1975	553	289	85	374
1976	603	289	86	375
1977	681	289	85	374
1978	685	312	97	409
1979	666	357	174	531

Table 1. Inmate Population and Full-time Staff Positions, 1956-1995 (continued)

FY Ending	Inmate Population	Uniformed	Staff Civilian	Total
1980	730	343	173	516
1981	819	474	158	632[b]
1982	990	571	168	739[c]
1983	1085	553	161	714
1984	1175	NA	NA	NA
1985	1250	485	162	647
1986	1345	530	153	683
1987	1381	625	160	785
1988	1527	750	198	948[d]
1989	1987	730	213	943
1990	2503	770	238	1008
1991	2468	931	277	1208[e]
1992	2862	1011	278	1289[f]
1993	2774	921	357	1278
1994	2937	862	373	1235
1995	3048	969	427	1396

Source: Personnel Supplements to the Rhode Island State Budget.

[a]Figures do not reflect the creation of the new Department of Corrections. These are more accurately estimated by the numbers for 1974.
[b]Opening of the High Security Center.
[c]Opening of the Intake Service Center.
[d]148.5 positions added to meet the requirements of the 1986 court order. Of this number, 122 were uniformed and 26 were civilian.
[e]Opening of the new medium security prison.
[f]Opening of the addition to the Intake Service Center.

Table 2. FTE Positions by General Function for Selected Years, 1956-95

| FY | Uniformed | | | Civilian | |
Ending	Supervisor	Other	Managers	Profession	Other
1956	13	121	9.0	2.5	13.0
1957	13	122	10.0	7.5	16.0
1965	17	151	12.5	12.8	22.0
1970	17	145	12.5	15.7	28.5
1973	24	170	15.5	24.6	27.3
1977	30	259	22.0	24.0	40.5
1978	44	268	25.8	28.5	60.7
1983	NA	NA	NA	NA	NA
1985	43	442	30.6	44.0	88.0
1990	63	707	21.0	96.8	121.0
1995	74	895	70.0	216.0	141.0

Source: Personnel Supplements to the Rhode Island State Budget. These totals may be slightly larger than those in Table 1 for some years due to the inclusion of part-time staff in this table.

Table 3. Expenditures, 1956-1995 (000's)[a]

FY Ending	DOC[b] Expends	Total	ACI Expenditures Personnel	Operating	Other[c]
1956	5 198	3 607	2 643	941	23
1957	5 873	4 156	3 171	957	28
1958	6 522	4 518	3 496	1 022	45
1959	6 744	4 637	3 580	1 057	66
1960	6 956	4 872	3 909	963	20
1961	7 729	5 323	4 338	985	42
1962	7 890	5 467	4 479	988	63
1963	8 114	5 998	4 940	1 058	508
1964	8 634	5 793	4 773	1 020	509
1965	9 742	6 268	5 286	982	614
1966	10 057	6 426	5 268	1 158	679
1967	11 811	7 509	6 295	1 214	578
1968	11 710	7 402	6 286	1 116	596
1969	11 408	7 417	6 204	1 213	555
1970	11 634	8 915	7 508	1 407	341
1971	12 017	9 186	7 764	1 422	474
1972	12 746	9 430	7 442	1 988	1 456
1973	16 305	11 634	9 286	2 348	610
1974	19 940	14 035	11 354	2 681	871
1975	21 884	16 491	13 330	3 161	869
1976	22 948	16 872	13 386	3 486	629
1977	26 776	18 112	14 144	3 968	554
1978	32 067	18 572	14 538	4 034	2 119
1979	30 641	19 722	16 293	3 429	1 475
1980	28 105	19 039	15 955	3 084	1 745
1981	29 962	21 203	18 100	3 103	2 254
1982	31 770	22 928	19 517	3 411	2 496
1983	33 676	25 204	21 826	3 378	2 684
1984	35 379	26 402	23 020	3 382	3 249
1985	36 697	28 226	24 610	3 616	2 515
1986	41 232	21 661	17 306	4 355	3 007
1987	44 924	33 303	28 290	5 013	2 781
1988	52 384	40 506	33 401	7 105	3 654
1989	63 399	50 495	40 104	10 391	3 789

Table 3. Expenditures, 1956-1995 (continued)

FY Ending	DOC[b] Expends	Total	ACI Expenditures Personnel	Operating	Other[c]
1990	75 743	59 199	46 375	12 824	4 251
1991	82 314	56 151	46 152	9 999	10 987
1992	86 390	56 914	45 582	11 332	10 062
1993	99 412	76 294	51 766	13 184	11 334
1994	1 003 5	87 079	59 800	15 737	11 542
1995	1 009 9	93 237	64 444	16 964	11 829

Sources: Program supplements to the Rhode Island State Budgets.

[a] In 1990 dollars.
[b] Prior to 1972, the figures are for the Division of Correctional Services within the Department of Social Welfare.
[c] The figures in this column do not include the costs of capital construction funded through bonds. They do, however, include debt service on those bonds and capital expenditures not requiring bond issues.

Table 4. Number of Homicides, Escapes and Serious Disturbances, 1956-1995

Year	Homicides	Escapes[a]	Disturbances[b]
1956	0	0	0
1957	0	0	0
1958	0	0	0
1959	0	0	0
1960	0	1	0
1961	0	0	0
1962	0	1	0
1963	0	0	0
1964	0	0	1
1965	0	0	0
1966	0	0	1
1967	0	1	3
1968	0	0	0
1969	0	0	4
1970	1	0	1
1971	1	1	0
1972	0	1	1
1973	3	1	4
1974	1	0	1
1975	2	1	8
1976	0	1	5
1977	1	0	3
1978	0	0	3
1979	0	0	1
1980	0	0	1
1981	0	0	0
1982	0	0	1
1983	0	0	0
1984	0	0	3
1985	1	0	0
1986	0	2	0
1987	0	0	0
1988	0	2	1
1989	0	1	1

Table 4. Number of Homicides, Escapes and Serious Disturbances, 1956-1995 (continued)

Year	Homicides	Escapes[a]	Disturbances[b]
1990	0	0	0
1991	0	0	1
1992	0	0	1
1993	0	0	0
1994	1	1	0
1995	0	0	0

Sources: U. S. Department of Justice, Bureau of Justice Statistics *Sourcebook of Criminal Justice Statistics*, 1975-95 (Washington, DC: USGPO, 1976-96); *Providence Journal-Bulletin*; Research and Planning Division "Inmate Deaths at the ACI, May 1974-July 1995" (Cranston, RI: R.I. Department of Corrections, 1996).

[a] Includes only escapes from within the perimeters of close custody units--high security, maximum security and medium security.

[b] A serious disturbance is defined as one involving three or more inmates and in which either someone is injured so seriously as to require medical treatment at a hospital and/or someone is taken hostage and/or there is property damage estimated to be in excess of $25,000 (1990 dollars). These figures are based on news reports and are undoubtedly an underestimate.

Index